HIKING TRAILS OF SOUTHWESTERN COLORADO

FIFTH EDITION

JOHN PEEL
& PAUL PIXLER

Library of Congress Cataloging-in-Publication Data

Names: Peel, John, author. | Pixler, Paul, 1920– author.
Title: Hiking trails of Southwestern Colorado / John Peel and Paul Pixler.
Description: Fifth edition. | Berkeley : West Margin Press, 2020. | Includes index. | Summary: "A trail guidebook to hikes and climbs in Southwestern Colorado, including areas around Durango, Silverton, Missionary Ridge, and Vallecito"— Provided by publisher.
Identifiers: LCCN 2020004215 (print) | LCCN 2020004216 (ebook) | ISBN 9781513262963 (paperback) | ISBN 9781513262970 (hardback) | ISBN 9781513262987 (ebook)
Subjects: LCSH: Hiking—Colorado—San Juan National Forest—Guidebooks. | Hiking—Colorado—Uncompahgre National Forest—Guidebooks. | San Juan National Forest (Colo.)—Guidebooks. | Uncompahgre National Forest (Colo.)—Guidebooks. | Colorado Trail (Colo.)—Guidebooks.
Classification: LCC GV199.42.C62 S265 2020 (print) | LCC GV199.42.C62 (ebook) | DDC 796.5109788--dc23
LC record available at https://lccn.loc.gov/2020004215
LC ebook record available at https://lccn.loc.gov/2020004216

Printed in China

24 23 22 21 20 2 3 4 5

Edited by Barbara Schultz

Indexed by Sheila Ryan

Cover image: Looking up through a profusion of wildflowers to the summit of Hesperus Mountain.

West Margin Press® is an imprint of

WEST MARGIN PRESS
WestMarginPress.com

Proudly distributed by Ingram Publisher Services

WEST MARGIN PRESS
Publishing Director: Jennifer Newens
Marketing Manager: Angela Zbornik
Project Specialist: Gabrielle Maudiere
Editor: Olivia Ngai
Design & Production: Rachel Lopez Metzger
Design Intern: Gloria Boadwee

CONTENTS

HIKES UP & ON MISSIONARY RIDGE

HIKES BETWEEN DURANGO & SILVERTON

HIKES OUT OF SILVERTON

VALLECITO AREA HIKES

THE AREA FOURTEENERS

PREFACE TO THE FIFTH EDITION

Welcome to what is a surprisingly hefty rewrite of this classic trail guidebook. It's been more than a decade since the fourth edition of this guide was published, and a lot has changed: Trailheads have moved; trails were built, modified, and made permanent by increased wear; roads deteriorated or were blocked off; private and public land-use restrictions were tweaked; avalanche debris forced detours; and fires altered the landscape. And that's just a start.

This edition adds a bundle of trails (including a new Vallecito section) and leaves out a few that aren't all that conducive to hikers anymore. Also, several hikes and sections are reorganized, plus new photos and maps have been added that we believe are much easier to use.

This update has certainly been a labor of love. Everything in here was painstakingly researched. Yep, it's a tough job wandering around in the wilderness, but someone has to do it.

The first person to create this marvelous compendium was Fort Lewis College philosophy professor Paul Pixler, whose first version came out in 1980. Paul wrote two more editions before deciding to find a successor. Through a mutual friend, Scott Graham, Paul invited me to carry on his work, and I wrote the fourth edition of this book, printed in 2006. Paul died in 2011 at the age of ninety, but a lot of his words remain in this book. This fifth edition started with me scribbling of notes in the margins of the fourth edition, but the bulk of the research was done in the summer of 2019.

There are always people who lend a hand in the creation of a guidebook such as this. Here are a few:

My father, Donald Peel, finished climbing all the state's fourteeners back in 1951, and was something like the thirty-seventh person that the Colorado Mountain Club recognized for doing so. He, and to some extent my mother, introduced me and my sister, Amy, to hiking. All those Life Savers candies he used to goad me from trail stop to trail stop in those early years paid off in the end.

Eventually, I started exploring the mountains with high school buddies Steve Chapman and Jim Wadge. We all survived our scrapes (usually it was me doing something like desperately clinging to a rope while stuck horizontally on a bridge, or needing dire help from above when stuck on a cliff), and we remain friends today.

More recently, my wife, Judy, and dog, Buda, have shared my adventures. Thanks, Judy, for your constant help, guidance, and editing on this time-consuming project. Friends David Buck and Peter Schertz joined me on several trails and challenging mountains. Leo Lloyd, search and rescue expert, helped to craft some of the gear essentials, safety tips, and first-aid information. One of Leo's first of countless wilderness rescues, incidentally, was catching Paul Pixler when Paul slipped on El Diente; that incident remains in the ensuing Introduction.

Can you find this spectacular waterfall, located near one of the hikes in this book?

Thanks also to the great team at West Margin Press: editor Olivia Ngai, designer Rachel Metzger, and marketing manager Angie Zbornik. Also, thanks to Jed Botsford with the Forest Service and Joe Lewandowski with Parks and Wildlife for lending their expertise; and to Mary Monroe Brown of Durango Trails 2000 for her consultation.

So pick a trail and refresh your wilderness IQ with the information in the Introduction and Ethics chapter. Use this book as it suits you, and go try to have as much fun as I did.

John Peel
Durango, Colorado

The shale-rock ridge leading to the Engineer summit. (Photo by Steve Chapman)

PIONEER TRAIL
OPEN TO
CLOSED TO MOTORIZED VEHICLES

INTRODUCTION

It's pretty basic, really: Stuff a few things in a small pack, arrive at a trailhead, don your chosen footwear, and start walking. The goal of this book is merely to add quality to that outdoor experience. It's to help match your mood and energy with the appropriate trail. It's to keep you on the right track.

This chapter will explain how the book is structured and the best ways to use it, with an explanation of the headings before each hike description. The next chapters have general information on coexisting with other trail users, facing potential hazards, proper gear and first-aid equipment, and preparation tips.

Many trails await. This book isn't designed to tell you exactly where to go, but it makes a good launching pad.

WHAT'S INCLUDED

The goal in creating this guide was to find the most enjoyable day-use trails in the Durango-Silverton corridor. It branches out a bit to include hikes out of Mancos and Vallecito as well. Most of these hikes are within an hour's drive of Durango or Silverton. Backpacking routes are not featured here, although you'll find several great ideas for backpacking trips, and some multiday routes are specifically pointed out within the day hike descriptions. Technical climbs are not featured, but a couple of the mountains in here will test your ability to rock-scramble.

Almost all of these hikes are on public land. Several cross private land, however, and that's noted. A few trails on public land are subject to seasonal closures and that's noted too; these are all near Durango.

The fourteeners of southwestern Colorado posed a bit of a dilemma for me. These overclimbed peaks get their own chapter, but not all twelve made the cut. Handies Peak via Grouse Gulch or American Basin is a 1-day route from as far as Durango with a reasonably early start. Mount Sneffels can be done in a day from Durango too, but it's a good idea to get a really early start. Wetterhorn, Uncompahgre, Redcloud, and Sunshine aren't so achievable in 1 day from Durango or even Silverton, but they are day hikes from nearby camping areas or from Lake City. The Needles and Wilsons didn't make the cut. The Needles are best climbed either by hiking down Purgatory Flats, up the Animas River to near Needleton, and up to Chicago Basin, or by taking the train to Needleton; plan to spend 2 or 3 days. Mount Wilson and El Diente are about as difficult as Colorado's fourteeners get and really are better to incorporate into a backpacking trip. Wilson Peak as a day hike is best from the north, but that's a long drive and still a *long* hike.

The top of Pioneer Trail reaches Nusbaum Road, the junction shown here.

HEADINGS

"Distance" is relatively straightforward. The more often you hike, the better you will know your capabilities. One caveat is that miles where you'll make a big elevation gain or where you'll be hiking at high altitude are more difficult than flat miles or trails at low altitude. However, as your body adapts to high altitude, those miles will become easier (note that I did not say "easy").

"Elevation" is also self-explanatory, again with a caveat or two. Some trails climb steadily and even though they don't seem all that steep, by the time you've gone a few miles you've gained a lot of elevation. Others are continually steep and you'll gain 2,200 feet in less than 2 miles. The most potentially frustrating trails climb steeply, lose altitude, and climb again. That aspect hasn't been figured into the total elevation-gain figures here, but it usually will be pointed out in the trail descriptions.

"Rating" is fairly subjective. The ratings used are Easy, Moderate, Difficult, and Very Difficult. One person's difficult hike is another person's very difficult hike. One hike that seems moderate in June may become easy for you by August. I tried my best to be consistent, but undoubtedly some you will return from a moderate hike and say, "That was *easy*!" So be it. Factors considered in the ratings were length, altitude, route finding, and degree of difficulty on the route.

"Time allowed" considers the entire trip, whether it's out and back, a loop, or a one-way, and is an estimate for an average hiker, but what is an "average hiker"? Also, if you're making frequent stops for photos, lunch, naps, or sightseeing, you'll need to add that time to the estimate. All factors considered, if you're moving at an overall speed of 2 miles per hour, you're generally keeping pace with the estimated time allowed.

"Maps"—the fold-up kinds you carry on the trail—are no longer included in this book's headings, but maps still appear in the book alongside each trail description. By all means, learn how to read maps and their topography. When you stop for a break, look at the map and make sure you know where you are. Many people use the maps function on their phones, and that can be helpful. Many hikers also download topographical maps onto a phone app. However, a phone screen–sized view makes it difficult to get an overall perspective on your location, and some hiking routes may not feature perfect cellular phone service. Not that long ago, the best resource for hikers was the US Geological Survey's (USGS) 7.5-minute series. You'd walk into an outdoor shop and buy the necessary "quad" maps that showed the features and topography of a specific quadrant, ranging about 7 by 9 miles. They're still available, and you can download and print any part of them yourself for free at usgs.gov/core-science-systems/ngp/tnm-delivery/. I still have a huge collection and use them, but that's no longer the norm. There are other printed maps available. *National Geographic* issues a popular set of maps calls Trails Illustrated, for instance.

TRAIL DESCRIPTIONS

Use the descriptions as you see fit. If you have a mileage counter—perhaps a phone app or GPS unit—follow along. Or just match the description with where you are (or think you are) to estimate how far you've come.

GPS coordinates and elevations are included at many trail junctions, passes, summits, and various other geographical points. These can help plan a route or allow you to double-check your location.

The road abbrevations should be obvious, but don't confuse CO and CR. CO is a Colorado (state) highway, and CR is a county road. US is a U.S. Highway, and FR is a Forest Service road.

A huge effort has been put into making these trail descriptions helpful and accurate, but it is possible that there is an error somewhere in this text. Lean hard on this book for accurate information, but if you find a mistake, please share that with me so that future printings can be corrected.

RESOURCES

In the back of the book you'll find a list of additional resources that provide further information. If you don't find answers to all of your questions in this book, one of these appended sources might help.

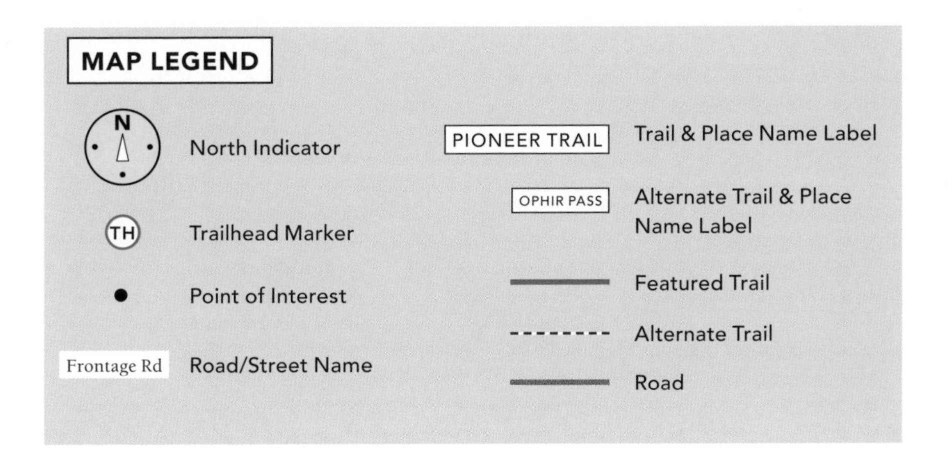

GENERAL INFORMATION

The following is a miniature survival guide, offering advice on dealing with conditions and elements you'll encounter on the trails. Use these tips to prepare for your hikes and so you'll know what to do when things go wrong.

OTHER TRAIL USERS

You will bump into other animals on the trails that aren't like you. Some, like dogs and horses, will be cheating by walking on four legs. Others will travel using two wheels, and some of those will be powered, either by gas engines or even electricity.

Do your best to get along with all of them. Be nice and smile, because mutual respect among all users goes a long way. (See Ethics on page 229.)

Dogs are great trail companions, be they yours or someone else's. If dogs are part of your group, be mindful of what they're doing. Don't let them harass and chase wildlife. In certain places, you could be fined. The legal precedent is a bit cloudy here, but ranchers can even go as far as to shoot your dog if it is endangering their livestock (cattle or sheep, for example).

Horses have the right of way, so look for a good spot to pull well off the trail and let them by, in the meantime talking to the rider (or horse) in a calm voice. And make absolutely sure that your dog does not get near that unpredictable horse's hooves.

Mountain bikers are usually very considerate, but they have their bad apples like any user group. As a hiker you technically have the right of way with bikers, but if it's easier for you just to step out of the way for a second to let the cyclist ride past, do it. Note to mountain bikers (including me): What irks hikers more than anything is when you don't even *act* like you're *thinking* of slowing down. If you're going downhill, it's easier for you to apply the brakes and pull over than it is for a hiker to dodge you.

Motorbikes are only allowed on a handful of trails in this book. Hikers, as much as the noise might bother you, it doesn't last too long. Let them by. It's generally pretty difficult for a motorbike rider to pull off the trail; that's a heavy, unwieldy beast they've got.

E-bikes are part bicycle, part machine, and their classification is unclear. However, they're becoming increasingly popular; look for them to show up soon on a trail or two near you.

Top: There is a worry that pika habitat may be dwindling with global warming as one possible cause, but the rabbit-related creatures are still prolific on rocky slopes in the high country. Bottom: Moose were reintroduced to Southwest Colorado in the mid-1990s. They're common around Silverton, and at least one has ventured near Durango.

HAZARDS: WEATHER, ALTITUDE, AND MORE

Hikers in higher altitudes in the Rockies must always be aware of the weather. It can change from beautiful to dangerous very quickly. This is especially true from early July to early September, when afternoon thunderstorms are frequent—the monsoon season. During this period, it is best to plan to reach the highest altitude in your hike by noon. These storms can be severe, even if they are short lived. They can bring wind, cold, rain, small hail, or all of the above. The greatest hazard, however, is **lightning**. This high-voltage static electricity can kill or maim in a split second. High points where the charged cloud is closest are the strike zones. This makes high or isolated peaks and ridges especially vulnerable.

Any dark cloud nearby in the summer should be considered suspect, even if it is small. There are additional signs of an imminent lightning flash. If you are on or near a high point and hear a buzzing in the rocks, or if the hair on your arms or legs or even your head begins to stand up, you're in prime territory; get down to lower levels as fast as possible—not so fast, however, that you trip and fall, which is a much more likely way to get hurt than a lightning strike. Also, if you seek shelter from rain under a tree, make it a tree that is lower than others nearby.

Lightning is the worst danger from storms, but it's not the only one. Rocks that call for scrambling can be very slick when they get wet. Lichens on them increase this problem. Paul Pixler related this story: "Once on El Diente, it began drizzling just after our party started down from the top; the rocks are near vertical and are very irregular in this area. I slipped on one that would have held easily when dry. Though I fell only 3 feet, that led to an edge where there was another drop, followed by another and another. Fortunately, two companions were at the edge of the first one and stopped me before I could go to the next drop. Though embarrassing, it served as a reminder to me to become more cautious, but it could have been disastrous."

Another danger from rainstorms is **hypothermia**. This is a condition in which the core body temperature begins to drop below normal. Cold fingers and toes are uncomfortable, but a cold body core is highly dangerous. Soaked clothes and some wind can bring this on quickly at high altitudes, even in July. If you begin to shiver violently, hypothermia is starting. Companions must come to the rescue and furnish heat immediately, because the victim soon becomes disoriented and may not recognize the danger. Extra clothing will help, as will a faster pace if possible. However, in more severe cases, skin-to-skin body heat transfer is likely to be the only answer. (Hopefully the victim is someone you like.)

High altitude is an unseen hazard, particularly to visitors from low elevations. Air at higher altitudes contains less oxygen; therefore, your heart and lungs work harder to oxygenate and circulate the blood. People with a history of heart problems or high blood pressure should probably consider only the easier and lower hikes.

Acclimatization to high altitude seems to basically involve an increase in red blood cell count, which makes for a more efficient use of the available oxygen in the thinner air. Different theories abound on how long this acclimatization takes.

Sometimes, snow blocks the road and thwarts early-season hiking plans. Usually you could drive from Silverton to Animas Forks by late May, but in 2019 it wasn't possible until August because of a huge avalanche from Grouse Gulch.

Altitude sickness brings on lightheadedness or headaches. Often symptoms will subside with a quick rest and slower pace. If these symptoms become severe, the way to recover is to hike to a lower altitude. Remember to stay hydrated; sometimes headaches are simply caused by not drinking enough water.

Snowfields and **scree fields** (loose dirt that you can basically slide down on your hiking boots) can help speed you down a mountainside or land you in deep trouble. Particularly with snow, the risk should be obvious: Get going too fast or out of control, and suddenly you're speeding down a steep slope on your butt. The landing is a rocky runout below—or worse. Broken legs and heads can result. Bring an ice axe and know how to use it if you're going to glissade down a snowfield. Know the runout zone. Be smart. Scree fields are generally a little safer. The problem comes when scree suddenly disappears and you find yourself on hard dirt, but you can't stop so easily, if at all. Be careful and think ahead.

It won't keep you from making bad decisions and getting hurt, but it's a good idea to have a Colorado Outdoor Recreation Search & Rescue (**CORSAR**) card. The fund it creates helps defray counties' costs for search and rescue expenses. Without it, those search and rescue teams you rely on may not be able to respond as quickly, or as well, to your emergency. The cards are available at many outdoor gear and fishing/hunting stores. La Plata and San Juan counties, by the way, have two of the finest search and rescue squads in the country.

GEAR ESSENTIALS

In addition to decent hiking boots, a day pack with adequate water and food for the day, and an extra clothing layer or two (depending on the altitude), there are a few pieces of gear that you should seriously consider packing. Some of these items will only be necessary in an emergency. If you start out the day with absolute certainty there will be no emergency, then I think the likelihood of your needing one of these items goes up.

RECOMMENDED GEAR:

These are what I recommend as essentials to have on hand when hiking.

- Headlamp.
- Bivouac sack/space blanket. This is extremely valuable in keeping an injured hiker warm, particularly if they go into shock. It's also handy for unplanned overnights.
- Water purification. Whether it's tablets or a UV "pen" or filter, don't head into the wilderness without it.
- Sunscreen.
- Matches, compass, knife, perhaps a whistle.
- Extra insulation. Synthetic is best. And don't forget rain gear. Sunny days turn cloudy quickly in the San Juan Mountains.
- First-aid kit. (Details on the contents are below.)
- Extra calories and water. Experience helps determine how much food and water you need, but it doesn't hurt to overestimate.
- A hiking partner. On easy and moderate hikes this isn't as important. But if you get hurt, you'll want some help.
- A small rope. Again, this isn't necessary for all hikes. But when you're on steep scrambles and exposed ridges, an 8-millimeter cord about 10 meters long can be a lifesaver. It weighs less than a pound.

FIRST-AID KIT

Not everyone will have an identical first-aid kit, and that's okay. Just make sure that whoever in your group is bringing one (someone must!) that includes the essentials. This is one example of a first-aid kit. It is carried by Leo Lloyd, a fire department paramedic who also serves with La Plata County Search & Rescue and is an international instructor with Rigging for Rescue.

- Baggie with an ibuprofen-Tylenol mix. A mix of three ibuprofen to two Tylenol pills works well for moderate to severe pain.

Leo Lloyd's first-aid kit includes gloves, Band-Aids, moleskin, an ibuprofen-Tylenol combo mix, gauze, wraps, tweezers, and scissors. (Photo by Leo Lloyd)

- Band-Aids.
- Moleskin for foot blisters.
- Gauze. This can be applied with pressure directly to a wound to stop bleeding.
- Triangular bandage. This can serve as an arm sling and has other uses.
- A pressure wrap over gauze to stop bleeding. This can be some sort of pressure wrap, such as gauze wrap, elastic wrap, or a triangular bandage.
- Tourniquet. In an emergency, this rubberized piece can stop serious blood loss or double as a wrap.
- Surgical gloves.
- Tweezers.
- Bandage scissors. Scissors will give you an easier, cleaner cut than you can get using a knife.

PLANNING AND COMMUNICATING

Perhaps the most overlooked aspects of an outdoor adventure, planning and communicating can prove critical in preventing or lessening an emergency situation.

- *Plan.* Have a plan, make sure everyone in your group knows what it is, and stick to it unless everyone is there to decide how to alter it.
- *Judgment.* This comes partly with experience, but it's important to evaluate your group members and know whose judgment to trust. If you're the

leader, make sure you don't involve others in situations they can't handle.

- *Communicate.* Before any trip, decide who's bringing the maps and the first-aid kit, and what the plan is. Don't wait till you get to the trailhead to discuss these important details. Also, communicate frequently during a hike or climb and stay together with your group; separating from the group commonly causes or compounds serious problems.
- *Navigation.* Bring maps, preferably physical rather than virtual ones. Cellular phones and GPS units can lose service, die, or malfunction. Personal locator beacons, preferably ones that can send texts, are becoming increasingly popular and useful. You can use one to send a distress message via satellite, and the receiver will show your location. A decent one goes for around $350.

Accidents happen, but there's a lot you can do to keep accidents from leading to life-threatening emergencies.

FINAL NOTE

I've wrestled often with the issue of how much to divulge in trail descriptions. The bottom line is: I just don't want to give away all the secrets.

I'll tell you some "well-known secrets" (I like that contradiction), but I'm not going to go out of my way to tell you everything. You wouldn't *want* me to give away everything. What fun is that? You want to discover things on your own. You want that element of surprise and delight when you see something unexpected. If you want someone to reveal every little detail—every waterfall, every swimming hole, every peak, and every flower you will see—then by all means, find a book or blog that does this.

Every hike is an adventure. Wilderness is out there to be explored, to captivate, and to surprise. My hope is you will use this book to capture that experience.

Pointing to a ridge that I'm not going to attempt between Wetterhorn and Matterhorn. (Photo by Steve Chapman)

TECHNOLOGY

In this day and age, I guess I would find this situation embarrassing: I'm lost or injured in the woods and have no phone even though I'm in cell range. Or I have a phone with cell coverage but can't tell anyone where I am because I don't know.

Of course, technology is continually changing even as I write this book, and I can actually be kind of a Luddite, but I'd be remiss if I didn't point out the ways that electronic devices can enhance your hike and help get you out of trouble. GPS (Global Positioning System) devices and phone apps are helpful methods of measuring and plotting your route, and communicating with others. Use your devices to your best advantage, but it's important to understand their limitations too.

Here's a brief description of some of the technology and apps out there.

GPS UNITS

To figure out where you are, this is still the best method. GPS is a method of triangulating your position on the planet using satellites hovering 12,000-plus miles above the Earth. Your GPS unit can determine within a few feet where you stand. If your GPS unit also has a downloaded map, then you're set for navigating. Even if it doesn't, you can still use it to get back to where you were—a previously tracked trail or waypoint, for instance. It's very handy.

Garmin dominates the GPS market, but there are other brands.

YOUR SMARTPHONE

With your Android, iPhone, or other smartphone, you can download several apps to help you navigate around the planet.

For hiking, GaiaGPS currently seems to be the go-to app. You can use the free version, or pay about $20 a year to download maps and have access to other helpful perks. Gaia acts much like a GPS unit. It tells you where you are and records your track so you can look at all the stats later and relive the hike, if that's what you're into. It's fun and informative. Strava is another app that uses GPS to determine your place and track your progress. It's a popular one among cyclists and runners, but there's no reason hikers can't use it.

To figure out what peaks you're seeing on the horizon, there's PeakFinder AR or PeakVisor, among others. Both of these work offline.

There are also apps for learning knots (Animated Knots by Grog), identifying flowers (iNaturalist), and showing the nearest spot where you can get cell phone reception (Cairn). It doesn't end there.

Here I am hard at work atop US Grant Peak. (Photo by Peter Schertz)

PERSONAL LOCATOR BEACON

This was also mentioned in the Introduction. These walkie-talkie–sized devices use satellites and will work to send out an emergency message where cell phones may not. The personal locator beacon (PLB) sends an SOS and your location to rescue agencies. PLBs have the capability to work around the world.

Satellite messengers are a step up from PLBs. These send distress signals and allow the user to send texts and have two-way communication. The more information rescuers have, the better off they and you will be. These aren't cheap. As mentioned above, the base price is about $350, and with satellite messengers you also need to be on a subscription plan, so that adds another expense.

There are many options with PLBs and satellite messengers, and the technology is expanding rapidly, so research your options to see what's current and to understand whether you truly need this.

Cave Basin Trail ventures into the Weminuche, Colorado's largest wilderness at 488,000 acres.

HIKES IN & NEAR DURANGO

It's obvious Durango is enthusiastic about trails. That enthusiasm started long ago, but the formation back in 1990 of Durango Trails 2000, the local trails advocacy group, really got things cooking. The nonprofit plans routes, energizes the community, and, with mostly volunteer labor, has built or maintains more than 300 miles of trails.

Thanks to the foresight of Durango Trails 2000, the Durango Parks and Recreation Department, La Plata County, the San Juan Mountains Association, and the San Juan National Forest and Bureau of Land Management (and perhaps others I've missed), Durango-area residents can hike—sometimes right out your back door—into the nearby hills and beyond into the high country on your way to explore a diversity of ecosystems. Durango Trails 2000 continues to be at the forefront of trail development, and serves as a model for similar organizations around the region.

If you are wondering why Durango is such a well loved and popular place, trails are a huge reason.

Left, top: Looking down the Barnroof Point trail toward the start, with Twin Buttes on the left. Below: A panorama taken from the Rim Trail shows, from left to right, the Hogsback, Perins Peak, the La Plata Mountains, and Animas City Mountain.

The **Telegraph Trail System** is one popular option. It's covered later in this chapter in the Raider Ridge hike (page 53) and the Meadow Loop/Telegraph Trail hike (page 56). Plenty of other trails exist, and the maps that accompany those hikes show many of the various trails.

There is a mile-long trail up **Smelter Mountain**, accessed near the start of CR 210. To get there: As you're leaving downtown heading south on US 550/160, after crossing the Animas River take a right at the next light. Then quickly take a right onto CR 210, then another right onto a paved access road that leads to the Animas-La Plata intake facility. Go 100 yards and park in the dirt lot on the left (N 37 15.200, W 107 52.726, 6,520 feet). Start hiking downhill briefly to cross a ravine, then steeply uphill to the northwest. Go 1 mile to reach a nice viewpoint just before the mass of communication towers and just as you hit the access road coming from that direction (N 37 15.763, W 107 53.354, 7,560 feet).

A couple of notes on Smelter: Between December 1 and April 15 it's only open from 10 a.m. to 2 p.m., and dogs are not allowed; this is to protect deer and elk. At all times, dogs must be on a leash to keep them from harassing wildlife. Parks and Wildlife asks humans and dogs to both respect wildlife from a distance.

Just north of the Smelter trailhead, the approximately 10-acre **Durango Dog Park** lies under the north shadow of Smelter Mountain, just west of the Animas River where US 550/160 crosses it. There is room for a few cars in a dirt lot near the park entrance (N 37 16.086, W 107 53.210), which is south of US 160 and just west of Roosa Avenue. It's also possible to access the dog park from the Smelter trailhead; follow an old road north about a half-mile to the park.

Several trails, or trail systems, appear on the map on the facing page. Here is a description of most of them:

Centennial Nature Trail is used by many Fort Lewis College students because it connects the lower town areas with the college campus and the Rim Trail. The Nature Trail can be found near the junction of East Sixth Avenue and Tenth Street. Through a series of switchbacks, the trail moves up some 250 feet to the campus mesa, coming out on the west side of the campus just south of the little chapel on the rim. At this same junction at Sixth and Tenth you'll find the "Sky Steps," 530 steps that go straight up the mountainside and are a favorite for athletes in training. At the top, you can catch the Rim Trail.

The **Rim Trail** takes a little sleuthing to follow, particularly on the southern end, but you can make a complete 2.7-mile loop around campus. If you go counter-clockwise from where the Centennial Nature Trail meets it, you'll cross Eighth Avenue (N 37 16.385, W 107 52.181), go south and then northeast, paralleling Goeglein Gulch Road for a while. You'll pass by the eleventh hole at Hillcrest Golf Club, cross Rim Drive near a three-way intersection (N 37 16.877, W 107 51.943), take a left,

CITY TRAILS

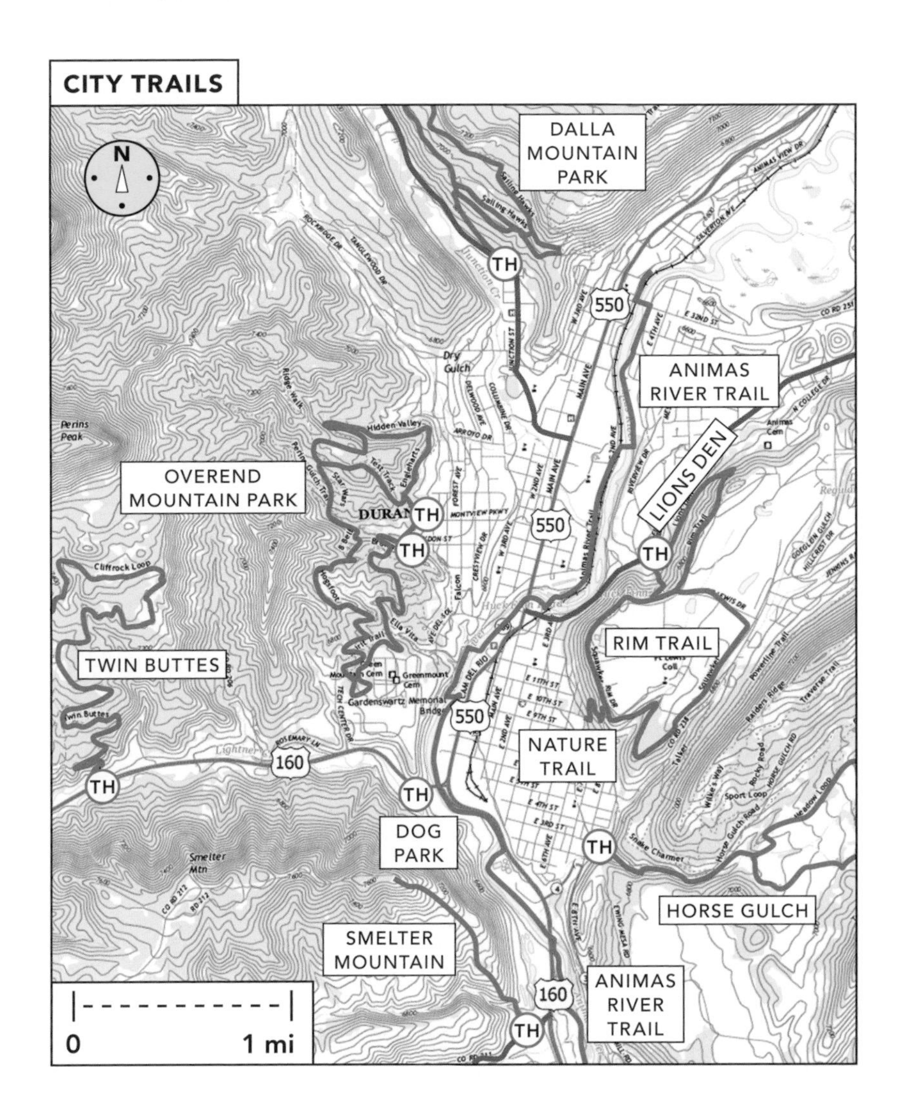

and then walk by the top of the city's Chapman Hill Ski Area. (Another good way to access the Rim Trail is to come up the Lions Den Trail from Chapman Hill.)

The west and northwest parts of the Rim Trail offer excellent views over town and the La Plata Mountains across the valley.

Chapman Hill–Lions Den Trails can be reached by going northeast 0.5 miles on Florida Road from the intersection of East Third Avenue and Fifteenth Street. Park in the Chapman Hill recreation area lot. Look for a trail just north of the skating rink; that's the Lions Den Trail (N 37 17.050, W 107 52.040). Take it about a mile uphill, then veer right at an intersection to contour the hillside (a left takes you up to the actual Lions Den and you meet Rim Drive at the golf course clubhouse).

It's another quarter-mile south, paralleling Rim Drive just west of the golf course, to the intersection with the Rim Trail. If you take the Rim Trail west from here a couple hundred yards, you can get back down to the Chapman Hill parking area via a steep road closed to traffic.

The **Animas River Trail** is an asphalt and concrete route that follows the river closely all the way from the north end of town to the south end. Planning and construction took twenty or thirty years, depending on who's counting, and it was ceremoniously finished in 2005. However, extensions on both ends and new crossings and connections remain in the works.

The River Trail is a bit over 7 miles long but will grow. On the north end, it starts at the intersection of Thirty-Second Street and East Third Avenue (N 37 17.702, W 107 52.203) on the north end of Memorial Park. A restroom open during warm-weather months and parking are available at Twenty-Ninth Street. In less than a half-mile, the trail crosses the river over a good footbridge. It continues south along the river around the east side of the high school grounds, crosses a bridge over Junction Creek, and goes behind the Durango Public Library. Then it crosses another footbridge, goes past a gazebo at Rotary Park, and heads under Main Avenue (N 37 16.838, W 107 52.701).

The trail continues behind businesses on the east side of the river to Iris Park. There, a nice bridge takes you across to the west side of the Animas River at the north end of Schneider Park and next to a skate park. After a couple blocks you cross the Animas again at the Ninth Street Bridge, then loop around and under the bridge.

Found along the Rim Trail, this metal sculpture molded in the shape of the surrounding mountains is part of the Peter Carver Geologic Overlook, a memorial for a young Durangoan who died in an avalanche in 2013.

A great view of Durango from Smelter Mountain.

After passing the DoubleTree Hotel, the trail goes under the US 160 bridge (N 37 16.125, W 107 53.150). It proceeds south along the highway about a mile to Whitewater Park, goes under another highway bridge, and crosses to the west side of the river over a rickety, wooden-planked bridge. It moves along a nice riparian area without any development for a half-mile until coming to a BMX track. (A bridge from the BMX track links to the Rivergate townhomes and Animas Surgical Hospital). The River Trail continues uphill another half-mile, and then continues on a neat cantilever over a steep section to begin its way around the Durango Mall. It again crosses the Animas near the highway, then goes past the Humane Society, Walmart, Escalante Middle School, and Home Depot before ending. Keep in mind there are numerous access points to the River Trail along its route.

Overend Mountain Park encompasses a series of hills and valleys in nearly 300 acres of wild land on Durango's western boundary that was acquired by the city in the 1990s. The lowest point of the park is about 6,600 feet at the city boundary; the highest point is the Hogsback (see page 33) at 7,484 feet, giving a net relief of 884 feet.

There is a network of approximately 15 miles of trails, providing some good short exploratory hikes. Some trails are steep and some are gentle. Winter also can be good for snowshoeing and ski touring, although most times snow just makes a mucky mess of things, particularly in the spring. You could get lost in the maze of trails, but not badly, because Durango is always to the east of you and is visible from various high points.

Overend Mountain Park is named for Ned Overend, who is not only the first official world mountain bike champion (1990 at Purgatory), but also was one of the landowners who agreed to sell this land to the city for a decent price. Ed Zink and Scott Fleming were among the others.

The area is composed of Mancos Shale: a gray, flaky soil that is usually soft at the surface. Some places are bare, while others have piñon pines and junipers along with some large ponderosa pines.

There are several access points. A primary one is at the west end of Leyden Street in the Crestview area (N 37 17.054, W 107 53.264). A map is posted on a sign at the trailhead. One trail sticks to the main gulch, known locally as Slime Gulch, but side trails begin branching off, one immediately to the right. Other options soon branch off to the left uphill.

There is also access off the west end of Montview Parkway, and Arroyo Drive at its intersection with North Glenisle Avenue. South of Leyden, you can cross the drainage ditch at the intersection of Kearney Street and Glenisle Avenue. This route goes up steeply at first. If you explore, you'll find other trails, and unofficial trails. Please honor private property signs.

Overend Mountain Park is very popular with mountain bikers, and hikers need to be on the lookout for sudden biker appearances around sharp corners. Bikers owe the right of way to hikers, but hikers should stay alert to their presence. Dogs must be on a leash in this park.

Dalla Mountain Park is another city-owned parcel with myriad trails. It's very popular with dog walkers and sport climbers. If it's popular with climbers, that means there are plenty of rocks and boulders, some of them huge, all of them sandstone. There are also trees (mostly piñons) growing out of these boulders everywhere, a reaffirming sign of the tenacity of life. To get there, go west off Main Avenue up Twenty-Fifth Street. Go 1 mile and look for the parking area on the right. There are several miles of trails winding about this 176-acre parcel the city of Durango purchased from previous owner Jake Dalla in 2005. This area, still known locally as "Sailing Hawks," abuts Animas City Mountain, and those trail systems are linked.

Located northeast of town off Florida Road is the 1.2-mile-long **Pioneer Trail**. It's popular with people in the Edgemont development nearby. From the intersection of CR 250 (East Animas Road) and CR 240 (Florida Road), go 3 miles up Florida Road. About 150 yards before the big sign for Edgemont Ranch (a subdivision), look for a gravel road on the left. Drive up that gravel road for 100 yards to a very small parking area (N 37 18.796, W 107 47.933, 7,360 feet), and there you'll find the trailhead. The trail begins by heading south, going right up to the Edgemont sign, then switching back northward, winding its way uphill through a ponderosa-dominated forest. At 1.2 miles it ends abruptly at Nusbaum Road (N 37 19.423, W 107 47.743, 7,900 feet). You've climbed 540 feet.

Pioneer is probably best for a quick out-and-back. But if you hike up Nusbaum, which turns into Silver Mesa Driveway, it's about a mile to the San Juan National Forest, at which point a barrier prevents cars from getting through. From the barrier, it's approximately 2.5 miles to the Missionary Ridge Trail, which you hit a mile or so north of the top of Haflin Creek.

Twin Buttes trail system also deserves a mention. This area is certainly a hotspot for mountain bikers, but the 12 miles of trails—built by Trails 2000 volunteer crews—

are multi-use. This marvelous system was created in conjunction with a development west of town that has been annexed by the city of Durango. Open space land was deeded to the city by the developers, and parts of trails actually wend through the subdivision or close to it. It's just 1.5 miles west of town on US 160. Go just past the gas station on the north side of the highway and turn right toward Animas High School, then quickly turn into a dirt lot on the right to park. The lower trails are open year-round, but the upper trails are closed from December 1 to April 15 to protect wildlife habitats.

HOGSBACK

DISTANCE: 2 miles round-trip

ELEVATION: Start at 6,660 feet, finish at 7,484 feet (824-foot gain)

RATING: Moderate, due to steep finish

TIME ALLOWED: 1¼ hours

Hogsback Trail is part of Overend Mountain Park, with the top on the far west side. It is distinct enough to deserve special attention. It is the most challenging and most rewarding hike in the park. It's possible to climb on a long lunch break.

From the top of the Hogsback, looking down at the ridgetop trail toward town.

APPROACH: Use the Leyden Street access. Reach Leyden from town by taking Twenty-Second Street west off Main Avenue. The street angles to the top of Crestview Mesa, where it becomes Montview Parkway; follow this west to Glenisle, then south one block to Leyden, and west again to the end of Leyden (N 37 17.054, W 107 53.264). Respect local residents while parking and starting your trek. As you drive up Leyden, you'll see both the Hogsback and Perins Peak beyond it.

HIKE: Take the trail over a large culvert and follow it along a usually dry gulch. In just over 0.1 mile a trail branches at a 120-degree angle left uphill. You can take this, or you can go another 0.2 miles to a second left, which is a little less steep (N 37 17.126, W 107 53.557). Both of these trails top out to join a larger, more gradual trail that goes west toward Hogsback.

The trail twists and turns through some brush, eventually reaching open shale. The last two pitches are steep and can usually be done standing up—the shale has good footholds—but if conditions are wet or very dry, you'll probably slide a bit. Near the top is a very narrow spot where you must be careful not to slip, lest you take a steep, unscheduled glissade in the shale for 150 feet. The steep area is on the left part of the trail; it is a good idea to hold onto the brush on the right side. On the top (N 37 17.063, W 107 53.954, 7,484 feet) at 1 mile there is a nice single slab of sandstone that becomes your reward for huffing and puffing. It is a good place to lie down and rest or to sit and study the scenery: the city below, Perins Peak to the west, the West Needles to the north-northeast.

You can return on the same route, or you can make a loop.

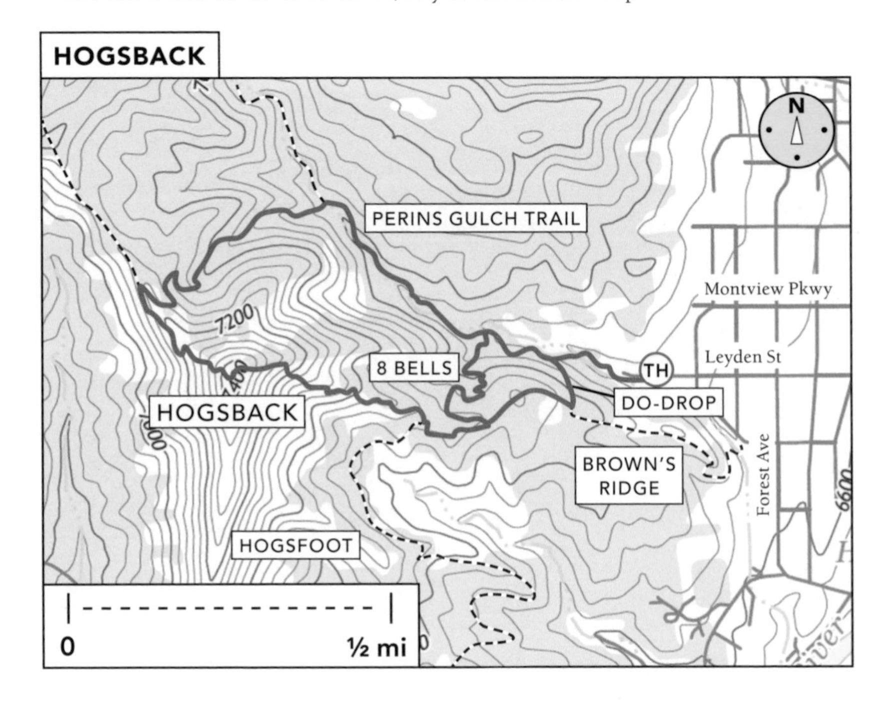

OPTIONS: A trail goes west off the Hogsback, and it's *really* steep for the first 30 yards. It's doable if you're careful. Follow this trail along a ridge for a quarter-mile from the top, then take a right (east) off the ridge (N 37 17.177, W 107 54.105, 7,100 feet) and drop down a winding trail about a half-mile, where the trail crosses Slime Gulch on a wooden bridge and comes to an intersection (N 37 17.286, W 107 53.781, 6,840 feet). Take a right, and follow this trail 0.6 miles to Leyden Street. Making this loop, which is all in Overend Mountain Park, adds 0.3 miles to the trip.

PERINS PEAK

DISTANCE: 5.4 miles round-trip

ELEVATION: Start at 6,885 feet, finish at 8,340 feet (1,455-foot gain)

RATING: Moderate

TIME ALLOWED: 2½ to 4 hours

With its distinctive profile, Perins Peak is a town icon. Its top has a sharp, pointed cliff that faces east and looks down over Durango like a guardian.

It was named after Charles Perin, a civil engineer who laid out the grid for the town when it was incorporated in 1881.

You can only do this hike during one-third of the year, from August 1 through November 30. The Perins Peak Trail goes through both state (Colorado Parks and Wildlife) and federal (Bureau of Land Management) land. The restrictions are there to protect the peregrine falcon, which was once an endangered species, as well as big-game species whose young are born in this area. But this is good hiking and it's worth waiting for the open period. Also, it has the advantage of starting right out from the city limits.

The first part is easy, but the last thousand feet of altitude gain are moderately difficult due to steepness. It is a vigorous hike, rewarding for the workout you'll get and for the nice view of both the La Plata Mountains and Durango.

APPROACH: From Main Avenue in Durango, go left (west) on Twenty-Fifth Street. After 0.5 miles, or two blocks past Miller Middle School, take a left onto Clovis Drive. At 0.9 miles Clovis continues into the Rockridge subdivision and becomes Rockridge Drive. Go up this drive and, just before reaching the end, go right briefly on Tanglewood and take another quick left that takes you back to a parking area.

HIKE: Locate the trailhead at a gate (N 37 18.394, W 107 53.809, 6,885 feet) and begin the hike. You'll quickly come to a fork. Take the path left, crossing Dry Gulch. The path right is the Dry Gulch Trail. The north massif of Perins looms above. You could also climb this, but this trail description is of the east massif overlooking town.

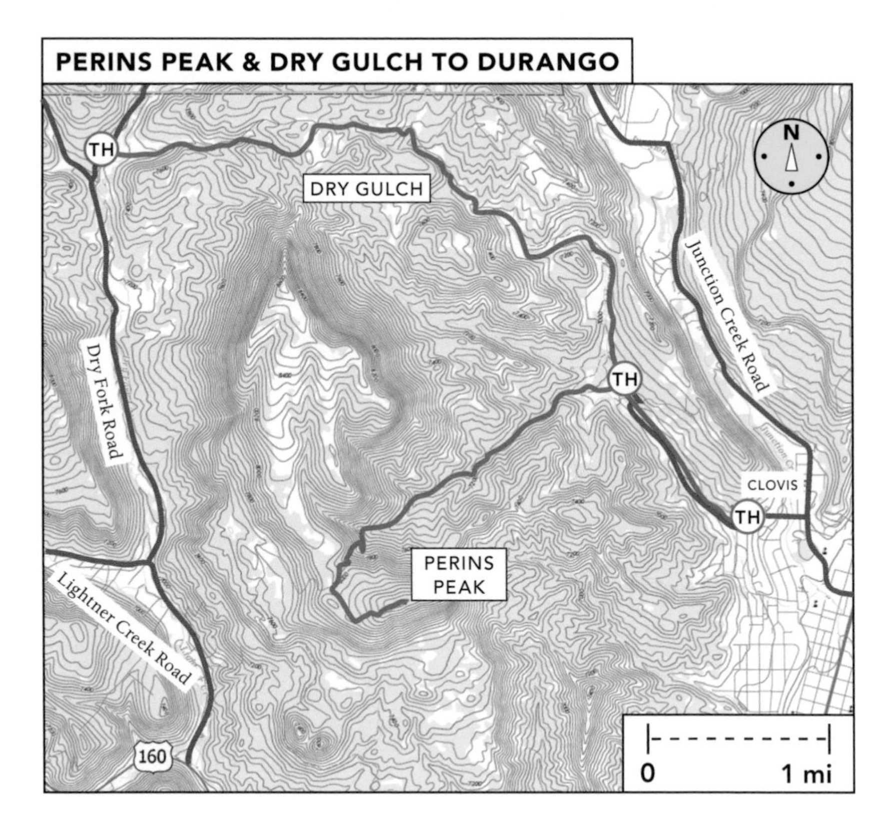

In 1.3 miles the climbing begins in earnest, and the trail switchbacks up the mountain. At 2 miles the trail has basically reached the mesa top, although it still climbs gently.

Reach an old road at 2.2 miles and go left (east) on it, steeply uphill again (N 37 17.475, W 107 55.341, 8,000 feet). Reach the high point of the climb at 2.7 miles (N 37 17.435, W 107 54.992, 8,340 feet).

OPTIONS: You may feel like wandering eastward over to the point where you get a better view of town. There's a little bit of downhill, and take care when you get near the ledge.

Another option—if you're up for an adventure—is to climb the north Perins massif. Return to the 2.2-mile mark and take the trail heading left. (Down to your left around here is the old Boston Coal Mine and Perins City, which you may find traces of.) From the 2.2-mile junction it's 2 miles along a path that is ill defined or nonexistent to this northern point, which ends in a serious cliff at 8,682 feet—340 feet higher than the peak we typically call Perins.

The impressive beak of Perins Peak, seen from the ridge just below the Hogsback.

DRY GULCH TO DURANGO

DISTANCE: 5.1 miles one-way

ELEVATION: Start at 7,315 feet, high point at 7,745 feet (430-foot gain), finish at 6,685 feet (1,060-foot drop)

RATING: Easy

TIME ALLOWED: 2 to 3 hours

Like the Perins Peak hike, this travels through land subject to wildlife closures. The Dry Gulch hike described here is all on Colorado Parks and Wildlife land, and is open for four months: August 1 through November 30. The closure is to protect breeding elk and deer in the winter, and nesting peregrine in the spring and early summer.

The peregrine has been officially delisted from the endangered species list, but the closure has remained in place to protect this still-rare bird that is said to reach over 200 miles per hour when diving at prey. If one swoops anywhere near you, you'll hear it. It's very cool.

Perins Peak's north summit, as seen from the Dry Gulch Trail.

Note that hunting season begins in late August for archery and extends nearly through the end of December, depending on the animal and location. It's a really good idea to wear a blaze orange vest, particularly during big-game rifle season in October and November. Check the Colorado Parks and Wildlife site (cpw.state.co.us) for specific dates.

The hike involves a vehicle shuttle. For the last mile of the hike you'll be walking on a good gravel pedestrian path through the Rockridge subdivision. If you want to avoid this part, take your waiting vehicle up to the Perins Peak trailhead (see Perins Peak approach on page 35).

APPROACH: Drive west of Durango 3.5 miles on US 160 to a right turn on Lightner Creek Road (CR 207). Follow it 1 mile north to where Dry Fork Road (CR 208), a gravel road, veers off it to the right (north). This puts you into the wildlife area.

Continue 2 miles north, and where the road splits in a Y go right. Go another 0.25 miles to a cattleguard. Turn right, and go downhill in front of the guard to a small parking area (N 37 19.442, W 107 56.576).

The hike begins here; it ends at the intersection of Clovis and Borrego Drives on the west side of Durango, where another car can be parked. To find this spot from Durango, take Twenty-Fifth Street west off Main Avenue 0.5 miles to a left-hand turn on Clovis Drive. Follow Clovis to the top of a hill, where you'll turn left onto Borrego.

The trail end is just south of that intersection (N 37 17.774, W 107 53.154).

HIKE: From the western trailhead (N 37 19.438, W 107 56.574, 7,315 feet), cross Dry Fork and start hiking east. There should be a semblance of a trail or old road in this area, or maybe just a path through tamped-down grass. If you can follow the old, overgrown road, stick with it. Head up a shallow valley. In about a mile the north buttress of Perins Peak comes into view.

At 1.2 miles you will reach the high point of the hike (N 37 19.554, W 107 55.486, 7,745 feet) in a cluster of big ponderosa pines. From here on it is downhill, tending southeast, alternating between tall pines and open meadows as you follow the approximate path of Dry Gulch (not to be confused with Dry Fork, by the way).

Soon you'll begin to see signs of civilization: a huge house to the north of Dry Gulch, then a couple of houses on the western outskirts of the Rockridge subdivision. You also may get lucky and see elk or deer, or bear, or even wild turkeys. Keep an eye open.

At 4.1 miles, pass through a gate and into a parking area for both this trail and the Perins Peak Trail (N 37 18.394, W 107 53.809, 6,885 feet). Hunters, of course, are frequent users of this lot. Continue down the road, cross Tanglewood, and find the gravel pedestrian path. At 5.1 miles, come to the intersection of Borrego and Clovis, locate your waiting vehicle, and try to remember where you placed your car keys.

BARNROOF POINT

DISTANCE: 5 miles round-trip

ELEVATION: Start at 6,960 feet, Barnroof's top is 8,723 (1,763-foot gain)

RATING: Moderate, due to difficult bushwhacking

TIME ALLOWED: 3 to 4 hours

Two things you should know before attempting this hike:

One, Barnroof is heavily vegetated, especially with ponderosa pine and oak brush. The brush is from knee-high to 10 or 12 feet. It can be a real thicket, hard to get through, and hard to see where you're going near the top as it flattens out. Because part of this hike will require bushwhacking, you should probably wear long pants. No, you should definitely wear long pants if you plan on reaching the top. The last half-mile is extremely thick.

Two, Barnroof Point is on Colorado Parks and Wildlife and US Bureau of Land Management property, and is closed to human traffic from December 1 (the end of hunting season) through April 15. Deer, elk, and grouse can often be seen on this mountain.

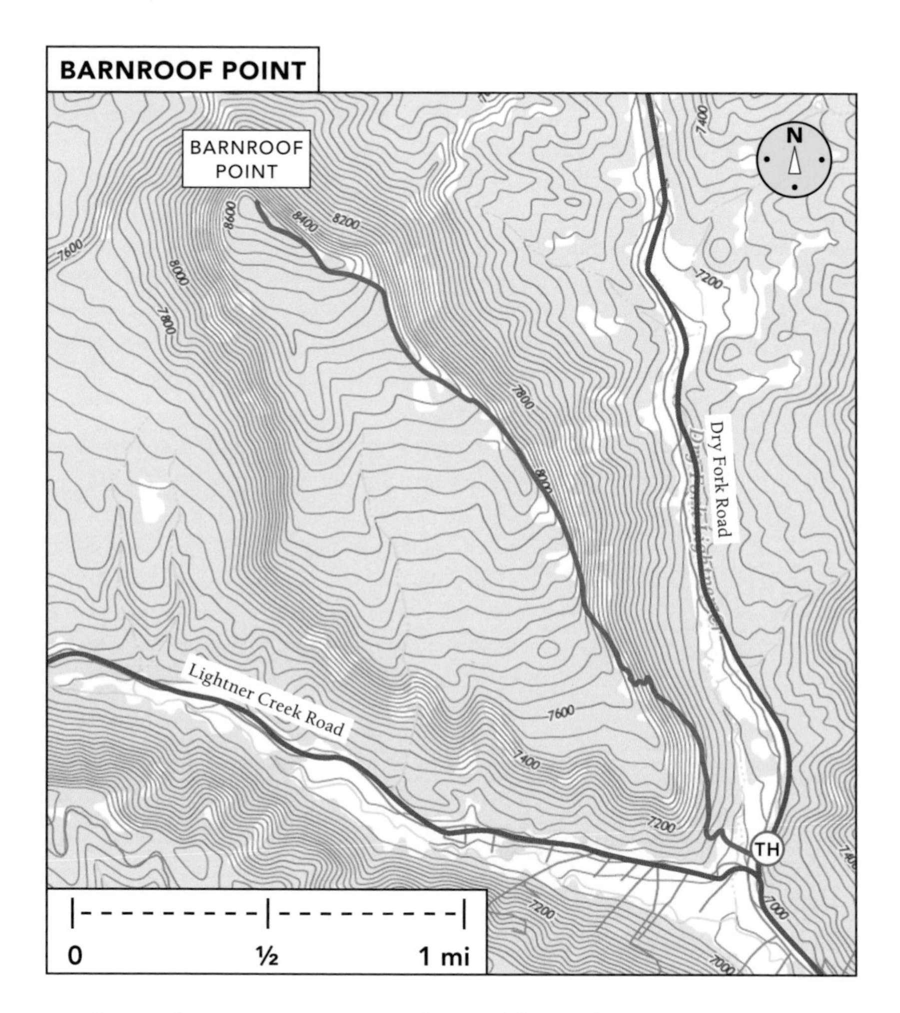

Barnroof is a low mountain southeast of the La Platas. It is interesting in that it stands as a single peak with valleys on all sides. This makes it a nice climb for presenting good views of surrounding territory, particularly the east side of the La Platas.

APPROACH: Drive west of Durango 3.5 miles on US 160 to a right turn on Lightner Creek Road (CR 207). Follow it 1 mile north to where Dry Fork Road, a gravel road, veers off it to the right (north). Turn onto this gravel road, then park immediately in a large parking area to the left (N 37 17.647, W 107 56.381, 6,960 feet). This is Parks and Wildlife land.

HIKE: Begin hiking by crossing Dry Fork, usually a very small stream or dry, and heading up the other side. Snake up an unmaintained path, and in 0.2 miles you'll hit an abandoned road that nowadays looks more like just a trail. Follow this uphill (north).

After 0.5 miles this road ends; follow a less obvious trail that contours along for about a hundred feet then goes very steeply uphill. You may need to use your hands along this stretch, and if it's muddy, it'll be slick enough that you may want to go do another hike. After this steep scramble you'll find yourself on the rim of what could be described as a gently uphill sloping mesa top (N 37 18.033, W 107 56.713, 7,630 feet).

Once on this rim, it will be easygoing for a while. The best bet is to stay close to the rim, but not so close that it scares the bejesus out of you—it's a long way down. There will be many fine views of the valleys below and the peaks beyond.

The farther you go, the tougher the going gets and the less of a trail there is. At 2 miles, after more than a mile along the rim, the brush becomes very dense, and it's very difficult to see where you're going. Just continue up, up, up, bearing northwest, pushing through the dense brush, and ultimately, in another 0.5 miles you'll find yourself at the top (N 37 19.008, W 107 57.693, 8,723 feet).

The view of the La Platas from the high point, the northwest corner of this sloping mesa, is fantastic. With a deep valley between, foothills sweep upward to the rocky high peaks, forming a majestic view.

The sights from atop the rim on Barnroof Point, looking down on Dry Fork Road.

COLORADO TRAIL: JUNCTION TO GUDY'S

DISTANCE: 8.6 miles round-trip to Gudy's Rest

ELEVATION: Start at 6,960 feet, Gudy's Rest at 8,000 feet (1,040-foot gain)

RATING: Easy

TIME ALLOWED: 4 to 5½ hours

If you hike much around these parts, it won't be too long before you bump into the Colorado Trail, a 486-mile tread that connects southwest Denver and the Durango environs. There have been pushes to lengthen the trail into downtown Durango, but those haven't gained traction, so for now it's about 4 miles by paved road from the town to the trailhead.

Southwest Colorado is fortunate to have a high percentage of these 486 miles, because the trail must do a lot of winding to get through the rugged San Juan Mountains. There are 78 miles of the trail in the Animas District (where Durango is located) of the San Juan National Forest alone.

This hike begins at the Durango trailhead. Other hikes on the Colorado Trail or parts of it are scattered throughout this book: Dry Fork Loop (page 45), Sliderock Trail to Kennebec Pass (page 68), Grizzly Peak (page 143), Hermosa Peak (page 149), Molas Trail (page 161), Sultan–Grand Turk (page 163), and Colorado Trail/ Molas Pass (page 166). Another option is to take 5 to 7 weeks and backpack the whole darn thing—Denver to Durango, or vice versa—but that's not what this book is about.

The Colorado Trail was conceived, and actually started, in the 1970s but soon languished. The idea nearly died until three groups got together and combined sponsorship: the US Forest Service, one of the originators of the concept; the Friends of the Colorado Trail, a group organized specifically to plan and promote construction of the trail; and the Colorado Mountain Club.

Gudy Gaskill (1927–2016) was appointed chairperson of the Club's Huts and Trails Committee. The plan was to use existing trails as much as possible and to work out new connections between them. Progress was still slow and doubt grew over the next decade that the trail would ever be completed. In 1985 the project received a huge boost from Richard Lamm, then governor of Colorado and an avid hiker and jogger. He and Gudy Gaskill got together and planned to complete the trail within two years with all-volunteer labor. Gudy put a prodigious amount of effort into organizing work teams and assigning them to trail sections. In the last full summer, nearly a thousand volunteers were at work. Those volunteers included old-timers such as Donald Peel (father of this book's author), a longtime Colorado Mountain Club member and president of the club in 1955.

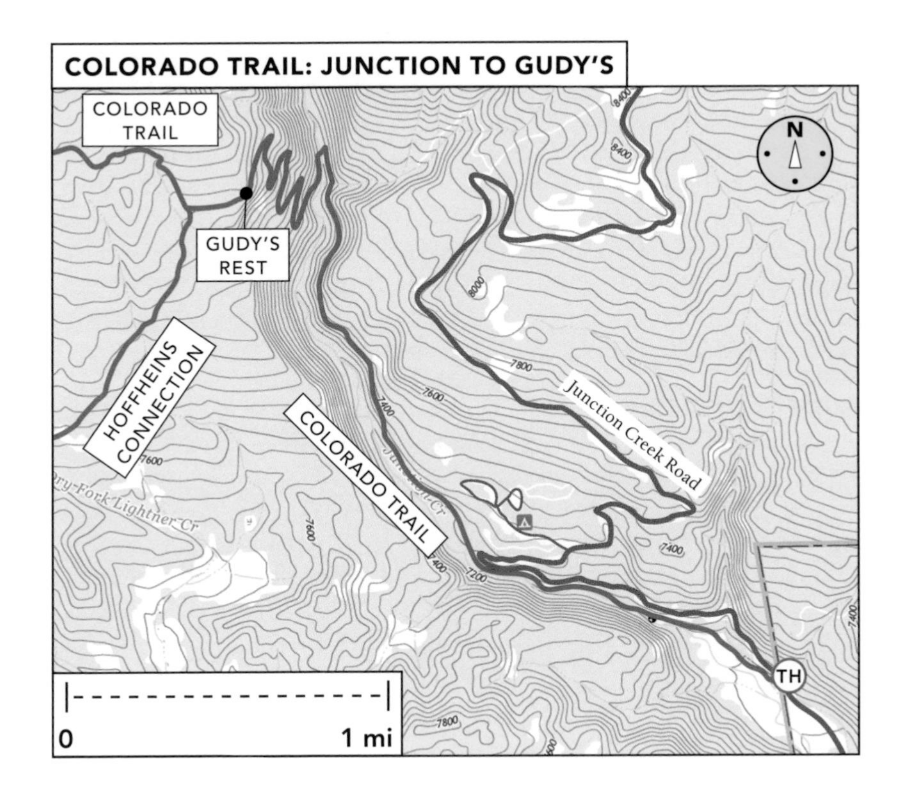

The trail was completed and ceremonies were held to mark the event in Durango and Denver in September 1987. Work has continued since then. Former longtime Durangoan Bill Manning has been director of the Colorado Trail Foundation since 2006. For more information, visit ColoradoTrail.org.

APPROACH: Take Main Avenue to Twenty-Fifth Street and turn left (west). At the edge of town it becomes Junction Creek Road. Follow it 3.5 miles from Main to the San Juan National Forest. Just as you cross the cattleguard that marks the forest boundary, and just as the road turns from pavement to gravel, there's a parking area and outhouse to the left, and the trail begins there (N 37 19.881, W 107 54.165, 6,960 feet).

Or to shorten the trip to Gudy's Rest, continue on the gravel Junction Creek Road for 1.2 miles, where there is a sharp switchback to the northeast; not too far beyond this is the Junction Creek Campground, so if you get there you've gone too far. You can begin hiking west here at this switchback, and in 100 yards (N 37 20.267, W 107 55.194, 7,200 feet) you will strike the Colorado Trail.

HIKE: At first the trail follows closely alongside Junction Creek. This is a popular spot for families and dogs, who have plenty of places to cool off on a hot summer day. At 1.2 miles the trail connects with the spur trail coming from Junction Creek Road (mentioned in the Approach to shorten the hike) and then begins to rise away from the creek. It continues to rise gradually as it contours above—sometimes dizzyingly high above—Junction Creek.

Then at 2.2 miles (N 37 21.024, W 107 55.626, 7,520 feet) the trail begins its descent downhill toward Junction Creek. At 2.7 miles it crosses the stream over a good Forest Service bridge (N 37 21.291, W 107 55.668, 7,410 feet). It then begins a series of switchbacks up the steep canyonside. From the bridge, it's 1.6 miles until the trail tops out at a nice rest area called Gudy's Rest (N 37 21.185, W 107 55.900, 8,000 feet); there's a bench there for you to take a break. It's a popular spot to enjoy views down the valley toward Durango and the college mesa above town.

OPTIONS: The trail past Gudy's Rest climbs gradually for 6.2 miles to what's colloquially become known as High Point (9,550 feet). From there it descends 4.1 miles and 1,000 feet back into Junction Creek canyon and crosses Junction Creek at a nice bridge (8,520 feet) that looks out of place in what is basically backcountry. From here on, there is quite a bit of up and down (mostly up); you'll arrive in 4.7 more miles at Champion Venture Road, the next possible road access. This is the beginning of the Sliderock Trail (see page 68).

A wintertime view down Junction Creek from the bench at Gudy's Rest.

DRY FORK–HOFFHEINS LOOP

DISTANCE: 8.5-mile loop

ELEVATION: Start at 7,390 feet, high point at 8,680 feet (1,290-foot gain)

RATING: Easy

TIME ALLOWED: 3½ to 4½ hours

This loop trail starts along a drainage, then splits and moves up through big timber. The upper portion has a much different feel to it—thick woods with big timber—than the lower, drier portion.

This is a very busy trail in nice weather and is used by hikers, bikers, and horseback riders, with bikers predominant. It is a pleasant hike on a good trail and is shady most of the way. It's close to town, and the added elevation takes a little edge off the summer heat.

If anyone's curious, Don Hoffheins is a former Forest Service employee who helped facilitate the building of his namesake trail.

APPROACH: Drive west of Durango 3.5 miles on US 160 to a right turn on Lightner Creek Road (CR 207). Follow it 1 mile north to where Dry Fork Road, a gravel road,

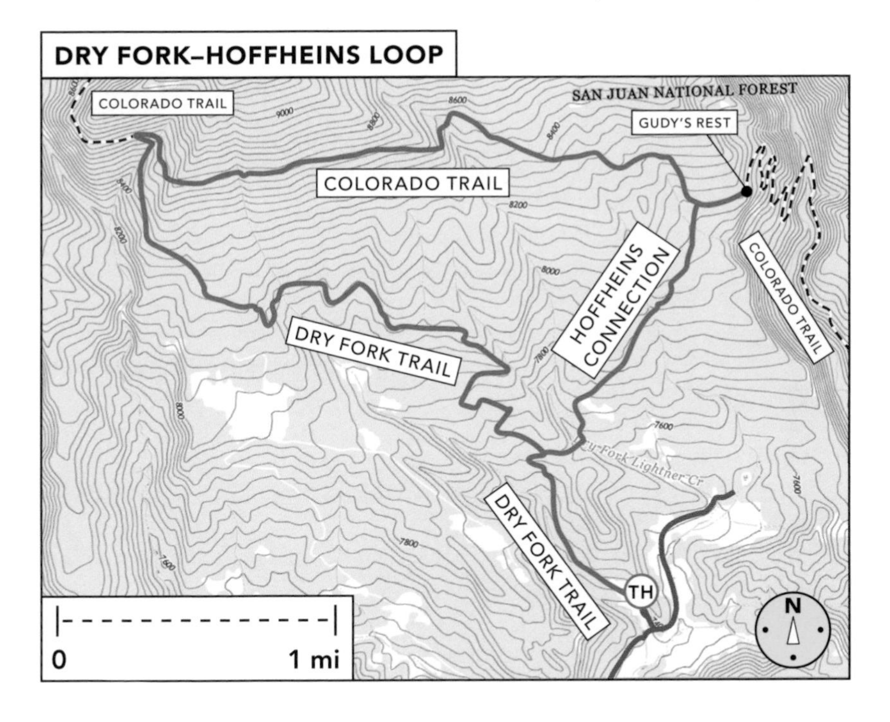

veers off to the right (north). Continue 2 miles north on Dry Fork Road; where the road splits in a Y, go right. Take the right side for 0.8 miles and make a left-hand turn toward the trailhead; there should be a sign directing you to the Hoffheins Connection or Dry Fork trail. In 100 yards you'll come to a large parking area (N 37 19.870, W 107 56.316, 7,390 feet), suitable to turn around a truckload of whatever you may be hauling (bikes, horses, cattle, etc.).

HIKE: Start by crossing through a stock fence over a cattleguard. It's 0.7 miles of mostly uphill trail to a second cattleguard, then uphill another 0.1 mile to a three-way intersection (N 37 20.355, W 107 56.717, 7,650 feet). Your choice—you can go either way. The Dry Fork Trail was built with the mindset of having a relatively easy grade; Hoffheins is steeper in places. For this description we'll go clockwise, heading up the mellower Dry Fork Trail.

Climb gradually, up through aspen and pine forests. At 3 miles you'll join an abandoned road that comes up from your left. At 3.5 miles there's a fork in this road, and it should be pretty obvious to veer right, continuing uphill. Intersect with the Colorado Trail (N 37 21.355, W 107 58.295, 8,580) at 3.9 miles. Take a hard right, now heading east.

Climb a bit more, and at 4.1 miles reach the hike's high point at 8,680 feet. This is a nondescript point, but you will be able to sneak a peek from here through the trees at Silver Mountain to the northwest. Although you're not quite halfway, it's all (almost all) downhill from here. It's 2.3 miles from the high point to where the Hoffheins Connection Trail (N 37 21.131, W 107 56.110, 8,010 feet) splits off to the right (south) at 6.4 miles. But if you have any energy left, you're going to want to make a short detour.

Just one-quarter mile east on the Colorado Trail is a spot called Gudy's Rest (N 37 21.185, W 107 55.900, 8,000 feet; see page 42). It is a beautiful overlook where you can admire the continuing Colorado Trail far below in Junction Creek valley as it nears its Durango terminus. A resting bench has been placed here (actually replaced many, many times due to vandals) to honor Gudy Gaskill (1927–2016), whose stubbornness and hard work helped to complete the Colorado Trail in 1987. This enormous project connects Denver to Durango by foot trail, a distance of 486 miles.

Back at the intersection, take the Hoffheins Connection downhill to the three-way intersection with the Dry Fork Trail at 7.7 miles, and continue the final 0.8 miles downhill to the parking area.

OPTIONS: It's not hard to make this a shorter or longer trip.

For a good short trip, just take the Hoffheins 2.1 miles to the Colorado Trail, and take the detour to Gudy's Rest.

For a longer trip, extend your stay on the Colorado Trail in either direction. Going past Gudy's Rest takes you down to Junction Creek in about 1.4 miles. You also lose about 600 feet elevation.

A cattleguard crossing sends you on the way at the Dry Fork trailhead.

Going west on the Colorado Trail at its junction with the Dry Fork Trail takes you as far as you'd ever want to go. Realistically, it's 3.5 miles of mostly uphill to a place called Road End Canyon, or High Point. From here the trail drops down several hundred feet to Junction Creek. Unless you're looking for an epic hike, it's time to head back.

ANIMAS CITY MOUNTAIN

DISTANCE: 5.5-mile loop

ELEVATION: Start at 6,700 feet, high point at 8,161 feet (1,461-foot gain)

RATING: Easy

TIME ALLOWED: 2½ to 4 hours

This is an easy half-day hike near Durango. It is especially appealing in the fall and spring when the higher country is too chilly or covered with snow.

One caveat, however: This Bureau of Land Management property is closed from December 1 to April 15. During this period the BLM, in cooperation with Colorado Parks and Wildlife, chains off all but the lower part of Animas City Mountain to give elk and deer a quiet place to go.

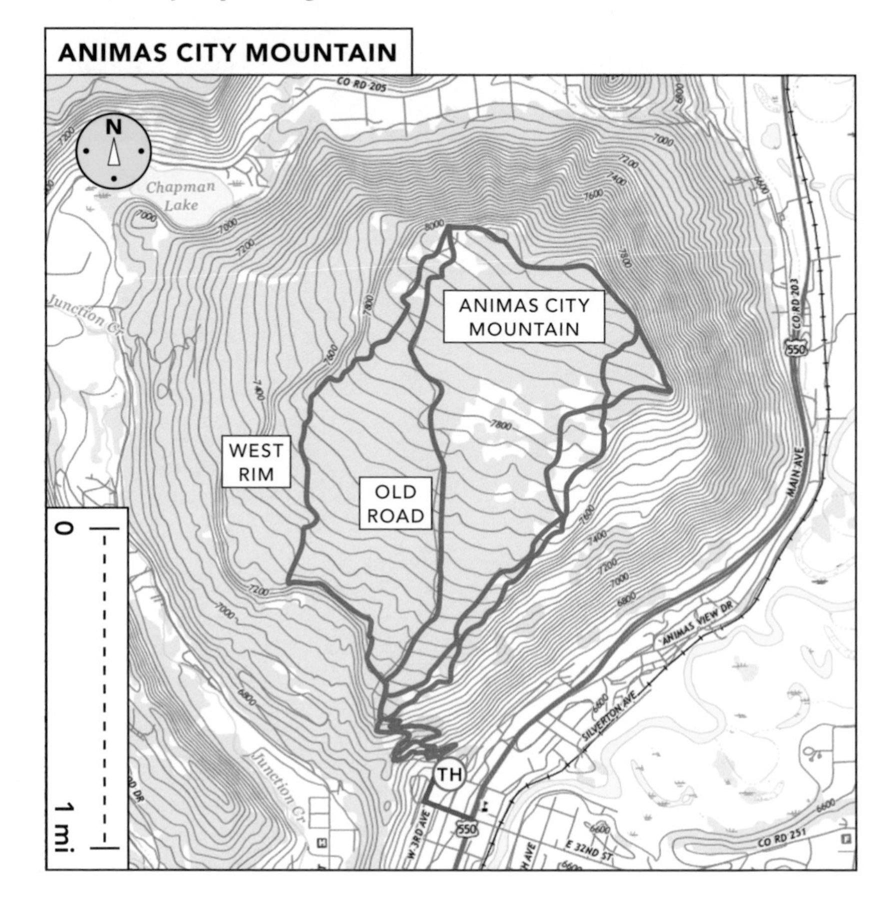

A morning view of Durango on the southeast side of Animas Mountain.

The east (right) side of the loop is two trails that parallel and occasionally cross each other. The west side of the loop is an old four-wheel-drive road that is quite rough on the lower part. There is another trail on the western rim that some prefer due to its gentler slope.

The route described here goes up the west side on the old road and does a clockwise loop.

APPROACH: Take Thirty-Second Street west from Main Avenue in Durango to its west end on West Fourth Avenue. Turn right here and follow West Fourth to its end, where there is an off-camber gravel area for several cars that tend to park willy-nilly (N 37 18.172, W 107 52.354, 6,700 feet).

The trailhead has a sign with a map of the loop, and maps are posted along the route at most of the many intersections.

HIKE: Go north from the parking area; just past a power station you can go either left (steep uphill) or right (gentle uphill). Let's say you go the easy way and go right. This route follows switchbacks uphill. Go right at the first intersection at 0.3 miles, but then stay left at the next one, 0.7 miles from the start. That takes you in about 50 yards to the old four-wheel-drive road, which tends north fairly steeply (N 37 18.303, W 107 52.567, 7,050 feet).

After a steady climb that eases the higher you go, at 2.4 miles you'll come to an impressive overlook with some sandstone outcrops (N 37 19.683, W 107 52.329, 8,080 feet).

At this point you can look down the mountain's steep north side into the Falls Creek Valley and northwest across the valley to the high La Plata Mountains. You can also see up the Animas River Valley to the town of Hermosa and well beyond, up into the West Needles.

To continue the loop from here, go east up the trail. It climbs almost another 100 feet of elevation before finally topping out at 2.6 miles (8,161 feet). The trail dips and rises back to the nearly identical top elevation, then at 2.9 miles it swings south. You'll begin to get nice views of the Animas Valley and the tortuous, winding river amid pastures populated with horses and cattle and homes. There are also some old turns of the river, now bypassed and disconnected, known as oxbows. These accumulate water during snowmelt season or floods.

At 3.1 miles you'll come to the first of three junctions where two branches of the same trail cross each other down the east side of the mountain (N 37 19.429, W 107 51.687). This probably goes without saying, but the views are better if you stay closer to the rim, and the distance is approximately the same. It's 1.9 miles from the first of the three junctions to the intersection near the old four-wheel-drive road. There are several return options from here, but if you go straight here, taking the steeper way down, you'll reach the parking area at 5.5 miles.

OPTIONS: There's a newer trail that goes up the western rim of this uplifted, mesa-like mountain. This trail offers good views of the Falls Creek drainage and the La Plata Mountains during the upper part of the climb. It's a little longer, but it's a little bit less steep than the other two options.

At the spot where you intersect with the old four-wheel-drive road (N 37 18.303, W 107 52.567, 7,050 feet), go up the road 0.1 miles and look for a trail taking off uphill to the left (N 37 18.387, W 107 52.575, 7,160 feet). Take that trail, which hovers around the rim, to a three-way intersection at the 1.4 mile mark (N 37 18.693, W 107 52.898, 7,351 feet).

Go right at the three-way and make your way up very steadily. At 2.9 miles, just as you connect with the other trail on the west side (to your right), you'll reach the rocky outcrop overlook described above.

LOG CHUTES

DISTANCE: 4.7 miles for the short loop, 6.3 miles for the long loop

ELEVATION: Start at 7,520 feet, high point of farthest trail is 8,400 feet (880-foot gain)

RATING: Easy

TIME ALLOWED: 2½ to 4½ hours

These trails, former logging roads reconditioned back in the 1990s, are not far from Durango in the Junction Creek area. Two main loops are discussed here, but there are several other options off these loops. A newer, eastern trail has become popular, particularly among the mountain bike crowd. This is on San Juan National Forest land.

APPROACH: Take Twenty-Fifth Street west off Main Avenue. This soon becomes Junction Creek Road (CR 204). It's 3 miles to a Y-intersection where you'll veer left; going right takes you up Falls Creek Road (CR 205).

In another 0.6 miles you'll reach the National Forest boundary at a cattleguard; at this same point, the paved road becomes gravel. Also here is the southern terminus for the Colorado Trail. The road soon turns into a twisting, climbing mountain road.

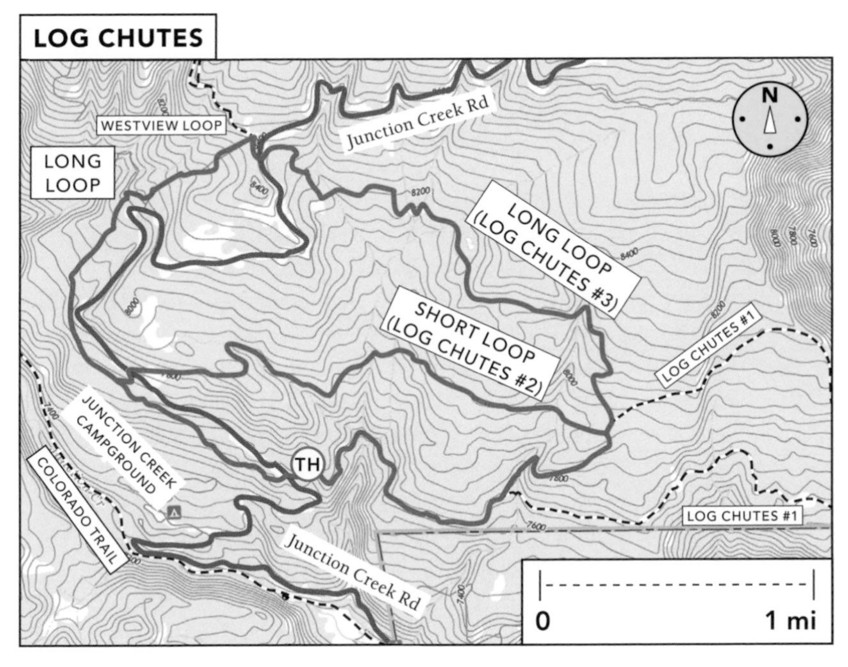

A view of the La Platas on the western side of the Log Chutes Trails.

From the boundary, go 1.8 miles (you'll pass Junction Creek Campground) and turn right into a parking area for the Log Chutes Trails (N 37 20.405, W 107 54.495, 7,520 feet). A closed gate bars the way to vehicles just past the parking area.

HIKE: Head east on a slight uphill grade on the closed-off road. You'll be using former roads of various widths most of the way. In 1.1 miles turn left off this road and go northeast uphill (N 37 20.343, W 107 54.753, 7,660 feet). At 1.7 miles, after 0.6 miles of mostly climbing, you'll reach a flat spot where the shorter trail loop splits off to the left (west) (N 37 20.534, W 107 53.337, 7,930 feet).

For the long loop, continue on another 100 yards to where another trail splits left (northwest) off the old road. This trail is marked "more difficult," to help mountain bikers decide the right route. From here the trail climbs to the north for a half-mile, then levels out and stays around 8,200 feet elevation for 1.3 miles as it again follows an old road. At 3.5 miles the trail takes off to the right (northwest) uphill on a single-track trail, and climbs 200 feet more before reaching Junction Creek Road at 3.9 miles (N 37 21.367, W 107 54.668, 8,350 feet).

Go left downhill on Junction Creek Road for only about 10 yards, locating the trail on the other side. This trail (actually an old road) heads slightly uphill for another 0.1 miles before coming to another old road, which you'll turn left onto and head steeply downhill (N 37 21.427, W 107 54.697, 8,400 feet). This trail has been used for downhill races, and it's possible that downhillers could be training on it. In any case, be aware that many mountain bikers use these trails.

From the road crossing it's 1.5 miles to a corral that's on the right side of the trail. At this point, 5.5 miles into the hike, the short loop trail joins the long loop. You're hiking on a two-track old road. A hundred yards past the corral, as you turn from going south-southeast to almost due east, there's a trail that heads south. This trail takes you to the Colorado Trail near Junction Creek Campground. Instead, go another 100 yards due east and find a trail that heads south-southeast off the two-track (N 37 20.647, W 107 55.106, 7,710 feet); if you suddenly reach Junction Creek Road you've gone too far.

From here it's 0.7 miles back to the parking area. At the end you'll cross the road one more time before arriving back at your car.

OPTIONS: The shorter option was pretty well explained on page 52. From the point where you go left off the longer loop, it's 2.2 miles to the corral. This trail dips and climbs a bit, but mostly remains at approximately the same altitude.

There are several trails to the east of the main loops that you could take and add some more distance or see a new piece of land. One goes out to a nice overlook of Falls Creek, although for much of this stretch those darn ponderosa pine trees kind of get in the way of your view.

RAIDER RIDGE

DISTANCE: 4.6 miles round-trip

ELEVATION: Start at 6,600 feet, high point at 7,480 feet (880-foot gain)

RATING: Easy

TIME ALLOWED: 2 to 3 hours

This is the first of four hikes that are part of the Telegraph Trail system, an interconnected set of trails just east of downtown Durango. (You can probably count the Skyline Trail on page 62 in here too.) Really, these four hikes are just suggestions and a way of introducing the hiker to this system, which also include Meadow Loop and Telegraph Trail (page 56), Carbon Junction Trail (page 58) and Sale Barn Canyon (page 60).

Raider Ridge is an easy hike out of Durango. It offers nice views down over parts of the city, the Fort Lewis College campus, the east side of the La Platas, and the south side of some of the San Juans.

The name "Raider Ridge" comes from the former mascot of the Fort Lewis athletic teams. At one time, students maintained a big "R" on the campus side of this ridge. The Raiders have been the Skyhawks since the 1990s, but the ridge often is still called the politically incorrect Raider.

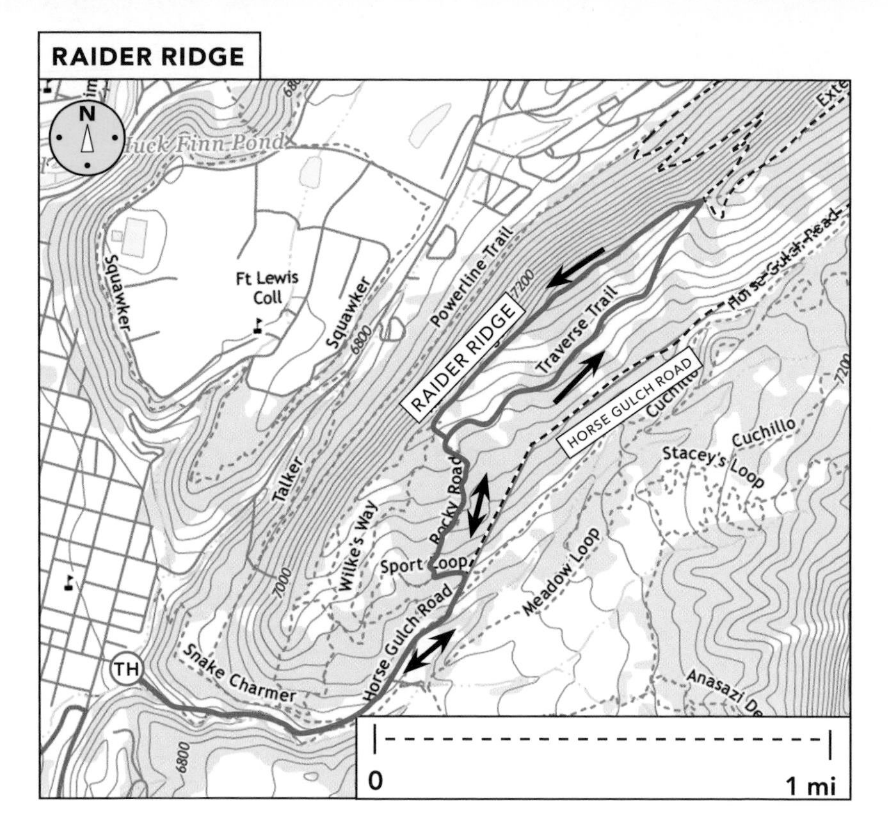

Some of this ridge is owned by the city of Durango; a good chunk of land is actually private property. The ridge is a steep sandstone uplift tilted 10 to 15 degrees to the southeast, known by geologists as a "hogback."

You can often hike or run this trail in midwinter without too much problem, although there can be some snow and, less conducive to decent hiking, mud. This route from Horse Gulch presents the sunny side of the ridge, where snow tends to melt fairly rapidly.

Many trails in the Telegraph system were built in the late 1990s and early 2000s with the impetus of Trails 2000, a local trails advocacy group. Raider Ridge, however, is an older trail. Mountain bikers are the main users of this system, but Raider Ridge does not get quite as many of them, particularly the "extended" ridge, which is the hike described here.

APPROACH: From East Eighth Avenue, head east on Third Street a block to a paved parking area (N 37 15.883, W 107 52.329, 6,600 feet). Don't park at the Horse Gulch Medical Complex just to the west. Third Street turns into a dirt county road, closed to public motor vehicles. There should be a porta-potty or two here.

HIKE: Hike up Horse Gulch Road 1 mile (0.3 miles past the Meadow Loop turnoff) to where an old unmarked road splits from the main road at a 120-degree left turn

Looking up the Raider Ridge Trail. The suggested route comes down from the background and goes downhill to the right here along the black dirt section.

(N 37 16.065, W 107 51.495, 6,940 feet). This trail heads west for 0.1 miles, where it splits again. Go right (north) uphill on what's called Rocky Road.

At 1.4 miles you'll reach another junction (N 37 16.314, W 107 51.573, 7,220 feet). Up ahead and to the left is a steep hillside of black dirt with a trail leading up it. This is the short way (about 100 yards from here) to the top of the ridge, and it's the route you'll come down if you follow these directions.

Instead of going up the black dirt hillside, go right, continuing on the remnants of the old road. At 2.2 miles, after a 200-foot gain, reach the top of the "extended" ridge, a saddle from where you'll get an excellent view (N 37 16.763, W 107 50.966, 7,420 feet). Straight north, the Animas Valley opens in front of you, and you can see all the way to the West Needle Mountains. The La Plata Mountains rise west above the city. Down below are the golf course and the SkyRidge development.

Take the trail that heads west, uphill briefly, along the ridge to the high point of this hike at 7,482 feet. Enjoy the many splendid views along the ridge. At 3.1 miles you'll come to the black dirt mentioned previously. From the black dirt, head downhill and retrace your route back to the trailhead.

OPTIONS: From the saddle at the top of the extended ridge you have several choices. You could turn right, continuing up the extended ridge to the northeast. You could go down the new SkyRaider Trail to the Powerline Trail and get back to the Horse Gulch trailhead that way. Or you could go downhill to the left in the ridge and make your way down from the black dirt.

MEADOW LOOP–TELEGRAPH TRAIL

DISTANCE: 5.1 miles round-trip

ELEVATION: Start at 6,600 feet, top of Telegraph at 7,480 feet (880-foot gain)

RATING: Easy

TIME ALLOWED: 2 to 3 hours

This hike heads up Horse Gulch, just like Raider Ridge, but this time you head east instead of north, cruising the east side of the Meadow Loop and up Telegraph Trail. Options abound, and this is really just a suggestion for myriad hikes in the area. You could hike this area for weeks and not do exactly the same loop. The trailhead is just a few blocks southeast of downtown Durango. It's accessible nearly year-round; the only time it's not a decent place for a hike is when muddy.

It's a very popular spot for mountain biking, which you'll notice quickly, so be on the lookout. However, most mountain bikers are courteous when they're not racing, and a smile goes a long way.

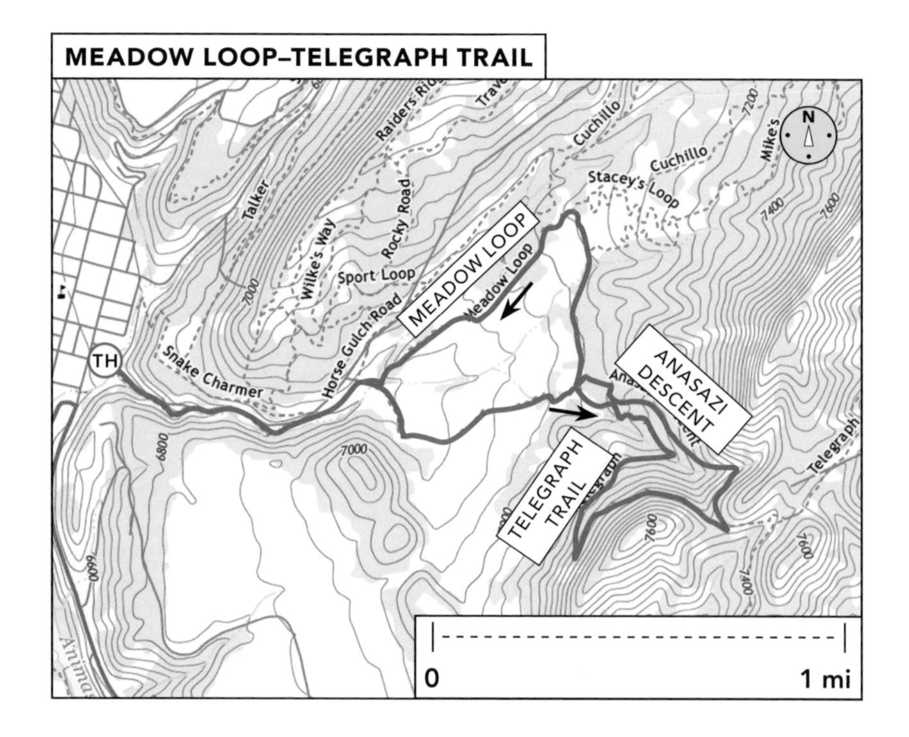

From Horse Gulch, the trail leads out toward Meadow. The Telegraph Trail can be seen snaking up the hillside in the background.

APPROACH: From East Eighth Avenue, head east on Third Street one block to a small parking area (N 37 15.883, W 107 52.329, 6,600 feet). Third Street turns into a dirt county road, closed to motor vehicles.

HIKE: Head up the dirt road, passing around the gate that shuts off the road to vehicles. In 0.7 miles turn right off the main road (N 37 15.850, W 107 51.681, 6,760 feet) onto the Meadow Loop, which follows the remnants of a road before veering off to the left at 0.9 miles and crossing the large meadow.

Keep right where there are trail options, and at 1.4 miles head up the Telegraph Trail. There should be trail maps posted along the way to help guide you. Telegraph climbs slowly as it contours east, west, south, and back east again, joining up finally near the top with the old telegraph road built early in the twentieth century. The distance from the parking area to the top of the Telegraph Trail (N 37 15.536, W 107 50.706, 7,480 feet) is 2.7 miles.

From the top go past the Bill Manning bench just a few yards and take a sharp left onto the Anasazi Descent. (Bill was the first director of Trails 2000 starting in the early 1990s; in 2006 he moved to Golden to take over as executive director of the Colorado Trail Foundation.) Veer right onto the Meadow Loop when you reach the bottom of the steep downhill. At the Stacy's Loop intersection at 3.7 miles (N 37 16.121, W 107 51.070, 7,040 feet), go left on Meadow, and take two more lefts to stay on Meadow; again, trail maps should help. At 4.4 miles reconnect with Horse Gulch Road; head on down to the parking area.

OPTIONS: There are so many options. Use the provided map, the posted trailside maps, or a free map that is provided by Trails 2000 and available at local bike shops to figure out the various combinations.

Stacy's Loop, Mike's Trail, and Cuchillo Trail are options in the Horse Gulch area. From the top of Telegraph the trail continues east, dropping into the Grandview area, and it's possible to make a loop involving Sidewinder and Crites Connection, or exit the trail system via Carbon Junction.

CARBON JUNCTION

DISTANCE: 4.2 miles round-trip

ELEVATION: Start at 6,460 feet, high point at 7,080 feet (620-foot gain)

RATING: Easy

TIME ALLOWED: 2 to 3 hours

This is another trail very close to town, offering yet another option on the Telegraph Trail system. It's a nice hike, particularly in the spring and fall, and even in the winter if it's not muddy or deeply covered by snow. Unlike Sale Barn, South Rim, and Big Canyon, this trail remains open during the winter.

The trail goes through a combination of easements through private land and Bureau of Land Management land.

APPROACH: Head south on East Eighth Avenue from College Drive. This turns into CO 3 in a few blocks. Go 2.3 miles to a small trailhead parking area on the left (east) side of the road (N 37 14.135, W 107 52.005, 6,460 feet). The trailhead is just before a T-intersection that connects to US 550/160.

You can also reach the trailhead from the southeast. Veer right onto CO 3 after passing the light at Dominguez Drive (Walmart turn). The parking area will be just ahead on the right.

HIKE: Begin uphill on the trail. It starts south but soon switches back; your bearing is generally east. It's a trail for a while, but soon you'll join an old road that heads briefly north. At the crest of this hill—0.5 miles from the trailhead—you'll top out next to a large, flat, open field. This is part of an 800-acre parcel to be developed as a multi-use public park, thanks to a donation from the Katz family, who purchased the land for this purpose.

The trail goes back south, away from the old road, and skirts this field. Soon you'll find yourself between an old gravel pit (left) and REA Canyon (right). At 1.5 miles

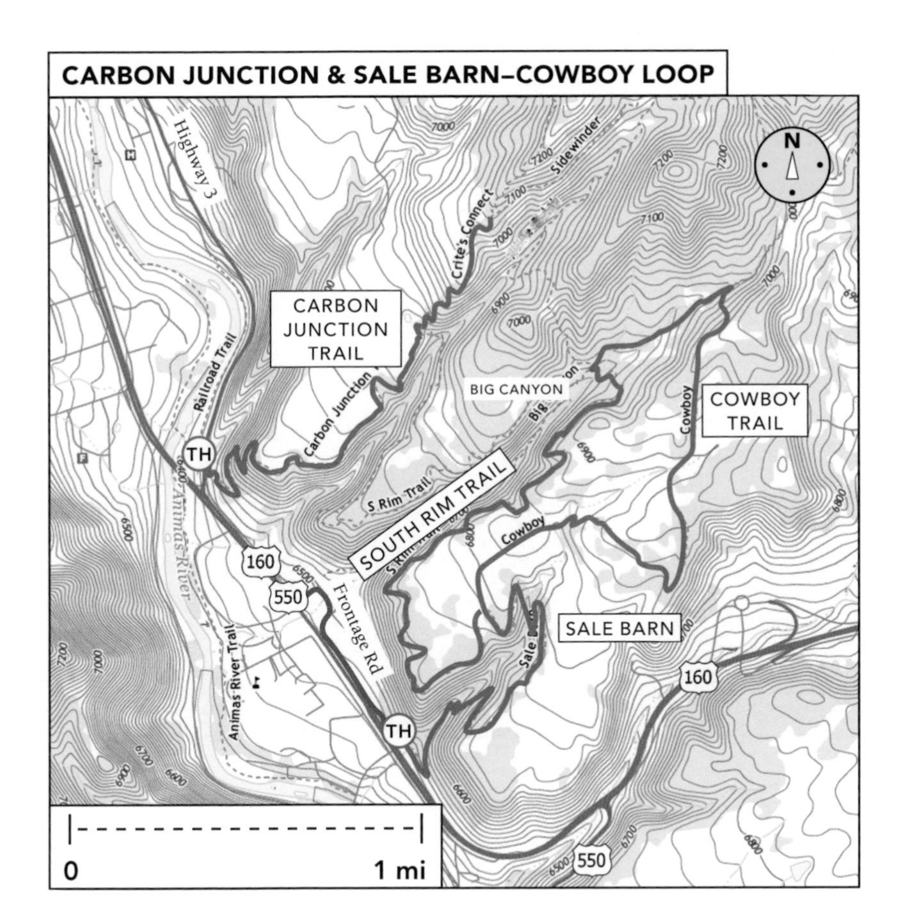

the trail splits, with Carbon Junction continuing left, and the South Rim Trail going right (N 37 14.444, W 107 51.347, 6,820 feet). This presents one of many options, but this description assumes you stay on Carbon Junction.

At 2.1 miles, after a half-mile of mostly gentle climbing, you reach a three-way intersection (N 37 14.732, W 107 51.136, 7,080 feet). At this point Carbon Junction and this trail description end.

OPTIONS: Where Carbon Junction ends, the Crites Connection goes left (north) and Sidewinder goes right (northeast). It's possible to add a 4.2-mile loop from here, going up Crites 1.7 miles, right on Telegraph Trail for 0.5 miles, then right on Sidewinder for 2 miles back to the three-way junction.

Another option: At the junction with the South Rim Trail, go right on the South Rim Trail about 2 miles, then go right onto Big Canyon Trail, which drops you in 1.1 miles onto a frontage road that parallels US 160. Hike along this frontage road about 0.5 miles back to the Carbon Junction parking area.

A view of Smelter Mountain, Perins Peak, and the La Plata Mountains.

SALE BARN–COWBOY LOOP

DISTANCE: 8.2 miles round-trip

ELEVATION: Starting at 6,480 feet, high point at 7,000 feet (520-foot gain)

RATING: Easy

TIME ALLOWED: 3 to 4½ hours

This is another Telegraph Trail system hike with various options. This one is located in the southeast part of the system. It offers views of the Grandview area, the La Plata Mountains, and even Walmart, if that trips your trigger.

There is some up and down to this hike, so the overall elevation gain is much more than 520 feet. This area is closed in the winter (December 1 to April 15) to protect deer and elk.

APPROACH: From the point where US 550 and US 160 join near downtown

Durango, take the combined highway 3 miles to Dominguez Drive. Go left onto Dominguez briefly. Just past the gas station, turn right onto a frontage road. Go 0.4 miles along the frontage road, and just as it's about to turn back toward the highway, continue straight up a hill on a dirt road. Park in the good-sized lot ahead of you (N 37 13.443, W 107 51.382, 6,480 feet).

HIKE: Take the path at the east end of the parking area. It soon crosses a ditch and heads north. It stays briefly in Sale Barn Canyon, then climbs above. You'll reach the canyon top 0.7 miles from the trailhead.

Skirt a gravel pit operation (it's on your right) through piñon-juniper forest. Note the variety of desert-type plants: sage, yucca, mountain mahogany, claret cup cactus. At 1.7 miles reach the end of Sale Barn Trail and a split (N 37 13.858, W 107 51.015, 6,780 feet).

Take the Cowboy Trail right (you'll return on the South Rim Trail, which goes left here). Follow the Cowboy Trail, crossing a gas well road at 2.1 miles, before coming to a nice overlook of the Grandview area at 2.5 miles. Here the trail heads northeast.

From the South Rim Trail you'll get a great view of the La Platas, including always prominent Silver and Lewis Mountains.

At 3.1 miles you'll come to a road; go right (north) on this road 50 yards and find the Cowboy Trail again on the left-hand side. From here it's another 0.3 miles to an intersection at 3.4 miles with the Big Canyon Trail (N 37 14.552, W 107 50.408, 6,900 feet), and you'll drop about 100 feet to get there.

Take Big Canyon left to an intersection at 3.9 miles under power lines (N 37 14.365, W 107 50.825, 6,800 feet). Go left onto the South Rim Trail. Hike uphill out of Big Canyon, then follow the trail as it winds along the mesa rim. Where the trail turns from going southeast to heading northeast above Sale Barn Canyon, there's a shortcut you could take down the steep hillside (N 37 13.567, W 107 51.361, 6,725 feet). But if you continue on South Rim, you'll reach the three-way intersection with Sale Barn and Cowboy Trails at 6.5 miles. Go right at the three-way and finish by hiking 1.7 miles back on Sale Barn to the parking area.

OPTIONS: At the first trail split at 1.7 miles, go left onto South Rim Trail. Follow it 2.6 miles, dropping down into Big Canyon. Take the Big Canyon Trail left (southwest) 1.1 miles to its terminus. Follow the frontage road back to the parking area for Sale Barn Trail. This whole loop is 6 miles, with the last half-mile on the road.

SKYLINE

DISTANCE: 4 miles round-trip

ELEVATION: Start at 6,970 feet, high point at 7,865 feet, for a gain of 895 feet

RATING: Easy but steep

TIME ALLOWED: 2 to 3 hours

Popular among residents along Jenkins Ranch Road, as well as mountain bikers, runners, and hikers from all over Durango, the Skyline Trail gets year-round usage. It's a good place for people to take kids and dogs. Even in the snowiest of winters, people snowshoe or hike up this trail for their daily exercise. Durangoans love their trails.

Against some opposition by a few local residents, but with plenty of enthusiasm from other local residents, Trails 2000 crews constructed Skyline in 2013–14 up the side of Raider Ridge. It's on a patchwork of City of Durango and Bureau of Land Management land. It connects with the Horse Gulch Trail system, and using this trail gives you many options for long and short loops.

APPROACH: From Goeglein Gulch Road in Durango, turn east onto Jenkins Ranch Road. Go through five roundabouts, and at 1.3 miles, just after that fifth fun

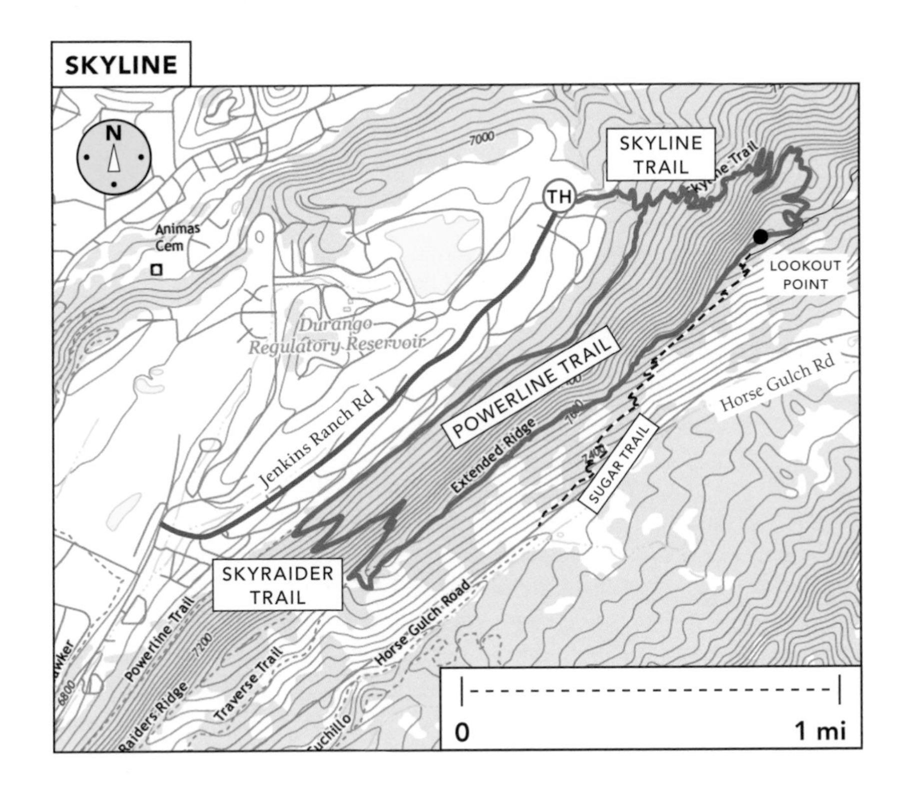

roundabout, park in the small paved and lined lot on the right (N 37 17.588, W 107 50.375, 6,970 feet).

HIKE: Just past the last parking space you'll find the trail and a dog poop bag dispenser. Head east on the scrub oak-lined trail, paralleling the road briefly as you skirt some homes. Quickly you get a nice view of the La Plata Mountains to the northwest.

Go left at a junction at 0.3 miles (7,040 feet). There are options, and you could go right here onto the Powerline Trail. Follow switchbacks up through the oaks; eventually you'll head toward a patch of fir trees on the steep slope. After a little more than a mile, the view north up the Animas Valley opens up, and you can see all the way to Pigeon and Turret Peaks, high thirteeners in the Needle Mountains. If you've never seen this view, it's an interesting perspective of the City Reservoir, Hillcrest Golf Course, and even the Smelter Mountain tailings pile.

At 1.5 miles come to a small plateau before beginning to climb again. At a junction at 1.9 miles you can go either way. Going right is a shortcut. But go left to a four-way junction (N 37 17.545, W 107 49.694, 7,845 feet) in about 50 yards, and take a right at the four-way, heading west along the ridge. At 2 miles there is a great lookout point on the right with a small flat rock. Lake Nighthorse is in view.

That's a mighty fine hike right there, but there are options.

OPTIONS: Another great loop option was being developed by the hardworking volunteers of the local trail advocacy group Trails 2000 just as this book was heading to press. The new SkyRaider Trail should be painstakingly dug out of the rock and oak brush along the northwest-facing slope of Raider Ridge and is slated to be ready to roll by the summer of 2020, connecting with the Powerline Trail below. This sets up a good 6-mile loop hike:

After completing the Skyline Trail, continue past the lookout point at 2 miles and make your way along the ridgetop trail. Watch your footing on the uneven and off-camber sandstone. At 2.3 miles you'll come to the junction with the Sugar Trail, which heads downhill to the left. Continue on the ridge and from here it's much of the same for a while, but that's not a bad thing. You hang close to the edge, and to your right are excellent views from your ridge in the sky.

At 3.6 miles you will reach a saddle (N 37 16.764, W 107 50.970, 7,420 feet); around here you should find the SkyRaider Trail traversing down a steep slope to the right. (Also at this saddle, the Rocky Road Trail goes down southwest to the left to connect with Horse Gulch; see Raider Ridge hike on page 53.) The distance of the SkyRaider Trail had to be estimated for this description; it's approximately 0.8 miles, which puts you at the Powerline Trail at 4.4 miles (N 37 16.854, W 107 51.156, 6,960 feet, or thereabouts). Go right (northeast) on the Powerline, and at 5.7 miles come to the intersection with Skyline. Take Skyline back to the parking area at 6 miles.

For another option, if you go east at the four-way junction, you're on the Smokejumper Trail, dedicated to Joe Philpott, a Durango native who was killed in an avalanche in 2013 at age twenty-six. He fought wildfires throughout the West for several summers with the Great Basin Smoke Jumpers out of Boise, Idaho. The trail leads to a plaque in Joe's memory. You can keep going along this trail for quite a distance, but eventually you'll hit private property. Plans are to develop it further.

Along the ridge between where the SkyRaider and Skyline Trails come up to meet it. That's the trail, right there, on the rock. The Animas Valley is in the background.

LA PLATA MOUNTAIN CLIMBS

The La Plata Mountains are a sometimes-overlooked gem of southwestern Colorado. They're visible from many vantage points in the area, including downtown Durango.

A few visits to the La Platas and you'll discover one truth: There is nothing flat about this relatively small range. Good luck finding a trail that isn't steep!

They have a lot to offer, including places to find solitude and some fun peak-bagging.

The La Platas are basically divided into east and west, separated by the La Plata River, which starts up high in La Plata canyon's northern reaches in the Cumberland Basin. Climbing opportunities are abundant, and not all climbs are covered here. Don't be afraid to do some exploring.

In this chapter you will find descriptions of climbs up Silver, Deadwood, Parrott, Madden, Gibbs, Diorite, Centennial, Sharkstooth, and Hesperus—the latter of which is the tallest at 13,232 feet.

No fourteeners. No huge lakes. A few remnants of old mines and old settlements that never amounted to a whole lot. You'll find some traffic on the main canyon road on summer weekends, but nothing has yet lured in the masses.

Left, top: The western approach to the La Platas, with Centennial Peak on the left and Hesperus Mountain on the right. Left, bottom: Looking east from the Hesperus summit, with Lavender Peak to the left, Mount Moss to right, and Silver and Deadwood Mountains in the distance. Below, left: Heading down the Colorado Trail from near Kennebec Pass. Below, right: Looking north from the Madden summit. After an unnamed bump are Star Peak, Gibbs Peak, Hesperus Mountain, and the Burwell-Spiller-Babcock combo.

SLIDEROCK TRAIL TO KENNEBEC PASS

DISTANCE: 4 miles round-trip, 7.6 miles round-trip including Taylor Lake

ELEVATION: Start at 10,360 feet, reach pass at 11,760 feet (1,400-foot gain)

RATING: Moderate

TIME ALLOWED: 2 to 3 hours

This is a relatively short hike following a long drive on a gravel road, but both the drive and the hike are well worth it. The gravel road drive starts at 7,000 feet and slowly winds its way up to the trailhead at 10,340 feet. It rises through piñon-juniper country, up through ponderosa. Eventually, tall aspen close in along the road, along with spruce and fir trees.

In early August, the wildflowers on this trail can be abundant. Open places display great patches of blue larkspur and alpine asters, punctuated with yellow daisies. Columbine are profuse up higher. In early October, the aspen trees are aflame with gold.

This is great deer and elk country. Your chances of seeing deer are quite good; elk occasionally appear, but they are more apt to stay farther away from the road. One foggy morning as we drove along, a bear ran across the road in front of us.

APPROACH: To reach the trailhead, take Twenty-Fifth Street west off Main Avenue in Durango. In a couple of blocks this curves off to the northwest and becomes Junction Street. Take this street out of town, where it becomes Junction Creek Road. The road follows Junction Creek all the way to the San Juan National Forest boundary, easily recognized for the blacktop stops here with a cattleguard. (It's about 3.5 miles to the cattleguard from the Main Avenue turnoff.) Driving on a gravel road from here on will be slow due to many curves, a steady uphill climb, and often a washboard effect in the surface.

Check your speedometer at the cattleguard. It's about 7 miles to Animas Overlook, where you can stop and get great views up the Animas Valley and to the mountains north. There is a nice wheelchair-accessible loop you can do here. At about 11 miles you come to Rands Point, where there is a turnout on the left side of the road. Stopping here is well worthwhile for you look far down into Junction Creek canyon and across its headwaters to the steep sides of Cumberland Mountain, Snowstorm Peak, and Lewis Mountain. Kennebec Pass, the hiking objective, is also visible between Cumberland and a high flat ridge north of it.

At about 17.5 miles (allow for some variation in speedometers), take a spur road to the left (southwest). This is called Champion Venture Road. There may be a sign

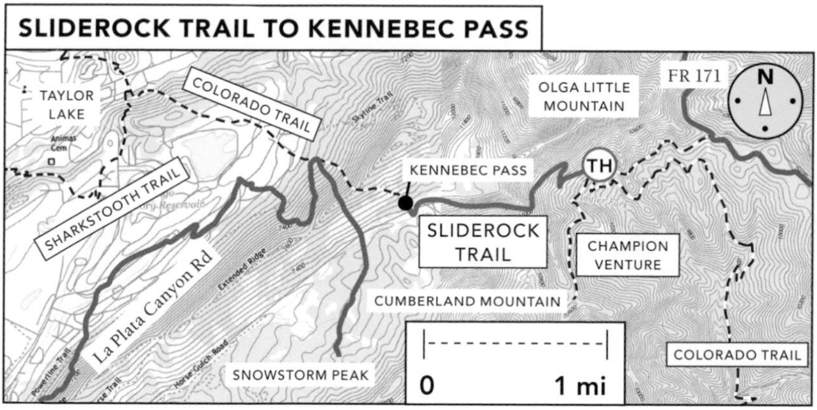

SLIDEROCK TRAIL TO KENNEBEC PASS

here pointing out that this is the way to the Sliderock Trail or the Colorado Trail. Follow this road 0.8 miles to the trailhead. The Colorado Trail is coming up from its origin west of Durango; it crosses the road at this point and joins the Sliderock Trail. A wide spot a few yards north of the trailhead provides suitable parking space (N 37 26.933, W 107 59.162, 10,360 feet).

HIKE: Begin by hiking uphill through a nice forest. As you near the pass at 1.5 miles, the trail traverses an open rocky area that yields a view southeastward down the entire Junction Creek canyon to Durango. The canyon is heavily wooded in dark green; a glance upward toward the pass and Cumberland Mountain shows the light green of tundra above the timberline. Every view from this trail is different and beautiful. At 2 miles you'll reach the pass (N 37 26.886, W 108 00.153, 11,760 feet). Here the views north and northeast give the best skyline panorama in Southwest Colorado. You can see the Needles, Twilight and the West Needles, the Grenadiers, Sultan, Engineer, Grizzly, and many others. If you hike 150 yards down the other side of the pass, you'll see around the west side of the ridge and more of the panorama opens up: Lizard Head, the Wilsons, Dolores Peak, and Lone Cone. Just as you go through the pass there, an unnamed ridge rises on your right (north) 300 feet in a quarter-mile. The view is enhanced even more if you climb it.

If you are interested in mining history, you can hike a quarter-mile southeast from the pass to an old mine, the Muldoon, that is in a better stage of preservation than some. It is in an exposed area above the timberline, so the views are excellent.

The 4 miles specified in the heading are based on a return from Kennebec to the starting point. This is a fairly easy hike, though a bit steep.

OPTIONS: Taylor Lake can also be included in this hike. It adds another 1.8 miles (3.6 miles round-trip) to the distance, but not much elevation change. To go to Taylor, continue from Kennebec Pass along the Colorado Trail, which uses a closed two-track road and briefly meets up with a four-wheel-drive road coming up through the La Platas. The trail goes on straight (west) to the lake.

Heading down the Sliderock Trail.

Trails continue southwest and northwest from Taylor Lake. The one going southwest climbs a ridge, drops down into Bear Creek Canyon, and goes up the other side to the pass between Sharkstooth and Centennial Peaks. This is called the Sharkstooth Trail and is approached from the west, a much shorter and easier route for that area. The one going northwest is the Colorado Trail, which soon joins Indian Trail Ridge for more excellent views.

Also, back at your parking spot on Champion Venture Road, Olga Little Peak (11,420 feet) is due north and 1,080 feet higher; it's named for Olga Little, who lived in La Plata Canyon in the early 1900s, and supplied miners with her string of twenty burros. The peak can be climbed from the vicinity of Kennebec Pass, but there's no trail and reportedly a lot of thick, skin-ripping vegetation to get through.

TOMAHAWK BASIN–DIORITE PEAK

DISTANCE: 5.2 miles round-trip to Diorite summit

ELEVATION: Start at 9,900 feet, summit at 12,761 feet (2,861-foot gain)

RATING: Moderate to difficult, due to steepness

TIME ALLOWED: 3½ to 4½ hours

This is another hike out of La Plata Canyon. You can chop some distance and altitude off the climb by driving up the rough four-wheel-drive road as far as 1.5 miles. Eventually the road becomes too rough for any vehicle, and you'll have to start winding your way on foot up the mountainside.

The hike is without benefit of trail but is easy to follow because it quickly gets above timberline, where everything is visible. Above the timberline, most of the hike is on loose talus rock and scree.

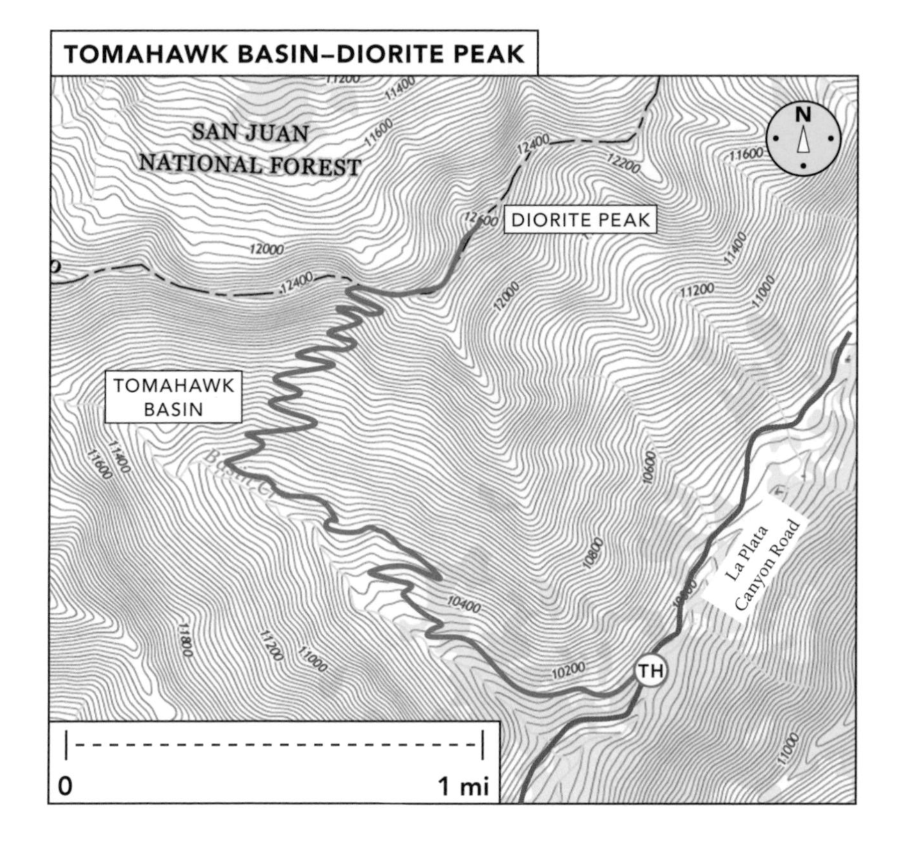

APPROACH: Take La Plata Canyon road 10.5 miles from US 160 to the Tomahawk Basin road. To break this down a little better, this road is 6.1 miles from where the pavement ends, or 1.3 miles up from the Lewis Creek turnoff. The Lewis Creek turnoff is the road that crosses La Plata River on a bridge. The last 1.3 miles to the Tomahawk Basin turnoff is very rough in spots, and high-clearance and/or 4WD (four-wheel drive) is recommended.

The Tomahawk turnoff (N 37 25.489, W 108 02.600, 9,900 feet) is a 120-degree turn uphill to the left. The Tomahawk road is very rough and narrow; two-wheel drives should not attempt it.

HIKE: Begin up the road. It'll be easygoing for a while, and steeper the higher you go. In 1.2 miles you'll come to the remnants of a huge old mill; it's very picturesque, especially in the fall (N 37 25.717, W 108 03.404, 10,550 feet).

Keep following what remains of an old road. At 1.5 miles it becomes too rough for vehicles. When you run out of road, hike north-northeast up the mountainside toward a low spot in the saddle at about 12,300 feet. A few hundred feet below the saddle is the site of an airplane crash from the early 1960s. This was a military flight in which two men were killed. The accident was all the more tragic because just 300 feet more of altitude would have allowed them to clear the ridge. The crash and many snows have scattered the wreckage over a wide area. Most of it has been salvaged, but climbers may see some scraps of aluminum skin, wires, and other smaller parts as they climb through the area.

Take a moment to check out the old mining ruins in Tomahawk Basin.

Once at the saddle at 2.1 miles (N 37 26.256, W 108 03.333, 12,310 feet), turn right, climb east to a high point on the ridge, and follow the ridge around northeast to Diorite. The summit (N 37 26.398, W 108 03.048) is a half-mile from the saddle.

The views from the top are breathtaking. Immediately below, steeply down on the west side, you look into Bear Creek Basin. On the far side of the basin, due west are Mount Moss and Centennial Peak. The connecting ridge between them, which includes Lavender Peak, is extremely rough and forbidding. Across this ridge and a little beyond is Hesperus

Peak, the highest point in the La Platas at 13,232 feet. North of Centennial, Sharkstooth rises steeply to a sharp point. To the north there is a complete panorama of peaks, including, from west to east, the San Miguels with their three fourteeners and the distinctive Lizard Head shaft, Grizzly Peak, Engineer Mountain, the Twilights, the Needles, and many more. To the east, near at hand, are La Plata Canyon and the east ridge of the La Plata Mountains, including Snowstorm Peak and Lewis Mountain.

Hikers should return by the same route they ascended.

CENTENNIAL PEAK & SHARKSTOOTH

DISTANCE: 4.4 miles round-trip to Centennial, 5 miles for both peaks

ELEVATION: Start at 10,932 feet, Centennial summit at 13,062 feet (2,130-foot gain); add 526 feet elevation gain if Sharkstooth (summit at 12,462 feet) is added

RATING: Moderate; difficult if you add Sharkstooth

TIME ALLOWED: 3 hours to Centennial, 4 hours if Sharkstooth is added

---

This description focuses on a climb of Centennial Peak. There is also an optional side trip to the top of Sharkstooth, which I will try my best to talk you out of climbing.

Centennial and Hesperus are characterized by bands of different-colored sedimentary rocks. Centennial, striped by these layers, was called Banded Mountain until its name was officially changed on July 30, 1976, in celebration of the Colorado state centennial. This was, of course, the same month in which the United States was celebrating its bicentennial.

A fairly long drive is involved; the last several miles are through tall aspen forest with occasional breaks in the trees to reveal the western profile of the La Platas. As you approach from the west, the glimpses that you get include Hesperus (at 13,232 feet, the highest peak in the La Platas), Moss, Spiller, Centennial, and Sharkstooth; all except Sharkstooth are over 13,000 feet. Although a bit shorter, Sharkstooth captures your attention because of its sharp triangular shape thrusting abruptly into the sky above the pass. From this angle it definitely looks like a shark's tooth.

APPROACH: From the intersection of US 160 and CO 184 in Mancos (you can't miss it—that's the town's only stoplight), go north on CO 184. In just a quarter-mile, turn right uphill on the road marked for Jackson Reservoir and Transfer Campground. This is known as the West Mancos Road.

A view of Centennial Peak from Hesperus Mountain. Sharkstooth sticks up below left.

At 10 miles on this road you'll pass Transfer Campground, and soon after the pavement turns to a good gravel road. In another mile at a road split, keep right on FR 561, continue past the Aspen Guard Station, and at 12.2 miles keep an eye out for FR 350, where you'll make a right off FR 561.

Continue east on FR 350 (Spruce Mill Road) for 6.4 miles to a turn slightly downhill to the right onto FR 346 toward Twin Lakes. At this point the road gets rough. You don't have to have 4WD, but high clearance is a must. It's another 1.5 miles to the end of the road and the trailhead, so you could hike this section if necessary. There is room to park several cars at the trailhead (N 37 27.709, W 108 05.701, 10,932 feet).

HIKE: Two trails begin here, and it should be obvious you want the Sharkstooth Trail. (The other is the West Mancos; see Hesperus Mountain on page 76.)

Start fairly gently uphill as the trail winds its way east through big spruce and fir. The climb steepens, and at 0.9 miles the trail passes through the old Windy Williams Mine site, which, as an interpretive sign explains, attracted miners beginning in 1912. Some ruins remain, and it makes for a nice short break (N 37 27.425, W 108 05.055, 11,315 feet).

The first goal is the saddle between Sharkstooth and Centennial, and you have some climbing to do. At 1.5 miles, you'll reach this wide pass, or saddle (N 37 27.429, W 108 04.577, 11,936). The main trail continues east and drops deeply into Bear Creek Canyon. To climb Centennial, turn right up the ridge. The way begins steeply up talus, then becomes a more gradual slope over tundra. Stay high on the ridge. Near the top it turns rocky again. It's 0.7 miles from the saddle to the summit (N 37 26.837, W 108 04.614, 13,062 feet).

This summit ridge may be windy and cold, so it's a good idea to have an extra layer or two, maybe even gloves and a hat.

From the top you can't quite see Durango, but look closely and you'll spot Fort Lewis College on the mesa above town. To the north you can see a large sweep of the San Juans, from the Needles northeast to the San Miguels north. Farther west are the Abajos in Utah, and Sleeping Ute Mountain is to the southwest.

OPTIONS: Return to the saddle, take a good look at Sharkstooth, and ask yourself: Do I really, really want to climb this?

What you're looking at is a huge pile of steep, loose shale. It's miserable stuff, and it's easy to dislodge a rock on a climbing partner. No foothold or handhold can be trusted without testing, particularly near the top. It's not a good idea to do this with a dog; most dogs will not bark a warning when they dislodge a rock.

You still want to proceed? Okay. The truth is, it doesn't take too long.

Head up the peak's south side. It begins over ordinary talus but gets continually steeper the higher you climb. Spread out horizontally so you're not climbing above anyone.

If you reach the top (N 37 27.593, W 108 04.378, 12,462 feet), enjoy the tiny summit perch. The north face drops precipitously. Then descend with even more care than you took on the ascent. Then vow never to do this again.

HESPERUS MOUNTAIN

DISTANCE: 5.4 miles round-trip

ELEVATION: Start at 10,932 feet, low point around 10,770 feet, Hesperus Mountain summit at 13,232 (2,462-foot gain)

RATING: Difficult

TIME ALLOWED: 4 to 6 hours

This is an excellent, rewarding climb that is not technical, but it'll get your attention in a few places. There's no great exposure, and this climb would probably be considered Class 2 with maybe a bit of Class 3, but just know you'll be using your hands some and picking your way up some steep spots with very loose rock. The hazard is higher for those below you.

This is the high point of the La Plata Mountains. One might think that makes it a magnet for climbers, and although it's visited often, you generally don't see hordes of folks climbing it on a given day.

The approach is fairly long, so expect a 1½- to 2-hour drive from Durango to the trailhead, an hour or more from Mancos.

APPROACH: From the intersection of US 160 and CO 184 in Mancos (you can't miss it—that's the town's only stoplight), go north on CO 184. In just a quarter-mile, turn right uphill on the road marked for Jackson Reservoir and Transfer Campground. This is known as West Mancos Road.

At 10 miles on this road you'll pass Transfer Campground, and soon after the pavement turns to a good gravel road. In another mile at a road split, keep right on FR 561, continue past the Aspen Guard Station, and at 12.2 miles keep an eye out for FR 350, where you'll make a right off FR 561.

Continue east on FR 350 (Spruce Mill Road) for 6.4 miles to a turn slightly downhill to the right onto FR 346 toward Twin Lakes. At this point the road gets rough. You don't have to have 4WD, but high clearance is a must. It's another 1.5 miles to the end of the road and the trailhead, so you could hike this section if necessary. There is room to park several cars at the trailhead (N 37 27.709, W 108 05.701, 10,932 feet).

HIKE: There are actually two trailheads here. The more traveled Sharkstooth Trail (see page 73) takes off to the east. The West Mancos Trail takes off toward the south and gets you closer to Hesperus Mountain, and that's the trail you want, because yes, you want to scale that big mass looming directly in front of you. Unfortunately this trail tends downhill. After 0.6 miles, cross the North Fork of the West Mancos on a nice set of logs. (N 37 27.364, W 108 05.435, 10,802 feet). After this crossing, it's time to start plotting your next move.

The best way up to the west ridge of Hesperus seems to be the grassy slope on the right of the photo. Hesperus's summit is at the left.

There are a couple of different ways to reach the top of Hesperus. If you look down the ridge from the summit and study the big slope, you'll see a couple of places where it's possible to access the ridge. One is up a steep dirt gully that sets you up quickly for the final ascent. Not far to the west, the more grassy slope seems to work out the best. Getting there takes some bushwhacking and trail finding.

You can look for some sort of path leaving the trail in the next 0.25 miles after the crossing. That's a crapshoot and means you may end up hiking through some difficult down timber. It seems to be better to leave the trail earlier and head up a less timbered slope, then get onto talus fields and contour your way around until you're set up under the grassy slope. Pick your poison. If you stay on the main trail, don't go any farther than mile 1, where the trail takes a sudden dive downhill to the right.

As you contour, as mentioned above, it's likely you'll find paths once in a while and maybe even cairns if you're lucky. Just don't count on this. Eventually you'll be hiking up that very steep grassy slope, one step at a time, pausing for a breath fairly frequently unless you're a superhero of some sort. Likely you will not find a well-established trail up this slope.

At around 1.8 miles you'll reach the ridge (N 37 26.796, W 108 06.026, 12,026 feet). The views had already opened to the north; now you'll start getting nice vistas to the west down the impressive cleft of the West Mancos Valley and to the south. Take a left (east) up the ridge, which rises slowly. At 2.2 miles (N 37 26.715, W 108 05.710, 12,272 feet), you'll reach the base of the true climb. We'll get back to this point later, but there's a good quick exit off the ridge here.

Follow the ridge as best you can. Over the years a fairly well-established path has developed along this route, and it tends to the south of the ridge pretty much all the way up, hitting the actual ridge only occasionally. As mentioned, there are a couple of tricky spots, mainly where there are large rocks balanced on even larger rocks. It's easy to kick one of these off, so those hiking in groups should be very careful and strongly consider going one at a time. (I nearly took out a good friend when I dislodged a boulder on this stretch.)

The current trail actually goes past the summit then curls back to reach the ridge, and you'll backtrack westward to the top at about 2.7 miles (N 37 26.694, W 108 05.333, 13,232 feet). Wahoo!

The summit is not large but it's big enough to support several people comfortably as they eat their well-earned sandwiches and absorb the great panorama. See how many of the La Plata peaks you can identify from here. You can see almost all of them including many on the eastern ridge, such as Silver Mountain. The Spiller-Babcock and Centennial-Lavender ridges look particularly fearsome.

You can return down the grassy slope the way you likely came, or you can head northward off the ridge at the 2.2-mile spot mentioned previously. This is the environmentally unfriendly but fun and fast way down. You can take huge, sliding steps down a black scree slope, and lose elevation rapidly. Early in the summer you can likely find a good spot to glissade down with an ice axe—the environmentally friendly and fun and fast way down. Be very careful.

Head north-northwest over talus and perhaps through the timber to get back to the trail.

OPTIONS: It's also possible to make this climb gentler by hiking all the way west to the end of the steepest part of the ridge and access the ridge there. This entails a longer contour and more elevation loss.

Once you've made it to the top, you may be tempted to cross the ridge from Hesperus over to Lavender Peak and perhaps onto Mount Moss. This is difficult due to some deep clefts that must be crossed, but it is possible. The final pitch on Lavender is a doozy, as it is close to straight up you can do it using breaks in the rock. Some people might want a rope. The ridge from Lavender to Centennial Peak looks impossible, but there are rumors that people have done it.

TRANSFER TRAIL

DISTANCE: 3.8-mile loop

ELEVATION: Start at 8,950 feet, low point at 8,240 feet (710-foot drop)

RATING: Easy

TIME ALLOWED: 2 to 3 hours

This hike begins on the Transfer Trail at the Transfer Campground northeast of Mancos, but it includes parts of four different trails. It's a gem in the western La Platas that has much to offer. If you do this in the fall, you'll want to bring a camera for gorgeous shots of the colorful foliage and the sheer West Mancos Canyon with the La Platas (already snow covered, if you're fortunate) in the background.

That's when you're up on the rim. When you drop down you'll feel the temperature drop, and you'll be hiking next to a noisy river towered over by tall spruce and fir. It's never flat and it's rocky in places, but it's a nice half-day trip.

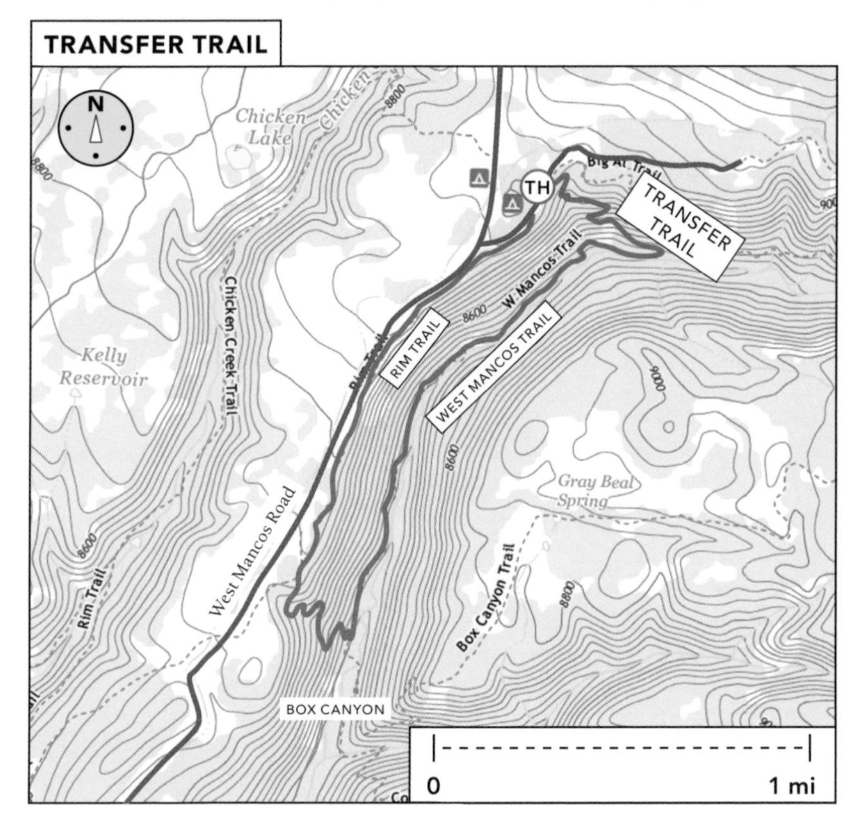

The western La Platas, as seen from the Rim Trail, with the West Mancos canyon below. From left are Sharkstooth, Centennial, which is almost obscured by Hesperus, then Moss, Spiller, and Babcock.

APPROACH: Take US 160 from Durango 28 miles to Mancos, and turn right at the town's one stoplight onto CO 184. Take CO 184 just 0.3 miles and go right (east) uphill on West Mancos Road (CR 42). It's 10 miles (even though the sign says 9 miles) on this paved road to Transfer Campground, where you'll veer right into the campground. Go 0.2 miles and park in the ample clearing next to the campground entrance on the left. Walk back across the road to the trailhead (N 37 28,100, W 108 12.476, 8,950 feet).

HIKE: Head southeast down the Transfer Trail. You'll already be hearing the river (west fork of the Mancos) below, assuming the ubiquitous cattle aren't too loud.

In 0.3 miles the Transfer Trail meets the West Mancos Trail (N 37 28.039, W 108 12.316, 8,760 feet). Go right, continuing downhill and downstream. At 0.6 miles you'll be walking right alongside the West Mancos River. The trail, as you'll soon learn, doesn't stick to the river but meanders above it and back down to it repeatedly. This shaded canyon holds its moisture, as you can see on the moss-covered tree trunks and rocks. Many places along the stream are excellent picnic or wading spots.

At 2 miles, just after passing water-project works, you'll join a two-track road. Another 0.1 miles brings you to the Box Canyon Trail (N 37 27.121, W 108 13.004, 8,240 feet). This is the low point (in elevation) of the hike. Turn right onto a single-track trail heading north uphill toward West Mancos Road. (If you continue straight, the Box Canyon Trail turns left off the road in 100 yards, crosses the West Mancos on a flattened log, and heads toward —of course—Box Canyon.)

The brunt of the uphill climb toward West Mancos Road lasts about 0.5 miles, with a gain of nearly 500 feet. At that point, 2.5 miles (N 37 27.264, W 108 13.134, 8,740 feet), the trail reaches the rim, joins a dirt road for 50 yards, and then veers right off the road, again as single track. This is the Rim Trail, and it's the finest stretch of this hike for photos of the La Platas. You'll see the sharp, but small, summit of Sharkstooth on the left, then Centennial, Hesperus (the most prominent), several others, and the smaller Helmet Peak on the right.

It's a little more than a mile along the rim to the Transfer Campground road, which you hit at 3.7 miles. Follow the road right for another 0.1 miles to the parking area.

OPTIONS: Transfer Campground can be a starting point for several hikes, large and small.

The Big Al Trail begins here; it's a 0.3-mile handicapped-accessible hike to a splendid overlook of the West Mancos Canyon. The trail's named after Al Lorentzen, a local Forest Service employee who was disabled by a falling tree while fighting a fire in Yellowstone National Park in 1988.

Or, after the first 0.3 miles on the Transfer Trail, you could take a left on the West Mancos Trail and go east to your heart's content. It's about 4.5 miles to Golconda, an abandoned town with virtually no remnants, and another dozen or so to join the Colorado Trail via the Sharkstooth Trail.

A final option: At the low point, take the Box Canyon Trail the other way, across the West Mancos on the flattened log. Go far enough (7 miles) and you'll connect with Echo Basin Road.

MADDEN & PARROTT PEAKS

DISTANCE: 5.6 miles round-trip on La Plata Canyon route, 4.4 miles round-trip on Madden Peak Road route, 12.6 miles round-trip on Old Gold Run route

ELEVATION: Start La Plata Canyon route at 8,989 feet, high point is Madden Peak at 11,972 feet (2,983-foot gain); start Madden Peak Road route at 10,098 feet (1,874-foot gain); start Old Gold Run route at 8,440 feet (3,532-foot gain)

RATING: Difficult for La Plata Canyon route, due to steep rock scrambling; moderate for Madden Peak Road and Old Gold Run routes

TIME ALLOWED: 4 to 6 hours for La Plata Canyon route, 2 to 3 hours for Madden Peak Road route, 5 to 7 hours for Old Gold Run route

---

Previous versions of this book have separated these two peaks, Madden and Parrott. Because they're on a ridge just 0.6 miles apart, perhaps it's easier to combine them. If you can bag one, it'll take you only about an hour to hike the other and return.

A big issue here is that there are multiple ways to climb these peaks, and each has its virtues and foibles. There's the steep and rocky way that involves bushwhacking, the long way with the shorter drive, and the short way with the longer drive. Read the detailed descriptions and decide what suits you.

I've chosen to give the La Plata Canyon route—the steep and rocky way—top billing here. The Old Gold Run route is great because it approximates climbing many

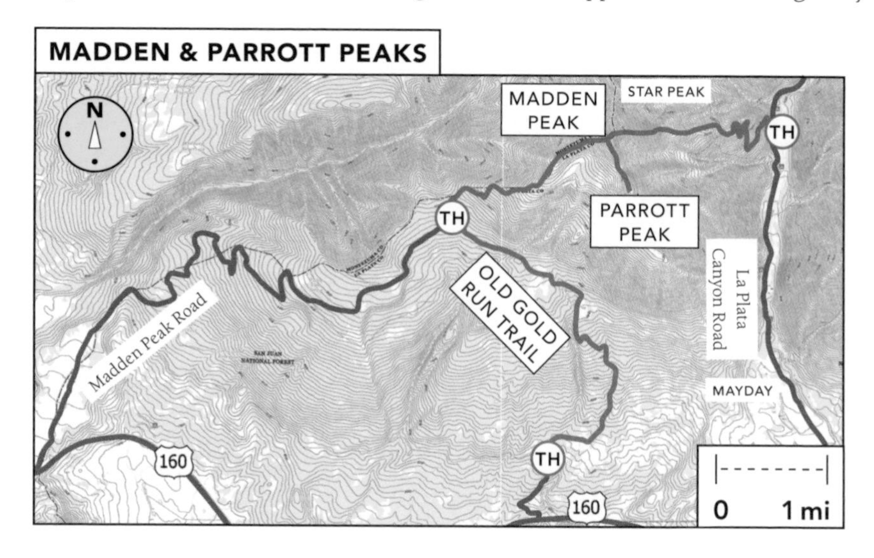

Colorado fourteeners both in altitude gain and distance. It's good training. The Madden Peak Road route is perfect if time is limited but you want to bag a peak or two and still feel you've earned it. Be warned that the drive in is a little rough.

Whichever way you choose, these peaks on the southwest corner of the La Plata Mountains offer fantastic views to the south and west. You'll be able to see four states. They're close to Durango and not exactly easy, but there's no technical difficulty. They're also not extremely popular, but on a typical summer weekend you'll likely see someone else roaming about.

LA PLATA CANYON ROUTE (STEEP & ROCKY)

This is my favorite way to climb these peaks, and although you'll have to do a little bit of route finding, it shouldn't be too difficult to find the summit. La Plata Canyon Road is impossible to miss if you do somehow lose your way and want to return.

APPROACH: From its split with 550, take US 160 west out of Durango about 11 miles (just past Hesperus) to CR 124, which heads north toward La Plata Canyon. In 4.4 miles, just after you've slowed to go through the tiny town of Mayday, the road turns to gravel. In 6.5 miles, just past Miner's Cabin Campground (on your right), look for a dirt road on the left heading steeply uphill. (Alas, the old blue bus that once adorned this spot is gone.) A small, rough area holds room for several vehicles (N 37 22.980, W 108 04.649, 8,989 feet).

The description assumes you will park here. It's possible to drive up this road at least the first 1.5 miles. However, the road is very rough and narrow, and it's no fun if you have to figure out how to get past an approaching jeep or Off Highway Vehicle (OHV).

HIKE: Hike up the road, which makes several long switchbacks as it heads steeply uphill. After 1.25 miles you'll reach a small saddle at a left-hand switchback (N 37 23.068, W 108 04.996, 9,874 feet) and grab some views of Star and Gibbs Peaks; there might be signs of mining activity here. The road levels off.

At 1.5 miles you'll reach a junction (N 37 22.975, W 108 05.159, 9,980 feet). Go right onto FR 791. When this road divides in 0.3 miles, go left uphill, and head toward the crest of a ridge. You should reach the ridge in about 100 yards. Continue on this ridge to the top. You'll encounter downed trees, some steep spots, and a long and steep rock field.

At 2.5 miles (N 37 22.958, W 108 06.060, 11,314 feet) you'll transition from sedimentary shale to volcanic shale. You're mostly out of the trees now, with just a few hearty pine trees braving the elements. Reach the wide-open summit at 2.8 miles (N 37 22.937, W 108 06.360, 11,972 feet) and enjoy the 360-degree views.

As promised, you can see four states from here. To the southwest, make out Shiprock, in New Mexico. Beyond Shiprock you can see the Lukachukai and Chuska

Looking up from the road into the north Root Creek basin between Parrott and Madden.

Mountains in Arizona. To the west are the Abajo Mountains of Utah. There's lots of Colorado to see: the town of Mancos, Mesa Verde to the west; Lewis, Silver, and other peaks on the eastern La Plata range; and Lake Nighthorse to the southeast.

OPTIONS: To connect to Parrott Peak, just follow the ridge to the saddle at 3.1 miles (N 37 22.657, W 108 06.292, 11,546 feet), and then on up to the Parrott summit at 3.4 miles (N 37 22.486, W 108 06.161, 11,857 feet). It's rocky but fairly easy.

From Parrott—named after Tiburcio Parrott, who in the 1870s financed the old town of Parrott City at the canyon's mouth—you have more options. Obviously, you can return the way you came. Or you can return to the saddle and head east into the drainage, the north fork of Root Creek. It involves bushwhacking down an avalanche path, but eventually you'll come to the semblance of a road through the skunk cabbage. Take that 0.3 miles to a dirt road and go left (N 37 22.743, W 108 05.549, 10,018 feet). It's another 0.5 miles to return to the junction you came to at the 1.5-mile mark of this hike.

Another option is to continue south down the ridge from the Parrott summit and look to connect with a forested ridge down lower that heads to the east. This is kind of tricky and only recommended if you're confident in your route-finding skills.

MADDEN PEAK ROAD ROUTE
(SHORT CLIMB WITH LONGER DRIVE)

The long, rough approach drive is certainly a turn-off. But if time is limited, this is the quickest and easiest method of reaching the top of Madden Peak. Heck, you could even drive up to the rough section, mountain bike the rough road, then lock your bike to a tree to do the hike. Might mean bringing a change of footwear, but this is certainly an option; unquestionably you would gain time on the mountain bike down.

APPROACH: Don't turn up La Plata Canyon but continue on US 160 another 10 miles past the CR 124 turn. At the top of Mancos Hill take a right onto the gravel Madden Peak Road (FR 316). The going is smooth until the 4.8-mile mark, when suddenly the road gets rougher. You probably want to park the family sedan here.

The road continues to get rougher and slower, with huge potholes and dips. You don't need 4WD, but high clearance is recommended. At 8 miles, you'll reach a meadow where you'll notice a trail heading off in a Y to the right (east). You might also see a Gold Run Trail sign. Park in this large meadow (N 37 22.209, W 108 08.095, 10,098 feet).

HIKE: From the meadow, hike up the dirt road, and in about 0.2 miles look for an abandoned road heading to the northeast that is gated off. If you miss it and come to the end of the dirt road in another 100 yards, no sweat; just find a path to the east from here and soon you'll join the abandoned road.

At 0.9 miles from the large meadow go left at the fork, up the really steep grade (N 37 22.478, W 108 07.552, 10,767 feet). In another tenth of a mile you'll break out of the forest. Make your way up to the ridge as you begin to get those four-state views. You'll encounter some abandoned mine shafts (man, those miners were tough!), and at around 11,500 feet you'll begin a scramble up loose shale rock, also called scree. You may want to use your hands in places as it steepens, and you'll definitely need to watch each step, but there's no technical prowess required.

At 2.2 miles you're at the summit.

OPTIONS: Parrott is within easy striking distance. See page 84.

Looking up at the western approach to Madden Peak.

Looking from the Madden Peak summit across the saddle to Parrott Peak and off into New Mexico.

OLD GOLD RUN ROUTE (THE LONG WALK)

This is also fairly easily accessible (though it helps to have 4WD) and straightforward. But yes, it's long.

APPROACH: Go past the La Plata Canyon turnoff at 4.7 miles and be ready for the Cherry Creek Picnic Area turnoff to the north (right). There's a small road sign on the left, but it'll come up quickly. Go up the hill and through the large open area and look for FR 320, which heads west at first but then tends north. After a mile of sometimes rough road (4WD recommended), you'll come to a T-intersection with an old railroad grade (8,440 feet). You can park around here or keep driving this bumpy, potholed road another half-mile to the trail. This description assumes you start at the T.

HIKE: From the T head east 0.5 miles. Keep an eye out for a fairly established trail, the Old Gold Run Trail, heading north off the road. There might be a sign, maybe just a pile of rocks, or maybe just the trail itself. These are the coordinates: N 37 20.337, W 108 06.572, 8,472 feet elevation. The trail climbs steadily. Continue 1.2 miles (1.7 miles from the T), and go through stock fences. You'll be hiking up through a thick aspen forest that should provide plenty of shade.

At a junction at 2 miles, go right (north) onto the Starvation Creek Trail (N 37 21.210, W 108 06.710, 9,445 feet). You'll likely encounter a couple of small stream crossings, the biggest of which occurs at mile 3.4 (N 37 22.486, W 108 06.161, 10,072 feet). Through this stretch there's a good chance you'll encounter cattle and motorbikes, or maybe horses or grouse. At 4.1 miles you'll come to the large meadow (N 37 22.209, W 108 08.095, 10,098 feet) described on page 85. Follow directions in the Madden Peak Road route from this point; it's another 2.2 miles to the summit.

OPTIONS: Wait! There are more options?

Sure. You can bag a series of four peaks in one day. Start at Gibbs Peak (see page 88) and work south over Star, Madden, and then Parrott. From the top of Parrott you can hike back down to La Plata Canyon and make a big loop, or you can go back to Gibbs the way you came.

Or you can park around Snowslide Campground and hike up Snowslide Gulch to access the top of Parrott. After about a three-quarters of a mile up the gulch, head right to access a ridge that tends basically northwest toward Parrott. You'll merge with another ridge just south of the Parrott summit. There's not much parking near this access; it's also hard to find the trail, and you'll need to do a bit of bushwhacking, but you wanted more options…

Looking down the western approach to Madden. You can see four states from here. That's Cortez, with Sleeping Ute in the distance.

GIBBS PEAK

DISTANCE: 7.8 miles round-trip

ELEVATION: Start at 9,080 feet, summit at 12,286 feet (3,206-foot gain)

RATING: Moderate

TIME ALLOWED: 4 to 5 hours

Compared with many La Plata hikes, Gibbs Peak is an easy one because it has a road most of the way up, at least a semblance of a trail from where the road ends, and only a few steep stretches to the summit.

Every hike in the La Platas is steep, and a drive up the canyon shows why. It's a narrow valley that rises steeply on both sides. The good news: The valley floor gets most of the traffic, so when you rise above it, you'll likely get some solitude, assuming that's what you seek.

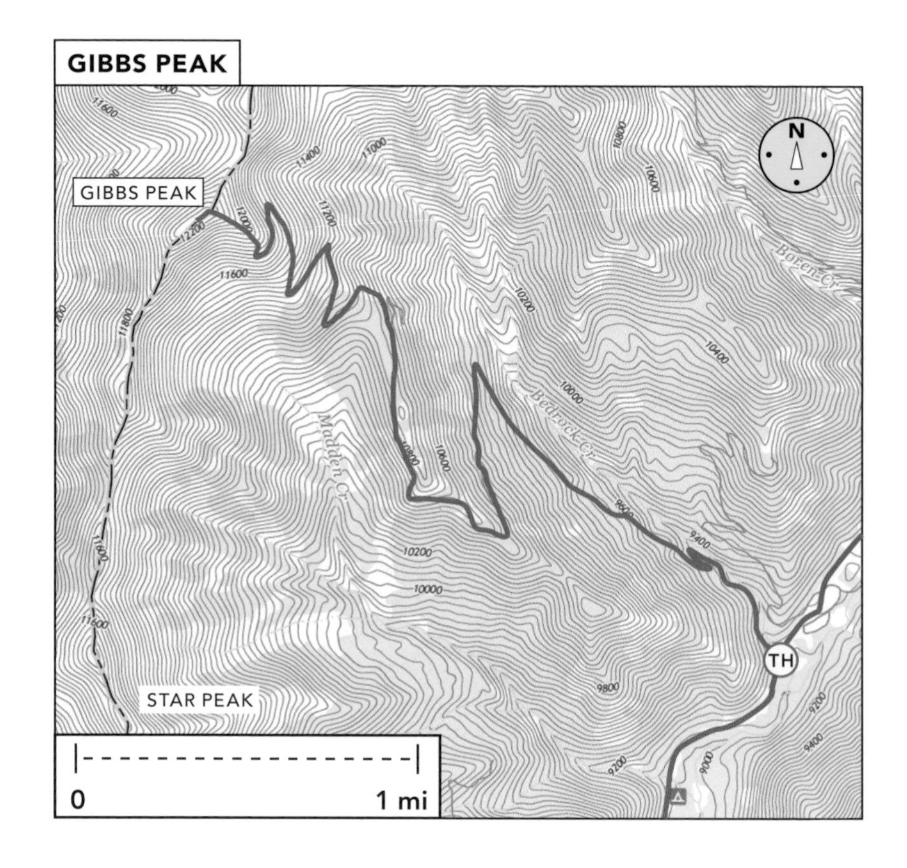

The top of Gibbs Peak offers a short section of fairly easy scrambling.

In the past there was an access issue with the owner of the cabin located early in the hike. Private property issues continue to crop up in the San Juans, particularly in the La Platas. Don't trespass, and if you have questions about private property lines, talk to officials with the Forest Service.

APPROACH: From Durango it's 11 miles on US 160 to Hesperus, then another 0.3 miles to the La Plata Canyon road (CR 124), which goes north off US 160. At 4.4 miles the road turns to gravel, just past Mayday. You'll pass Snowslide and Kroeger campgrounds. At 7.6 miles the four-wheel-drive Gibbs Peak road heads up northwest to the left (N 37 23.495, W 108 04.294, 9,080 feet). Park here. If you cross Bedrock Creek on the canyon road, you've gone too far.

HIKE: Begin up a four-wheel-drive road (officially the Bedrock Creek OHV trail) that varies between sections of steep climbs and sections of gentle rises. At the first big switchback at 0.5 miles, it's possible to take a shortcut to reach the road above. The mileage here assumes you don't cut this switchback.

In 1.4 miles you'll come to the next major switchback (N 37 24.256, W 108 05.270, 10,100 feet), with the road going uphill (south) to the left and a less obvious road continuing straight to the Allard Mine. Go uphill left, and at 2 miles a major switchback (N 37 23.814, W 108 05.154, 10,460 feet) changes your direction to west, then northwest. The road becomes a bit rockier for a while.

After a flat section that heads north-northwest, the road heads west and begins to climb up the mountain. At a point where downfall blocks the road (3.3 miles from the start of the hike), it's best to begin hiking west and southwest of the mountainside. There should be a hint of a trail here. Soon you'll again turn northwest and climb a rocky ridge toward the summit (N 37 24.590, W 108 06.132, 12,286 feet). You may have to use your hands in a couple places, but there's little exposure.

OPTIONS: If you can find it, there's a little trail that leaves the road just north of Madden Creek. You can follow that trail and eventually end up going north, then southeast briefly, on a little-used road that connects with the Gibbs Peak road, described above, at 10,700 feet. It's a nice trail and allows you to avoid the road.

SILVER MOUNTAIN

DISTANCE: 9 miles round-trip to Silver Mountain summit

ELEVATION: Start at 9,080 feet, Deadwood at 12,285 feet, Silver at 12,450 feet (3,370-foot gain)

RATING: Moderate, with a few short and steep climbs

TIME ALLOWED: 5 to 7 hours

Silver is the marquee La Plata Mountain for many Durangoans because you can see it from most places in town. (Don't do anything stupid on the summit; they can see you down there.) There's a river to cross and some elevation to gain, so it's not a breeze, but you'll be rewarded by a great view of the local landscape.

The route follows the Neptune OHV Road until a few hundred vertical feet west of the Deadwood summit, at which point a ridgeline trail will take you the rest of the way. A previous route began close to the intersection of Lewis Creek and the La Plata River, and followed Tirbircio Creek on the northwest side of Silver Mountain. However, private land issues have made this route untenable, so use the hike described here; there are no additional options.

APPROACH: From its split with 550, take US 160 west out of Durango about 11 miles (just past Hesperus) to CR 124, which heads north toward La Plata Canyon. At 4.4 miles, just past Mayday, the road turns to gravel. At 7.5 miles, turn right and downhill into La Plata City Campground. You're looking for a road that runs into the La Plata River, and if you see signs for Neptune OHV Trail #797, follow them. There is room for several cars just before the road meets the river (N 37 23.587, W 108 04.152, 9,080 feet).

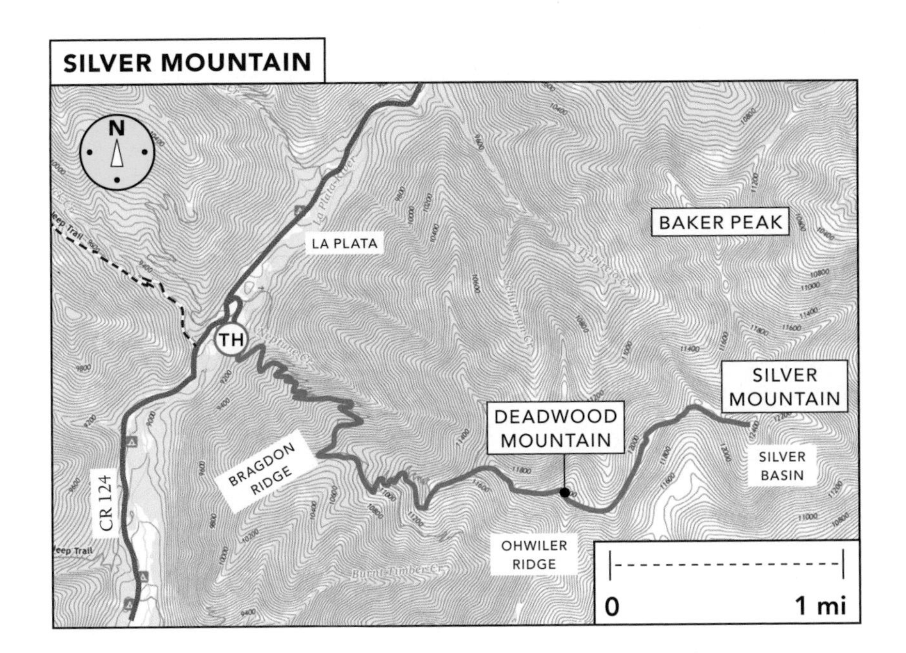

HIKE: The first task is to cross the river. Bringing sandals and shorts for this task is a good idea, particularly early in the hiking season and following heavy winter snows. The current might be running so swiftly that you'll decide not to attempt it. By July in most years it shouldn't be a problem though, and by August it's likely you won't even get your feet wet.

Once across, the path is the OHV road. You may encounter some four-wheelers, but this route isn't for beginners, so there probably won't be too many. The path snakes up the mountainside, and you'll begin to get views of the western La Platas, particularly Gibbs, and the spiked triumvirate of Burwell, Spiller, and Babcock.

At 1.8 miles, you'll meet up with Bragdon Ridge (N 37 23.116, W 108 03.681, 10,744 feet). An abandoned private road joins from the right. Continue up the main road. It makes more switchbacks, hits the ridge again, and soon Deadwood Mountain appears dead ahead. At 2.9 miles (N 37 23.039, W 108 03.056, 11,622 feet) the official road ends (abandoned roads head both left and right here). There will be a steep hiking trail straight ahead; take it.

This obvious trail stays close to the ridge. It's a bit rocky at times, but it's not very difficult. At 3.4 miles, you'll reach the Deadwood summit (N 37 22.976, W 108 02.609, 12,285 feet). A large expanse of the Needle Mountains is visible between Lewis and Silver Mountains to the northeast. Durango can be seen nearly 6,000 feet below.

Next, follow the zigzagging ridge over to Silver Mountain, beginning southeast toward Lake Nighthorse, which you've undoubtedly noticed by now. Again, there's nothing terribly tricky along this ridge, although you will find some exposure to one side or another at times, and it can get windy up here. The ridgetop rolls over several

Cross the La Plata River to begin the climb. This is along the Neptune OHV road. There's hardly a trickle when this was taken, but early in the season, it won't look this easy.

bumps and drops down to near 12,000 feet before the final 400-foot steep push up to the Silver Mountain summit (N 37 23.214, W 108 01.769, 12,450 feet).

Enjoy views nearly due north to the three Wilson fourteeners, a unique view of Engineer Mountain, the Needles in all their glory, and down southeast toward Perins Peak, Twin Buttes, Barnroof Point, and more.

Along the ridge heading down from Deadwood, a view of the western La Platas. From left to right: Madden, Star, and Gibbs Peaks.

HIKES UP & ON MISSIONARY RIDGE

This area changed in 2002 when a fire started on a hot, dry June 9 at a switchback along Missionary Ridge Road. The blaze swept quickly through a tinder-dry forest, making its way east all the way past Lemon and then Vallecito reservoirs. It ultimately burned an estimated 73,000 acres.

All the hikes in this chapter were affected, excepting Mountain View Crest, which is north of the main burn area and mostly above timberline anyway. Many of the ponderosa, fir, spruce, and other big trees in the fire's path were destroyed, although some nooks and crannies were spared. Where the fire didn't burn so hot, some trees survived.

By now the area has turned green again, and the ubiquitous aspen has taken hold in much of the area. Many blackened trees remain standing, just waiting for dead roots to disintegrate and a strong wind to come along. Be wary on a breezy day.

The trails remain, the creeks still flow, and the hiking is fine. Many of these trails begin at lower elevations. If you're looking for something close to town or something for an early spring or late fall day, these hikes might be just the ones you need.

Top: After a few miles on the Burnt Timber Trail the view opens up, with the Florida River valley to the east, and Organ Mountain (13,032 feet) in the distance. Bottom: Shearer Creek in the early fall, just above where the trail crosses the creek for the first time.

HAFLIN CREEK

DISTANCE: 7.6 miles round-trip

ELEVATION: Start at 6,620 feet, high point at 9,500 feet (2,880-foot gain)

RATING: Moderate, due to altitude

TIME ALLOWED: 4 to 5½ hours

It's not hard to spot changes wrought by the 2002 Missionary Ridge fire, which started not far from here, headed east, and scorched 73,000 acres, much of it National Forest land. That means you're going to see a combination of black tree trunks, many of them fallen, as well as small aspen trees and other green undergrowth.

It's still a nice hike, particularly in early summer and early fall, when temperatures are a little cooler. It's a great early-summer warmup for fourteeners. The elevation and mileage gained on this hike are similar to that of climbing a mountain; the big difference, obviously, is the altitude.

Haflin is a small creek in a deep and rugged canyon that breaks through the west steep side of Missionary Ridge. You start near the creek, hike high above it, later come even with it, cross it, and finally rise through an open brushy area to the top of the ridge above the stream source. In this brushy area, you can get good views to the west of the Animas River valley and the La Platas beyond.

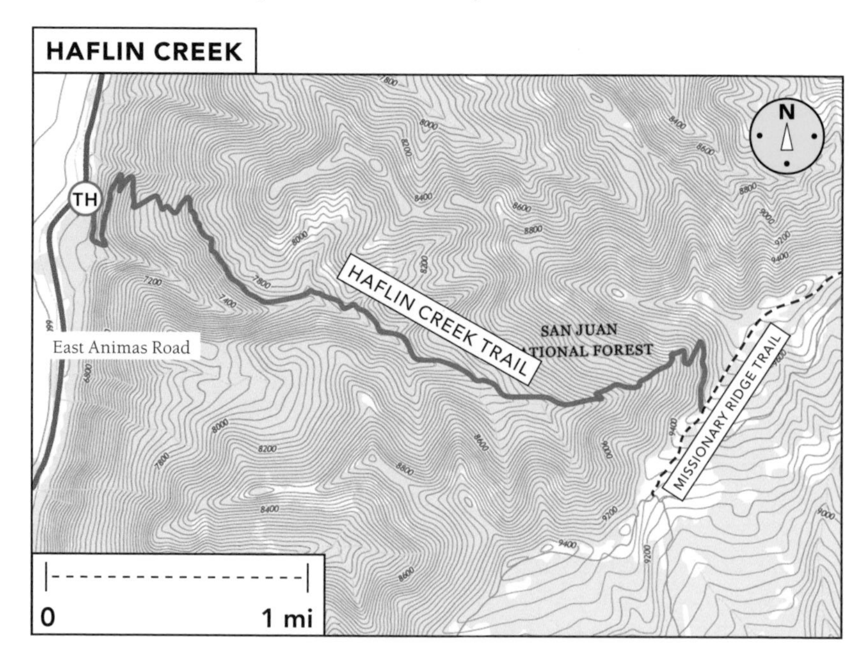

A winter solstice run down the Haflin Creek Trail.

Before the fire, this hike illustrated very well the different climatic zones. At the bottom, you start among piñon, juniper, oak brush, and yucca. Soon you'll reach a level of ponderosa pine; this gave way to quaking aspen and the beginning of spruce and fir. But the fire devastated this canyon, leaving few areas unscathed. It'll be decades before the burned conifers return. Aspen are already making a comeback: the first stage of succession.

Note: It's a good idea to stay out of this area during hard rains (flash floods and mudslides are possible) and high winds (if you see a falling tree, think fast).

APPROACH: From Main Avenue in Durango, take Thirty-Second Street east 1.2 miles and make a left turn on East Animas Road (CR 250). After 5.3 miles on CR 250, you should see a sign on the east side of the road for Haflin Creek Trail. A few off-road parking spots are available here (N 37 22.075, W 107 50.356, 6,620 feet). A fenced-off Forest Service maintenance yard is just to the south.

HIKE: The trail starts off slightly uphill in an easterly direction but soon launches into a series of climbing switchbacks, some of them a bit steep. The first switchback goes north in 0.25 miles; if you miss it, you'll find the going gets rougher fairly quickly.

Continue climbing switchbacks and distancing yourself from the canyon bottom. At about 0.4 miles you'll really start to notice the burned ponderosa. The good news is you'll get views across the valley; you'll be able to see evidence of the Valley Fire, which occurred during the 2002 Missionary Ridge Fire but was not related to it.

At 1.1 miles from the start, the steep switchbacks end and you'll head southeast. (The trail rises only moderately for the next 1.5 miles.) At 1.5 miles from the trailhead you'll begin to hear a waterfall. This will tempt some people, but it's very difficult to get to a place where you can see it. Best advice: Don't try. Enjoy the creek before it falls; there are several access points.

At 2.8 miles the trail again steepens. It'll remain steep until the final switchback, after which the trail traverses south up an open hillside. At 3.8 miles you'll hit the Missionary Ridge Trail (N 37 21.412, W 107 47.945, 9,500 feet). Enjoy views of the La Platas; Silver and Lewis are the most prominent mountains from here.

No part of this hike is difficult, but it is rated moderate because of the relatively large amount of altitude gain.

OPTIONS: This is listed as a half-day hike, but you could lengthen it by going either north or south on the Missionary Ridge Trail.

Going south, the hiking is good for a mile or so, and you soon come to the Durango Hills subdivision.

Going north on this trail brings you to two easterly descents and one westerly descent within 6.2 miles. All three descents offer the possibility of making this a point-to-point hike. In 1.7 miles you'll come to the First Fork Trail, and 3 miles after that you'll reach Red Creek (see page 105); both of these go east off Missionary Ridge. In 1.5 miles after Red Creek you'll come to the Stevens Creek Trail (see below), which heads west toward the Animas Valley.

STEVENS CREEK

DISTANCE: 11.4 miles round-trip

ELEVATION: Start at 7,750 feet, high point at 10,050 feet (2,300-foot gain)

RATING: Moderate

TIME ALLOWED: 5 to 7 hours

This is called Stevens Creek, but you stay way above the creek and never really see it or even come close enough to hear it. You are in the Stevens Creek valley, so that's good enough, right?

This hike, like the Haflin Creek hike, is up the west side of Missionary Ridge and connects to the Missionary Ridge Trail, but it is much longer because the route is less direct and the ridge trail swings east quite a distance here. The Stevens Creek Trail

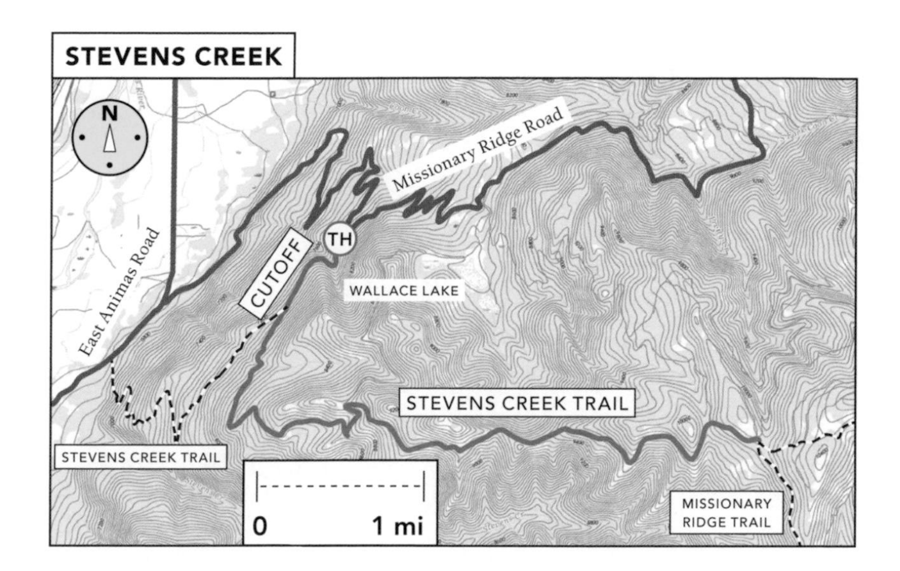

passes through big-timber areas of pine, aspen, fir, and spruce, as well as through some open meadowland with streams in the valleys. But like the Haflin hike, this travels through areas scorched by the 2002 Missionary Ridge Fire. Some of it isn't all that pretty, but it does increase the view.

The route follows constructed trail and several old mountain roads, most of them closed to cars and trucks. Very little of it is rocky. There is nothing difficult about it except its length.

Access is a little tricky. There is a trailhead off CR 250, but it's *very* difficult to find and there's little to no parking. Instead, this description bypasses the lower part of Stevens Creek Trail and takes you up Missionary Ridge Road to a cutoff trail.

Also, be aware that this trail has been popular with downhill mountain bikers; they use it for practice. That shouldn't be a problem, because they stay mostly on the lower section, but it's definitely something to keep an eye out for.

APPROACH: Take US 550 north of Thirty-Second Street and Main Avenue for 6.5 miles, then turn right onto Trimble Lane (CR 252). Take Trimble Lane 0.9 miles and veer left (north) onto East Animas Road (CR 250). Take East Animas Road 3.2 miles and veer right onto the gravel Missionary Ridge Road, heading uphill.

The Missionary Ridge Road winds its way uphill. To find this trailhead, it's a good idea to use your odometer and your memory; it's 3.7 miles to the trailhead, which you'll find at the third sweeping left-hand switchback in the road. There is not a whole lot to mark the trail, but after close inspection you should (hopefully) see a brown plastic stake, or something, that tells you this is the cutoff trail to Stevens Creek Trail.

There's room for a couple of cars in a pullout off the switchback (N 37 25.460, W 107 46.982, 7,750 feet).

Indian paintbrush, not far from the Stevens Creek Trail near Wallace Lakes.

HIKE: Go south over a berm and find the trail heading slightly uphill. Contour in and out of one drainage, then turn south and join up with the Stevens Creek Trail at 0.5 miles (N 37 25.175, W 107 47.238, 7,900 feet). Go left uphill on an old road grade (still heading south). You're meeting the Stevens Creek Trail 1,200 feet above the other trailhead along East Animas Road. You're welcome.

The trail continues south for another 0.25 miles before it does a jog to contour the Elkhorn Canyon drainage. After another 0.5 miles south, at 1.3 miles, the trail turns east and heads generally east up to Missionary Ridge. Also, during this stretch the trail will widen as it joins another old road.

At 2.6 miles, and after a short climb north-northwest, you'll come to a junction (N 37 24.681, W 107 46.915, 8,810 feet). The trail left takes you to Wallace Lakes and back to Missionary Ridge Road. Continue right (east) on the trail. From here it's another 3.1 miles to the Missionary Ridge Trail (N 37 24.507, W 107 44.392, 10,050 feet); for the last 0.5 miles you again join an old logging road.

The total hike from where you parked to the junction with the Missionary Ridge Trail is 5.7 miles. At the junction with Missionary Ridge, the trail goes below the top on the west side; therefore, there is no view across to the valley below to the east side. If you want that view, you can go either right or left on the Missionary Ridge Trail, but it's about a half-mile to the left and a mile to the right before you get decent views eastward. Or you can just be satisfied with the good views looking west toward the La Platas.

OPTIONS: You could attempt to find the Stevens Creek trailhead off East Animas Road. It's between 0.4 and 0.5 miles south of where Missionary Ridge Road begins.

From here, it's 2.8 miles and 1,200 feet elevation gain to the junction mentioned above, where Stevens Creek Trail meets the cutoff trail that goes south from Missionary Ridge Road.

MOUNTAIN VIEW CREST

DISTANCE: 9.2 miles round-trip

ELEVATION: Start at 11,480 feet (or 11,080 feet), overlook at 12,998 feet (1,518-foot or 1,918-foot gain)

RATING: Moderate, due to length and altitude

TIME ALLOWED: 5 to 7 hours

The trailhead is northeast of Durango and is reached via 24 miles of gravel road (which can be washboarded and dusty) and 2 miles of four-wheel-drive road. It'll take 1½ to 2 hours of driving from Durango. The end of the trail offers some of the most fantastic scenery in Colorado. Several variations will affect your time, mileage, and altitude. The statistics given above are from the end of the four-wheel-drive road to Overlook Point and back by the same route. Once you're in the area, you will want to take advantage of the full range of views. You can make this hike in a half-day, but a long, full day is much better to allow you to appreciate its riches.

APPROACH: Take US 550 north from Thirty-Second Street in Durango 6.5 miles to Trimble Lane, where you'll take a right. Take Trimble (CR 252) 0.9 miles to East Animas Road (CR 250), then turn left (north). From there it's 3.2 miles to Missionary Ridge Road, a gravel road that veers right and uphill off of CR 250. This climbing gravel road (FR 682) has many switchbacks and goes through areas that were badly scarred by the 2002 Missionary Ridge Fire.

Follow FR 682 about 19 miles and take Henderson Lake Road when it branches off to the right. In 2.9 miles there's a large parking area on the right. Most cars should be able to make it another 0.3 miles, where the road becomes four-wheel drive. From here it's 2.1 miles to where the road ends at the wilderness barrier and you will find plenty of parking space (N 37 31.828, W 107 40.857, 11,480 feet).

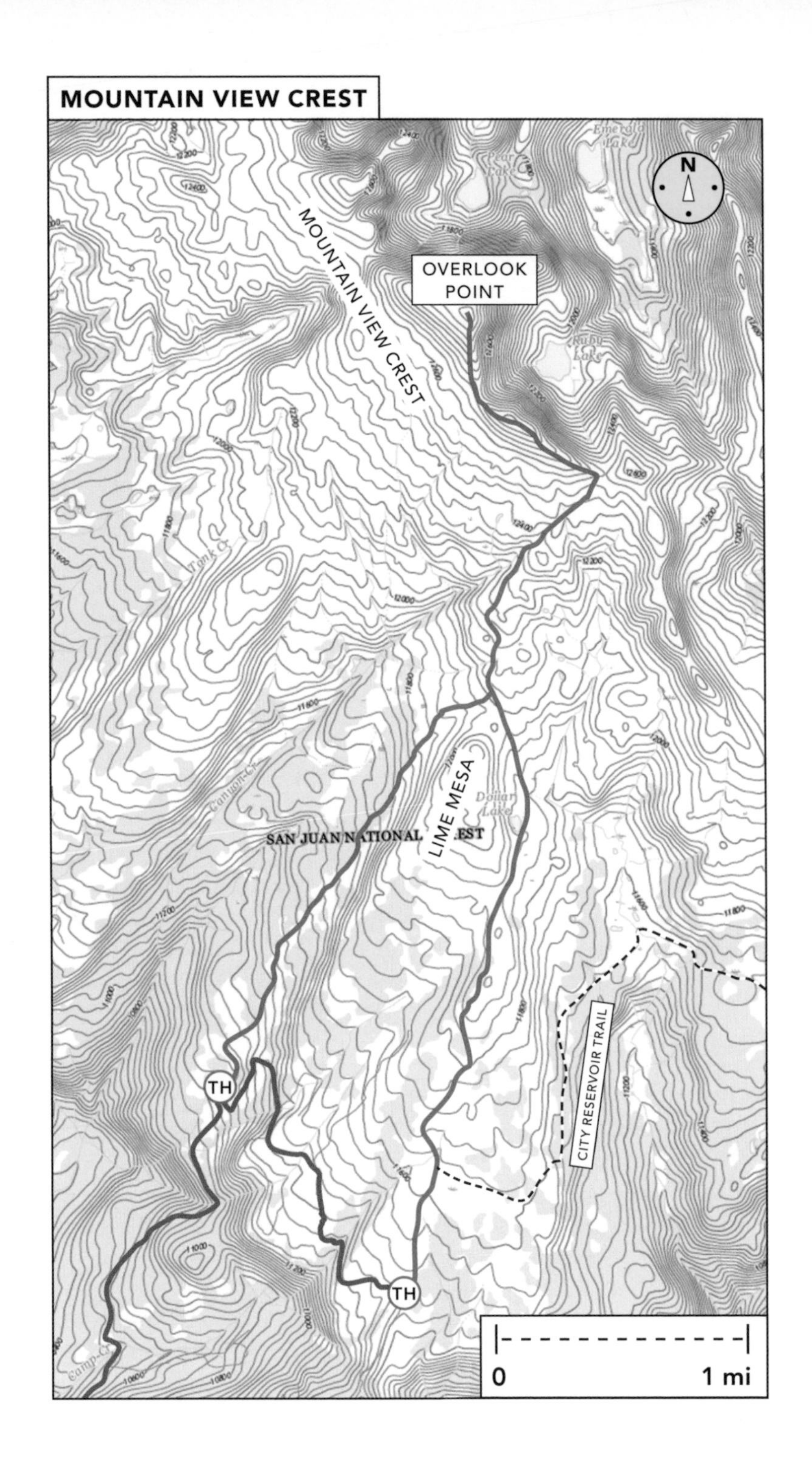
MOUNTAIN VIEW CREST
N
MOUNTAIN VIEW CREST
OVERLOOK POINT
LIME MESA
SAN JUAN N ATIONAL .EST
CITY RESERVOIR TRAIL
TH
TH
0
1 mi

From the saddle before the climb up to Overlook Point, Ruby Lake lies below, with Pigeon and Turret Peaks in the not-far distance.

From the point where the road turns to four-wheel drive, it's only 0.4 miles to the spot where the alternate trail route leaves the road; described below, this route skirts the west side of Lime Mesa. Driving to the wilderness boundary takes 15 to 20 minutes more and gains you about 400 feet elevation.

HIKE: From the end of the road, cross into the Weminuche Wilderness and hike straight north along the east side of Lime Mesa, following the old, rutted-out jeep road. The trail is right at the timberline, and in a while you'll begin to get wide-open views. It's 1.9 miles to Dollar Lake (N 37 33.327, W 107 40.367, 11,860 feet). At 2.9 miles, the trail turns northeast and steepens.

At 3.5 miles, to the south of a ridge, two trails split (N 37 34.414, W 107 40.075). One goes right, almost due east. Take the one going left (north) uphill to the ridge, and in 0.1 miles you'll reach a saddle at the east end of Mountain View Crest. Don't let the view take your breath away.

The views become even more dramatic as you climb left along the ridge a half-mile to the top of the first rise (12,802 feet). The second rise, another half-mile beyond, is called Overlook Point, and it stands at 12,998 feet (N 37 35.020, W 107 40.577).

The drama is below and beyond, in the form of four beautiful lakes. To the right and below Overlook Point lies, first, Ruby Lake; a little farther north and lower is Emerald Lake. Walk northwest and down from Overlook Point, and you'll see both Pear and Webb Lakes almost due north. All of these provide excellent trout fishing. To go down to them commits most people to an overnight stay; they're farther away than they appear.

But the view down to the lakes is only the start of the scenery. Far below them, Needle Creek is too far down to see, but across Needle Canyon, and abruptly above, rise Pigeon and Turret Peaks. These two miss being fourteeners by a small margin, but there is no more dramatic view in the San Juan Mountains. Viewing the east face of Pigeon can send shivers up and down your spine.

The Needles fourteeners are easy to spot if you know what you're looking for. The Wilsons, to the northwest, dwarf Engineer Mountain in the foreground. Almost due north on the far horizon is the unmistakable summit of Sneffels, another fourteener.

OPTIONS: You don't have to drive all the way to the wilderness barrier. From where the road turns rough (see Approach on page 101), it's 0.4 miles to a switchback. Just where this sweeping switchback begins climbing toward the south, look for a blocked-off road heading north (N 37 32.454, W 107 41.612, 10,080 feet). This road/trail heads north-northeast and meets up with the trail described north of Dollar Lake, just north of Lime Mesa.

The route becomes less defined the farther you go, but it should be fairly easy to follow. It's best not to stray too far from Lime Mesa. If you veer west into the trees too far, you'll get bogged down. In 1.7 miles you'll come to the north end of Lime Mesa and reach the timberline; swing right (east) here across the tundra. In about 0.2 miles, you should intersect the trail described above. Take it left another 1.1 miles to the saddle at the east end of Mountain View Crest.

If you take this alternate route along the west side of Lime Mesa and begin from the switchback, it's about a half-mile shorter, with 400 feet more elevation gain than the route described from the end of the road.

Also, it's possible to climb Mount Kennedy. From where the trails split at mile 3.5, take the trail going east and hike 3 miles. You can end up climbing north off the trail to the top of Kennedy. It has a double top, with the farthest being the highest (13,125 feet). Either top will give about the same view.

The view here is to the north into Chicago Basin, surrounded by the Needles fourteeners. They are, from west to east, Eolus, Sunlight, and Windom. This is one of the most popular backpacking areas in the state. People ride the Durango & Silverton Narrow Gauge train to Needleton and hike 6 miles up Needle Creek, where a base camp can be established to climb all three peaks.

RED CREEK–FIRST FORK

DISTANCE: 7.2 miles round-trip

ELEVATION: Start at 7,820 feet, high point at 9,800 feet (1,980-foot gain)

RATING: Easy, except for the steep last 0.5 miles

TIME ALLOWED: 3 to 4½ hours

Red Creek Trail is a nice hike any time the snow is not too deep. But it is especially good on a warm summer day; for most of the way, it follows a nice gurgling stream at the bottom of a narrow canyon in the shade of big fir, spruce, and aspen trees. Like other Missionary Ridge hikes, this route shows evidence of the 2002 fire. However, the east side of the ridge was not so severely scorched as the west side (Haflin and Stevens Trails, for instance). So there are places you'll see no damage at all, and some spots of severe damage.

The trail is easy to follow. It climbs quite gradually for 3 miles, then heads steeply up a series of switchbacks the last 0.5 miles to the top of Missionary Ridge.

APPROACH: Take East Third Avenue north to its end and turn right (northeast) onto Florida Road. Take this road 9.7 miles to a left-hand turn onto CR 246; this is also the way to Colvig Silver Camps.

Follow this gravel road past the camps; in 1 mile the road becomes FR 599, gets much rougher, and heads into the 2002 burn area. This road can get very potholed and difficult to negotiate, especially when it's been raining a lot; you can probably do it in any car, but 4WD is not bad to have if you get into a jam. In another 0.3 miles you'll have to go through a fence and likely will have to open a large swinging gate.

At 0.4 miles beyond the gate the road is blocked off and there is parking available for several vehicles (N 37 21.149, W 107 44.382, 7,820 feet).

As you can deduce from the above description, it wouldn't be the end of the world to park your car when the road gets too rough and walk from there.

HIKE: Start northwest up the road. At 0.2 miles, you'll come to the First Fork Trail, which is across Red Creek to the west. An out-and-back on First Fork makes a great half-day hike. In the spring and very early summer it can be a little difficult to cross Red Creek, but for most of the year, it should be manageable.

To get to Red Creek Trail stay on the road, and at 0.5 miles you'll come to what used to be a good-sized parking area (N 37 21.552, W 107 44.590, 8,020 feet). Find a trail going northwest through a forest of tall aspen and fir that escaped the 2002 fire. You'll cross to the west side of Red Creek in the first 0.1 miles and continue to cross and recross it.

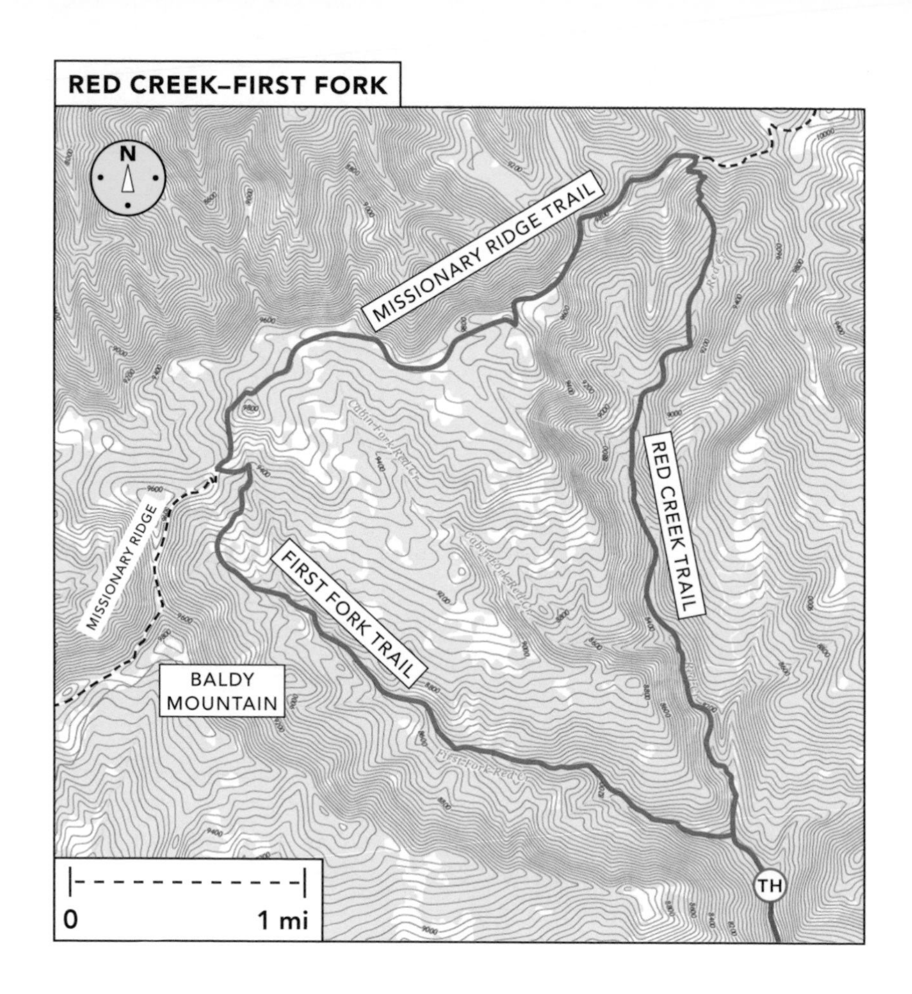

This area didn't fare badly in the fire, but it is prone to flash floods because of rough road conditions. You may notice a few places where the trail has been washed out and repaired.

At 1.4 miles from the start you'll pass through a Forest Service gate on the west side of the creek. At about 3.1 miles the trail is overgrown and can be hard to follow; in other places the trail is a deep trench. At 3.2 miles the trail steepens noticeably, and a quarter-mile beyond that you come to a clearing from where you can look back south and get a nice view into the distance. You can also look up from this clearing and see the ridge that is your destination.

It's another 0.1 miles from the clearing (3.6 miles from the start) to the top of the ridge, where you'll meet the Missionary Ridge Trail, here going east-west on the ridgetop (N 37 23.739, W 107 44.716, 9,800 feet). The distance of 7.2 miles round-trip in the trail description assumes turning around at the union with the Missionary Ridge Trail.

OPTIONS: This hike can be extended into a 10.1-mile loop that brings you back to the starting point via First Fork Trail. From the junction of Red Creek and Missionary Ridge Trails, go west (left). There's a lot of up and down, some of it steep. In 0.8 miles you drop to a low point on the ridge (9,600 feet), then climb back up immediately. From the low point it's 0.7 miles to a thick aspen forest where, curiously, trees were badly burned on one side and left unscathed on the other.

In all it's 3.1 miles along Missionary Ridge, from Red Creek to First Fork Trail. You'll find First Fork Trail taking off to the east at a low point on the ridge. The sign here doesn't exactly scream at you, but you probably won't miss it (N 37 22.616, W 107 46.886, 9,500 feet).

Take First Fork downhill, making sure in a little over 0.1 miles to take the switchback going right (south). Another trail goes straight (east) here, and people have been known to wander for a while. In 1.5 miles from the top the trail levels out a bit and begins a set of numerous creek crossings. In another 2.2 miles from the first creek crossing you'll come to the end of the trail and will have to ford Red Creek to reach the road (N 37 21.314, W 107 44.527, 7,890 feet). Go right here on the road and walk 0.2 miles back to the parking area.

Obviously, another loop option is to go up First Fork and down Red Creek. Amazingly, this is also a 10.1-mile loop.

Another option from the Red Creek Trail junction with Missionary Ridge is to go out and back northeast along the Missionary Ridge Trail. It's only 1.6 miles along the ridge to the junction with Stevens Creek Trail (N 37 24.507, W 107 44.392, 10,050 feet), opening the possibility of a point-to-point hike (consult the Stevens Creek description on page 98 for more details, but it could make about a 10.4-mile hike). Along the stretch from Red Creek to Stevens Creek Trail, the spruce-and-fir forest is well burned. Chances are you'll be okay, but dead trees have been heard falling. It's best not to travel along here when it's windy.

SHEARER CREEK

DISTANCE: 16 miles round-trip

ELEVATION: Start at 7,560 feet, high point at 10,200 feet (2,640-foot gain)

RATING: Moderate, due to length

TIME ALLOWED: 7 to 9 hours

This is an interesting, but long, hike to the top of Missionary Ridge from a southeasterly approach. It starts out climbing a hill above Florida Road and in 1.3 miles joins Shearer Creek, which it follows closely almost all the way to the top. The rise is quite gradual most of the way, except at the top.

Because of its access directly off Florida Road, this route gets some winter use too. Just take care to stay along the trail because it is an easement through private land for 2 miles.

APPROACH: From the intersection of East Third Avenue and Fifteenth Street in Durango, go northeast on Florida Road (CR 240) 11.9 miles to a turnout and trailhead parking area on the north side of the road (N 37 20.797, W 107 42.199, 7,560 feet).

HIKE: As stated above, the first 2 miles are through private property, so you must stay on the trail and keep dogs on a leash. The Forest Service has legal access for the public through this area. The first few miles of trail are well marked and fairly easy to follow uphill through the large ponderosa pines still standing after the 2002 fire.

Begin uphill through a latched gate. You'll climb, passing through two or three more gates that you'll have to open and shut. As the trail drops 150 feet to the creek you'll begin to pass through the burned section. In 1.3 miles from the start, the trail crosses the creek (N 37 21.654, W 107 42.059, 7,830 feet) and takes a sharp left onto a dirt road. The trail crosses and recrosses the stream many times. It is a gurgling, pleasant little stream in the summer and fall and is easily crossed on the rocks. In the spring and early summer during the snowmelt, the stream is higher and much harder to cross, so this trail is not recommended until the major snowpack is gone at levels of 10,000 feet and lower.

The trail eventually joins a fairly level road (at about N 37 24.485, W 107 42.697, 9,910 feet). From here you'll head north and west on a side ridge that leads in about 2 miles to the top of Missionary Ridge. The point of this side ridge overlooks Lemon Reservoir 2,000 feet below, but it is heavily wooded, making it hard to see the lake.

The return is by the same route as the climb. There is one problem on the return: In the last mile after you leave the stream there are enough cattle paths to obscure the main trail. Keep a close eye on the trail and head southwest, and you should make it back to the parking area, happy but tired.

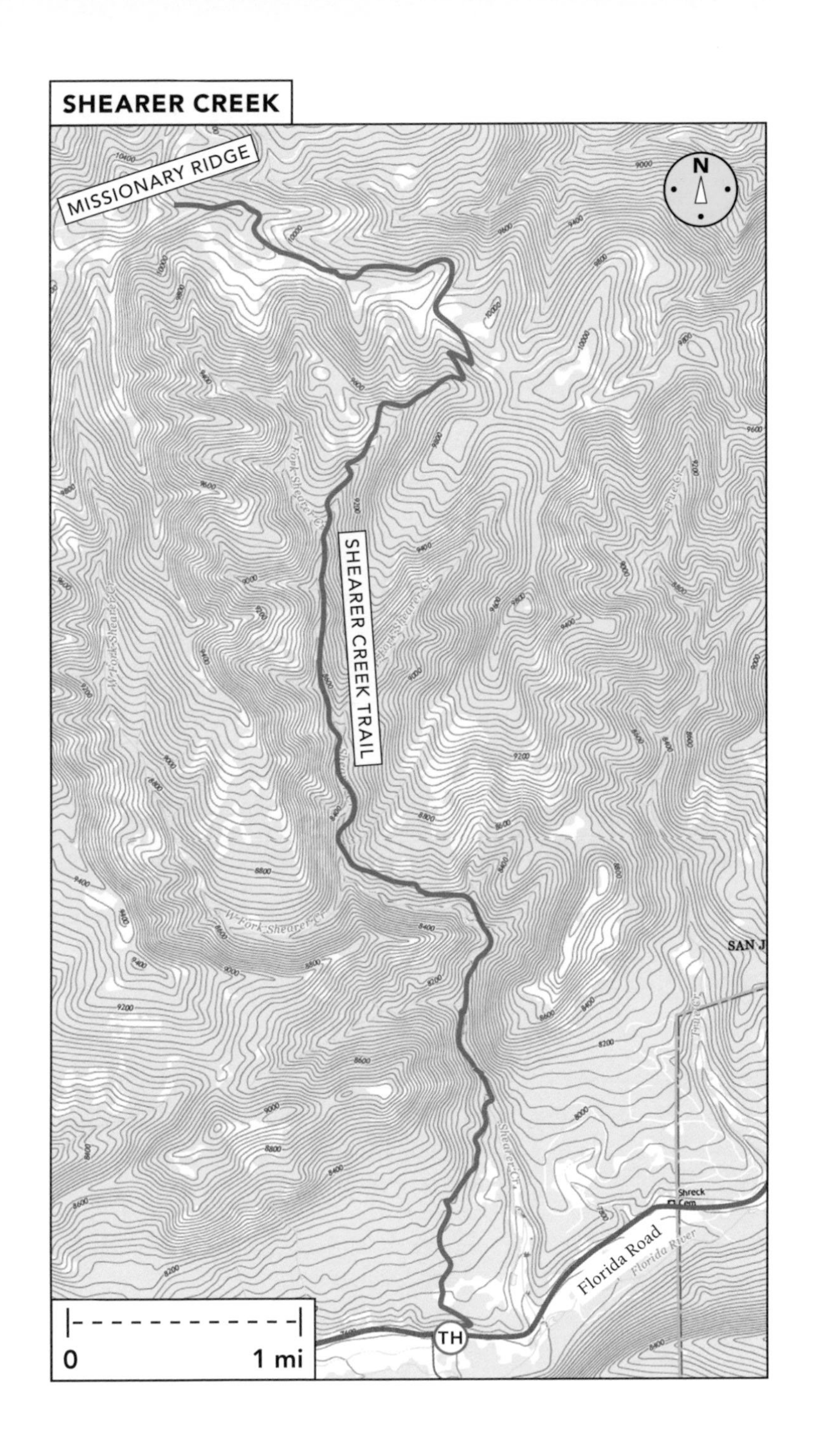
SHEARER CREEK
MISSIONARY RIDGE
N
SHEARER CREEK TRAIL
SAN J
Shreck
Cem
Florida Road
Florida River
TH
0
1 mi

Shearer Creek in the early fall, just above where the Shearer Creek Trail crosses the creek for the first time.

OPTIONS: Returning via the Stevens Creek or Red Creek Trails is possible. These options assume you have a second car waiting to pick you up at the bottom of these trails.

From where Shearer Creek Trail reaches the top of Missionary Ridge it's about 1.5 miles west (left) to the junction with the top of Stevens Creek Trail (see page 98). It would be another 5.7 miles on Stevens Creek, taking the cutoff toward Missionary Ridge Road. Total distance for this hike is 15.2 miles.

You could also continue south past the Stevens Creek junction another 1.6 miles along the Missionary Ridge Trail to the Red Creek Trail (see page 105), then 3.6 miles on the Red Creek Trail to a second vehicle. Total for this hike is 12.7 miles.

BURNT TIMBER

DISTANCE: 7.6 miles round-trip to old road and back

ELEVATION: Start at 8,500 feet, old road at 10,840 feet (2,340-foot gain)

RATING: Moderate, due to rocky trail and climbing

TIME ALLOWED: 3½ to 4½ hours

This rewarding hike traverses genuine backcountry and stays near the rugged upper Florida River canyon. The east side of this canyon presents a high, imposing wall of timber and rock.

There is no great turnaround point, as the trail continues for many miles. This trail makes a good start to a backpacking out-and-back or loop. Horse riders and hunters also use this trail, which quickly heads up into the Weminuche Wilderness.

The description below offers some suggestions for turnaround points to make this a half-day or all-day hike, as well as one method to scramble up to the top of Missionary Ridge.

APPROACH: From the intersection of East Third Avenue and Fifteenth Street in Durango, go northeast on Florida Road (later CR 240) for 14 miles until you get to Lemon Reservoir Road (CR 243). Go straight here, while CR 240 goes 90 degrees right and heads over to the Vallecito drainage.

From the CR 243/240 intersection, go 1.6 miles to the dam, behind which is impounded beautiful Lemon Reservoir. This is an irrigation supply filled by melting winter snows. It is peaceful and inviting, nestled at the base of high wooded hills on each side. Lemon is a favorite fishing and picnicking spot with several good sites along its banks. You may find boaters and paddleboarders here as well.

You'll drive well past the reservoir, and 5.2 miles from the dam take a 90-degree turn left onto FR 596 toward the two National Forest campgrounds. Go through Florida Campground and continue 1.6 miles to Transfer Campground, where you'll find a large parking area and the trailhead to the northwest (N 37 27.816, W 107 40.938, 8,500 feet). This is also the parking area for technical climbers who make the short hike along the north end of the campground to access rock walls above the Florida River.

HIKE: Head up this braided trail etched into a rocky limestone base. At 0.2 miles enter the wilderness, and at 0.5 miles you'll come to a rocky outcrop with a nice view if you head eastward 50 yards or so.

The trail climbs steadily with a few breaks, heading almost due north. At 2.1 miles hike down a short way to cross the main branch of Burnt Timber Creek in a thick aspen grove (N 37 29.449, W 107 40.747, 9,950 feet). Just before heading down to

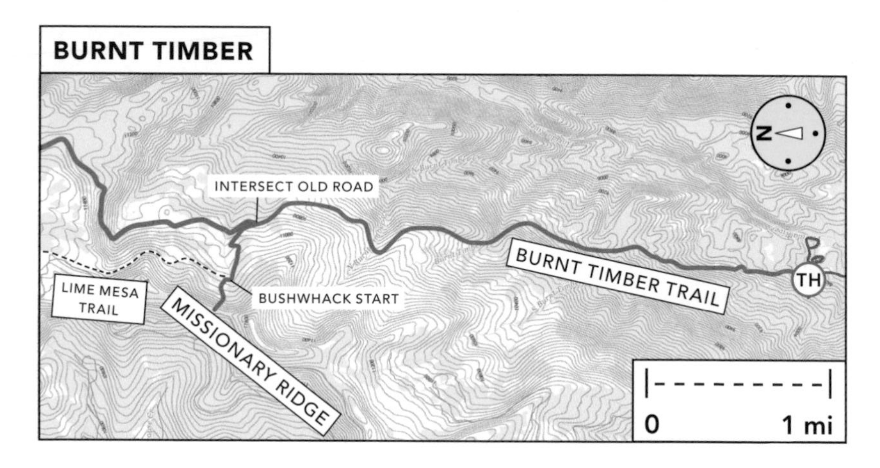

this crossing a fainter trail heads uphill to the left on the south side of Burnt Timber Creek; take it if you feel like exploring, but this description continues north. For a short hike, this marks a good turnaround spot.

The trail steepens for the next half-mile after crossing Burnt Timber Creek. At 2.6 miles at the top of one steep rise, a nice view of the Florida River valley and rocky peaks beyond comes into view. You're looking up into the City Reservoir area, and the rounded rocky mountain is Organ Mountain (13,032 feet).

Cross North Burnt Timber Creek at 3 miles (N 37 30.111, W 107 40.847, 10,570 feet) as the trail begins to contour along the mountainside with more good views down toward the Florida River drainage.

After a quick climb, at 3.8 miles you will come to a sort of intersection with an abandoned road, likely with a good-sized cairn marking the spot (N 37 30.643, W 107 40.616, 10,814 feet). The trail joins this old road and heads north on a fairly level grade. This intersection is the nondescript turnaround point. But there are plenty of options.

OPTIONS: You can continue along the main trail to your heart's content, all the way to West Virginia and Virginia gulches, or all the way to City Reservoir, which is approximately 13 miles from your trailhead. You can connect with the Lime Mesa Trail via a couple of different routes and continue to the Mountain View Crest area. Again, it's a long way.

Do you want to get to the top of Missionary Ridge? Here's a suggestion: At the intersection with the old road at the 3.8-mile mark, take the abandoned road uphill to the left. In about half a mile, head up off this track to the left (west) and bushwhack your way very steeply up to Missionary Ridge at 4.7 miles (N 37 30.920, W 107 41.213, 11,492 feet). This is one method to reach the ridge, but there are other ways. Once you get to the ridge you'll probably have to walk a little way on one of the abandoned roads up there to get a decent view through the trees, but you should be able to see north toward Lime Mesa and west toward the Animas Valley.

The rocky route along the Burnt Timber Trail.

HIKES BETWEEN DURANGO & SILVERTON

Not far from US 550—along that paved strip that cuts through the San Juan Mountains between Durango and Silverton—a spectacular variety of hiking options await the eager adventurer.

From long, relatively easy trails to mountain climbs of all difficulty levels, you should be able to find something that suits your ability and your risk level. There is the mellow myriad of trails in the Chris Park area. There are expert-only climbs up Snowdon and North Twilight Peaks. And there is just about everything in between.

The trails in this chapter are organized south to north, generally. Some will take you quite a way off US 550, but most begin near or at the highway itself.

This stretch of road begins in the Animas Valley just north of Durango, the historic Durango & Silverton Narrow Gauge Railroad at its side. It climbs up toward Rockwood, near where it leaves the train tracks and makes its own way. The geologic wonder of Engineer Mountain soon captivates the eyes, and no doubt the Needle Mountains (Pigeon and Turret most prominent from this angle) will as well. Just past Purgatory Resort you may notice impressive Grizzly Peak; then it's time to head up to Coal Bank Pass at 10,610 feet.

The West Needles (the Twilight Peaks and, north of there, Snowdon) come into view next as you drop down Coal Bank and your engine strains up the next pass, Molas at 10,912 feet. This same route between Durango and Silverton, as you may be aware, is that of the annual Iron Horse Bicycle Classic.

And once you have completed these trails and drop down from Molas Pass into Silverton—no requirement to do the hikes in order, of course—you will be ready to tackle the next chapter.

Left, top: Crater Lake with North Twilight Peak looming above. Left, bottom: Looking southeast along the ridgeline toward the Grayrock summit after an early fall snow. Below, left: A double-log crossing was set up in the summer of 2019 at Dutch Creek along the Hermosa Creek Trail. The Forest Service hopes to rebuild the burned-out bridge in the near future. Below, right: The top of Goulding connects with the Pinkerton-Flagstaff Trail.

HERMOSA CREEK

DISTANCE: 10.2 miles round-trip to Dutch Creek confluence with Hermosa Creek

ELEVATION: Start at 7,700 feet; high point at 8,040 feet (340-foot gain), but a 530-foot drop follows and you'll have to regain that

RATING: Easy

TIME ALLOWED: 4 to 6 hours

Hermosa Creek Trail is one of several trails on the western side of the highway between Hermosa and Purgatory where you'll be walking through areas ravaged by the 416 Fire, which burned 53,400 acres during the tinder-dry summer of 2018. Others in this book are Jones Creek (page 119) and Goulding Creek (page 121). Elbert Creek (page 127) comes very close.

Although the fire was devastating to the landscape, much of the land was beginning to regenerate in the summer of 2019. The burn was of "mixed severity," meaning most areas were not irreparably damaged for our lifetimes. You'll see a mosaic of green and blackened slopes. Fortunately, only about 5 percent of the area was deemed to be of "high severity" burn, where soil is toasted so badly that seeds cannot germinate, sometimes for many years or decades. The soil is now hydrophobic in

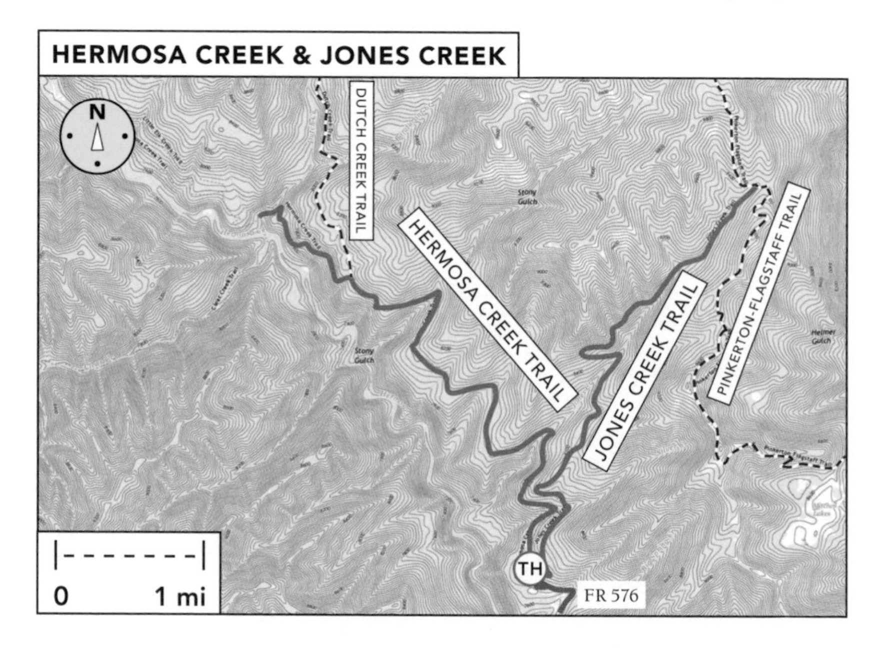

A year after the 416 Fire, flowers were already blooming along the Hermosa Creek Trail.

places, meaning that water washes right over it, and that produces flash floods during heavy rains. You'll find sloppy mud washing over various parts of these trails in places, making for gooey going when it's wet.

You'll be witness to this burn, and the fascinating recovery, as you hike along any of these trails. Keep in mind that dead trees fall eventually, particularly in high winds. Be careful out there.

The hike described here stays in the burn area, but if you continue up Hermosa Creek, the upper several miles of trail are not in the burn area. You may no longer be walking in a pristine forest, but this remains one of the gems of the San Juans. The largest known blue spruce, a so-called "champion" tree, can be found just a little way into the trek. Another blue spruce, formerly a "co-champion," was burned near the confluence of Hermosa and Dutch Creeks, where the fire burned intensely.

This is an excellent hike, but just know that it's unlikely you will be alone. This is a world-renowned mountain bike trail, usually accessed from the Upper Hermosa trailhead. Motorbike riders love this trail, as well as the Jones and Dutch Creek Trails. You may also encounter cattle on the trail or near the campground.

APPROACH: From Main Avenue (US 550) and Thirty-Second Street in Durango, head north 8.8 miles on US 550 and turn left onto the northern terminus of CR 203. It's 0.4 miles past the little enclave of Hermosa and just past Hermosa Creek. A sign to

Lower Hermosa Road should point the way. Just be careful as you make this left turn; there's no turn lane and highway drivers are sometimes oblivious.

You'll go just 100 yards or so on CR 203, then take a right onto CR 201, which will become FR 576 when it enters the designated forest. From the turn off the highway, it's 2.1 miles to the end of the pavement and a total of 4 miles to the trailhead at Lower Hermosa Campground. Turn left into the campground; note the trailhead at the entrance to the campground, and go find a parking spot in the designated area for non-campers.

HIKE: Start from the trailhead, and in 0.1 miles veer left at the junction with the Jones Creek Trail (N 37 27.363, W 107 51.433, 7,720 feet). At 0.5 miles go uphill to reach an intersection with a trail coming from the right. This trail comes down from the end of the road, which is now closed just beyond the campground entrance.

At 1.4 miles cross Jones Creek, which usually has at least a trickle (N 37 28.096, W 107 51.335, 7,925 feet). You'll cross another two or three likely small trickles in the next couple miles (including Stony Gulch at 3.3 miles), and at 4 miles you'll reach the junction with the Dutch Creek Trail, which takes off up to the right (N 37 28.961, W 107 52.684, 8,040 feet). By now you're heading downhill; continue downhill to the left.

Continue down, down, down, losing about 500 feet in elevation to where Hermosa Creek Trail crosses Dutch Creek at 4.9 miles (N 37 29.323, W 107 53.201, 7,510 feet). If you've been on this trail in the past you'll be seeing a completely changed landscape, views of Dutch Creek you've never seen, and scarred and dead trees as far as the eye can see. The bridge over Dutch Creek was burned out in the 416 Fire, so in 2019 the crossing was a couple of long logs spanning the creek. The Forest Service plans to replace the bridge, likely by 2020. The trail was damaged by flooding and mudslides in many places, particularly here at Dutch Creek, but trail workers have been trying to reclaim the trail. It may be a long process.

Just past the Dutch Creek crossing, at 5 miles, the Clear Creek Trail takes off downhill to the left. It's another 0.1 miles to Hermosa Creek. This spot, the Dutch Creek confluence with Hermosa Creek, makes a good lunch stop. Fording Hermosa Creek here takes you into the Hermosa Creek Wilderness, and you can continue on Clear Creek Trail. Fording is not recommended, but it's possible.

OPTIONS: You can continue up Hermosa Creek Trail as far as you like. The trail doesn't spend much time near the creek, but you do get some nice vantage points of it from above. Mostly the trail winds in and out of various side drainages for the next several miles before finally dropping back down to creek level and crossing it a couple of times. In all it's another 14 miles to the Upper Hermosa trailhead if that's your goal.

JONES CREEK

DISTANCE: 8.8 miles round-trip

ELEVATION: Start at 7,720 feet, high point at 9,310 feet (1,590-foot gain)

RATING: Moderate

TIME ALLOWED: 4 to 6 hours

As with the Hermosa Creek Trail, this one goes through an area that was heavily scarred by the 416 Fire of 2018. Unlike the Hermosa Trail, this one climbs, heading up to a ridge that separates the Hermosa and Animas Valleys. From the top of Jones it's possible to take a connecting trail to some nice viewpoints toward the Animas Valley.

Jones Creek Trail is an old trail that was rebuilt in the 1990s, taking out the steepest and most rutted sections. Where it isn't going through a burn area, the trail travels through big timber, ponderosa pine, fir, and spruce, with a small meadow at its terminus.

There is a lot of wild, roadless area west of US 550. You will be walking in the 70,600-acre Hermosa Creek Special Management Area, which was created in 2014 along with the 37,200-acre Hermosa Creek Wilderness, which is west of Hermosa Creek in this large drainage area. It's all roadless. The top of the ridge in this hike is the eastern border of the special management area.

APPROACH: From Main Avenue (US 550) and Thirty-Second Street in Durango, take US 550 north 8.8 miles and turn left onto CR 203. This turn is 0.4 miles past Hermosa village and just after the highway crosses Hermosa Creek, before the railroad crossing. Go 100 yards to a T-intersection and turn right onto the Lower Hermosa Road, which parallels the highway briefly.

Follow this road uphill 4 miles to the Lower Hermosa Campground. Turn left into the campground, note the trailhead at the entrance to the campground, and go find a parking spot in the designated area for non-campers.

HIKE: Start from the Hermosa Creek trailhead, and in 0.1 miles veer right at the junction onto the Jones Creek Trail. (N 37 27.363, W 107 51.433, 7,720 feet). Cross the closed-off road and find the trail going uphill, southeast briefly before tending more north and east, on the other side.

The trail climbs rapidly through switchbacks at first, then it levels out, climbs again, drops some, and then mostly climbs after it meets up with and crosses sometimes-dry Jones Creek at 2.4 miles (N 37 28.536, W 107 50.832, 8,370 feet).

The trail makes a couple of switchbacks away from the creek, then returns to hug the creek's west bank. It climbs steeply along the creek and ends in a large clearing, where it meets the Pinkerton-Flagstaff Trail at 4.4 miles (N 37 29.464, W 107 49.931,

Be careful of falling trees in the burn areas. This warning sign was posted at the beginning of the Jones Creek Trail.

9,310 feet). An abundance of shade in a thick forest used to make this a good hot-weather hike. Now you'll see plenty of charred trees interspersed with some areas of remaining forest. When you do get views, you can see down into the rugged Hermosa Creek area.

The trail is fairly popular with mountain bikers and motorbikers. You'll hear the motors, but the engine-less bikes can pop around sharp corners suddenly. Most bikers are very courteous and slow down immediately. Generally, if you're friendly, they'll be friendly.

With nearly 9 miles in the round-trip route, many hikers will be satisfied by just going out and back, but several other options are available for those who want a longer hike.

OPTIONS: At the top you'll meet the Pinkerton-Flagstaff Trail, which goes along the top of the ridge in basically a north-south direction. This is the spine of the main high ridge east of Hermosa Creek. The trail runs along much of the top west above the Hermosa Cliffs with the Animas River to the east. On the ridge, the trail spends most of its length higher than 9,400 feet, going up to 9,661 feet at one point.

Turning left on the Pinkerston-Flagstaff Trail takes you in several miles up to the Dutch Creek Trail. The right fork is more practical: For 2.6 miles, it tends south and parallels Jones Creek at a higher level and at a gradually widening distance. There are several good, long-distance viewpoints along this ridge, either west toward the high peaks of the La Plata Mountains or east toward the top of Missionary Ridge and beyond. Any of these spots is a good place to take a well-earned rest from the climb and drink in the splendor.

At 2.6 miles the trail dives off the ridge toward the east, heading down toward Mitchell Lakes. Keep going and in 4.4 miles you can reach US 550.

GOULDING CREEK

DISTANCE: 6 miles round-trip to Pinkerton-Flagstaff Trail

ELEVATION: Start at 7,920 feet, finish at 10,080 feet (2,160-foot gain)

RATING: Easy to moderate, with a fairly steep climb on a good trail

TIME ALLOWED: 3 to 4 hours

There are a couple of breaks through the Hermosa Cliffs north of Hermosa, and this is one with a good trail heading up through it. (Elbert Creek on page 127 is another.) This area was very close to the start of the devastating 416 Fire, which burned 53,400 acres in the summer of 2018. Signs of the fire will last for decades, perhaps outliving the lifespan of this book.

Be prepared for a good, steep climb. There is nothing technically challenging; it's just pretty steep at the beginning, and you'll earn your altitude.

Goulding Creek Trail approaches the Hermosa Cliffs, which run north along US 550 for about 16 miles, from an aspect that looks difficult from below. Goulding Creek is easier than it looks though, thanks to a series of switchbacks and that gap in the cliffs. Very possibly you'll encounter cattle along the trail in the summer. This is a beautiful hike any time, but it's especially nice during late September and early October, when the aspen leaves are at their golden best.

APPROACH: From Thirty-Second Street and Main Avenue in Durango, go north on US 550. After 15 miles you'll pass the Glacier Club (still called Tamarron by locals), a resort and golf course on the east side of the highway. It's almost exactly 1 mile past the Glacier Club entrance to the poorly marked dirt road that heads left (west) and uphill off the highway. This is a tricky turn because there might be anxious traffic behind as you slow to seek this hidden road. If you miss it, go a little over a mile to the Haviland Lake exit and turn around.

Once you locate the road, drive up it about 50 yards and turn left at a T-intersection. Go downhill 0.2 miles to the end of this bumpy road and park at the trailhead (N 37 30.706, W 107 49.191, 7,920 feet).

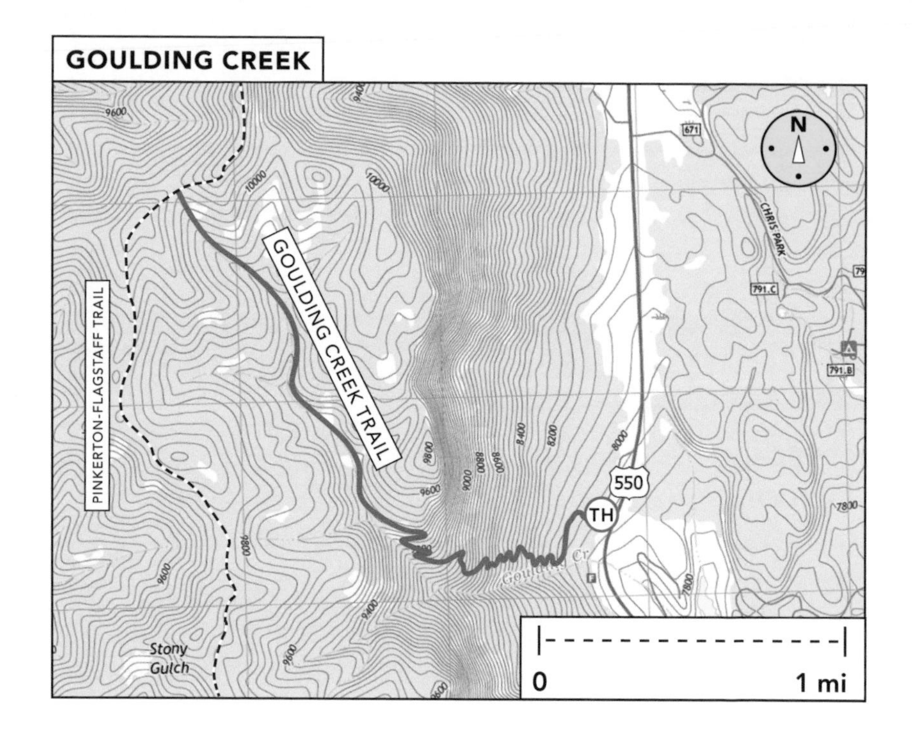

HIKE: Head briefly uphill to the west before turning south. Trees here are blackened but just one summer after the fire, oak brush galore and aspen shoots were greening the forest. The shade those trees provided is gone now, making that sun just a bit hotter.

When the trail turns back toward the west it begins its steep rise, and the views improve of the Animas Valley. In front of you are the Glacier Club, Rockwood to the southeast—you might see the train before it hits the Highline—and Missionary Ridge across the valley.

At 1.6 miles you'll reach a gate, and you've already gained 1,500 feet (N 37 30.680, W 107 49.847, 9,400 feet). The trail levels off a bit from here, climbing much more gently as it connects with Goulding Creek. Goulding can become a trickle or even dry out completely in the summer. At this point the atmosphere changes; you're in a peaceful, green valley in an area hardly touched by the fire.

As you continue, a couple of open valleys look intriguing to the north, but the main trail hangs near Goulding Creek. There is a potentially confusing spot at 2.6 miles with several trails going hither and thither (N 37 31.351, W 107 50.332, 9,680 feet). Try to stay near the creek, bearing generally west-northwest. At 2.9 miles you should reach a cattleman's cabin that is still used sporadically. Head up for the final push to the ridge above, where the Goulding Creek Trail ends and you'll connect with the Pinkerton-Flagstaff Trail, running north-south (N 37 31.582, W 107 50.602, 10,080 feet).

The lower section of Goulding Creek Trail was badly charred by the 416 Fire in 2018.

Don't be surprised to hear the whine of motorbikes up here, and see some along the Pinkerton-Flagstaff. It's part of a popular loop that includes Jones Creek, Dutch Creek, and Hermosa Creek Trails.

OPTIONS: Those who want a longer hike have a couple of other options. Either of these would mean coming out at or near the end of the Hermosa Road, where you would need another car or someone to pick you up, because you would be nearly 15 miles by road from the original parking place.

The first and shortest route is to go left down to Jones Creek Trail (see page 119). To do this, first follow Pinkerton-Flagstaff south for 3 miles to the top of the Jones Creek Trail and take Jones Creek on down another 4.3 miles to the Lower Hermosa Campground. Or continue south beyond Jones Creek on Pinkerton-Flagstaff another 2 miles and head down the Mitchell Lakes Trail on the east side. This would reduce the highway distance between parking places to only 5 miles.

The second option is via the Dutch Creek Trail. The easy but long way to join this trail is to go right (north) up the Pinkerton-Flagstaff Trail 1.5 miles to where the Dutch Creek Trail joins it from the west. It is about 6.5 miles down this trail to the Hermosa Creek Trail and another 5 miles down (left, or southeast) that trail to the Lower Hermosa Campground.

CHRIS PARK

DISTANCE: 0.25 to 4 miles or more; really, it's whatever fits your mood

ELEVATION: Start at parking area at first gate at 8,170 feet, low point at Chris Park at 7,900 feet, high point at Haviland View Trail at about 8,250 feet

RATING: Easy

TIME ALLOWED: 10 minutes to 2 hours

This is an easy-to-access, easy-to-hike trail system about 20 minutes north of Durango. It's a very popular winter spot for snowshoers, hikers, and fat-bikers (mountain bikes with really fat tires). It's good in the summer too, but it can get a little warm as the sun hits its zenith.

Some of the trails are popular with horseback riders, so use caution. When you come upon a horse, announce your presence from 200 feet away, if possible. Move off the trail, but remain visible and let the horse know where you are.

APPROACH: From Thirty-Second Street and Main Avenue in Durango, take US 550 north 17.5 miles to a right turn (east) on the Haviland Lake Road. Haviland Lake is a lovely larger lake with a nice Forest Service campground and good fishing. Some people put in their kayaks.

From the highway it's 0.1 miles to a parking area on the right (south) side of the road, just past the commercial horse corral, which offers summer horse rides and winter sleigh rides. Just a few feet past the parking area is a gate, which is closed to the public in the winter. You can park here year-round (N 37 31.740, W 107 48.984, 8,170 feet). Walk along the road less than 0.1 miles to find a trail access point.

There are several places to access this trail system. Another good one is down at Chris Park. Go another 0.2 miles past the gate to a Y-intersection, and go right on a gravel road toward Chris Park. Take this road 0.9 miles and find ample parking in the Chris Park group camping area. Just as you take a right into this parking area, there are two trail access points (N 37 31.200, W 107 48.264, 7,900 feet).

HIKE: Pick a trail and get moving. There's nothing really steep here, but there are quite a few ups and downs, and if you're out for a while you'll get some good exercise.

One suggestion: Take the Aspen Loop to Hermosa View, use the Cave Connector to Chris Park Trail, down to Chris Park, up Wagon Trail, and over to Haviland View, then back to the start. That should take you a couple hours or so. Enjoy.

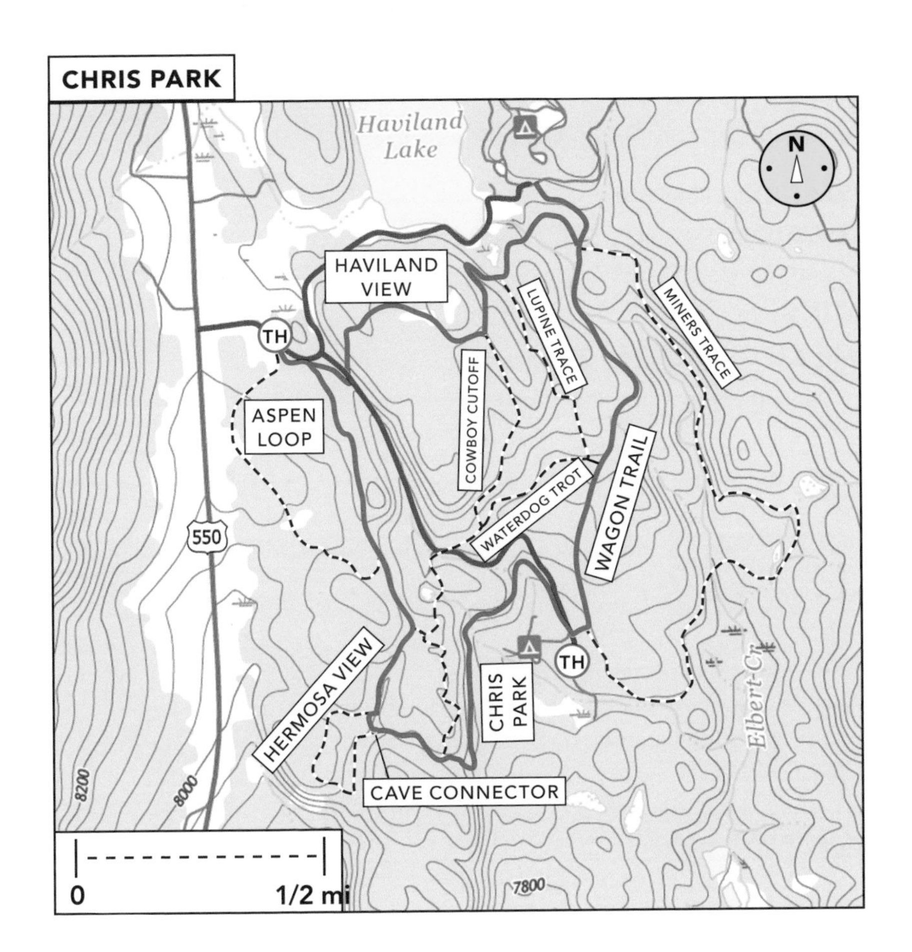
CHRIS PARK
Haviland
Lake
N
HAVILAND
VIEW
TH
ASPEN
LOOP
COWBOY CUTOFF
LUPINE TRACE
MINERS TRACE
WATERDOG TROT
WAGON TRAIL
550
HERMOSA VIEW
CHRIS
PARK
TH
Elbert Cr.
CAVE CONNECTOR
8200
8000
7800
0
1/2 mi

FOREBAY LAKE

DISTANCE: 3.4 miles round-trip

ELEVATION: Start at 8,150 feet, high point at 8,370 feet (220-foot gain), Forebay at 8,300 feet

RATING: Easy

TIME ALLOWED: 1½ to 2½ hours

This is a very easy hike that is good for the whole family, with little elevation change. It follows a four-wheel-drive road most of the way through rather dense vegetation, which makes it a bit unique in this part of the state. Forebay Lake is a good fishing spot. You'll follow a big suspended pipe and cross under it, which is interesting too.

APPROACH: From Thirty-Second Street and Main Avenue in Durango, take US 550 north 17.5 miles to a right turn (east) toward Haviland Lake. Make sure to take a left at the first Y-intersection, staying on the paved road toward Haviland. The road crosses the dam at a single-lane bridge. Veer right twice, the second time onto a gravel road at 0.9 miles from the highway. Go a short distance and park (N 37 31.974, W 107 48.334, 8,150 feet).

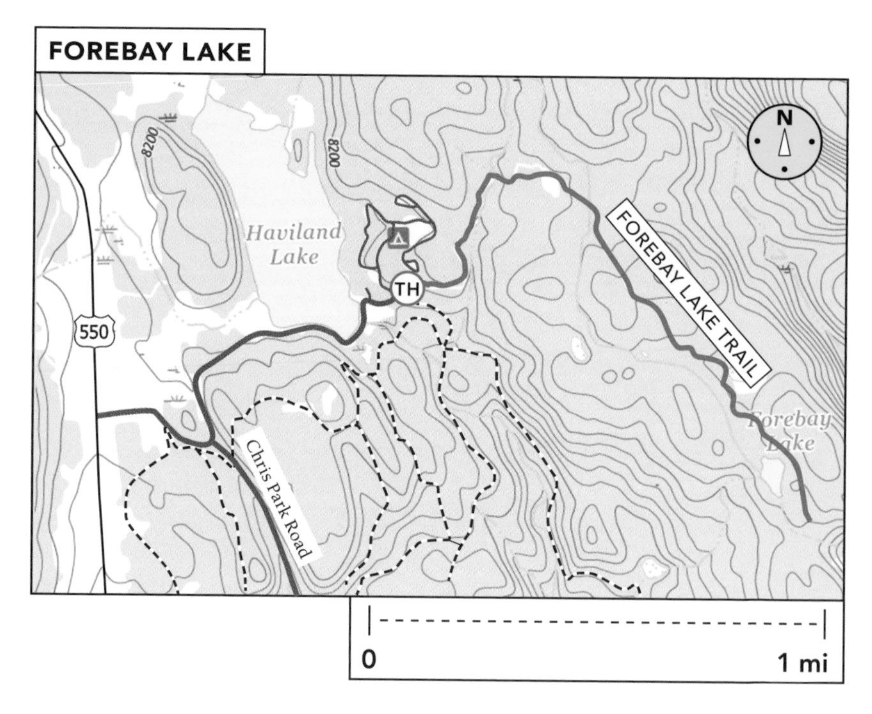

HIKE: Head east up the road, which was closed off a decade or more ago and has gradually become overgrown. In 0.4 miles you'll have to ford Elbert Creek as it comes down from Electra Lake to the north (N 37 32.224, W 107 48.115). It's usually possible to do this without getting wet; there's a log or two that should get you across, but poles are nice for balance.

It's a little difficult to follow through this section, but just after the crossing look for a trail heading east. The trail cuts through a meadow under a power line, then rejoins the old road.

From here you will be following a big pipe that carries the water supply for the Tacoma power plant from Electra Lake, a mile farther north. (Tacoma is down by the Animas River. Electra Lake is a large and attractive place, but is a private area.)

In about 1.4 miles from the start you'll hike past a small lake/pond on your left (east). This is not Forebay; continue on 0.3 miles to Forebay (N 37 31.640, W 107 47.390, 8,300 feet) where a huge round metal tower looms above the lake.

Just southeast of Forebay you can stand at the top of the bluff overlooking the Animas River and the power plant a thousand feet below. At the right time of day in the summer you might even see the little narrow-gauge train at the bottom of the canyon carrying sightseers between Durango and Silverton. Across the Animas Valley the view is up the steep, high western side of Missionary Ridge.

The road stops at Forebay, so you must return the way you came.

ELBERT CREEK–CASTLE ROCK

DISTANCE: 9 miles round-trip

ELEVATION: Start at 8,800 feet, finish at 10,450 feet (1,650-foot gain) on Elbert Creek or at 10,400 feet (1,600-foot gain) on Castle Rock Trail

RATING: Easy to moderate, with a fairly steep but short climb to Castle Rock

TIME ALLOWED: 4 to 5 hours on Elbert Creek, 2½ to 3 hours to Castle Rock

---

The Elbert Creek Trail breaks through the Hermosa Cliffs a couple miles south of Purgatory Resort. The trail is not very far from the ski area as the crow flies. Cattle and horses are frequent users of this trail, so be prepared to step aside for the latter and avoid the former.

The shorter and perhaps more popular hike heads up to Castle Rock for a dominant view of the land and valley below. This trail's popularity increases when aspen change in the fall.

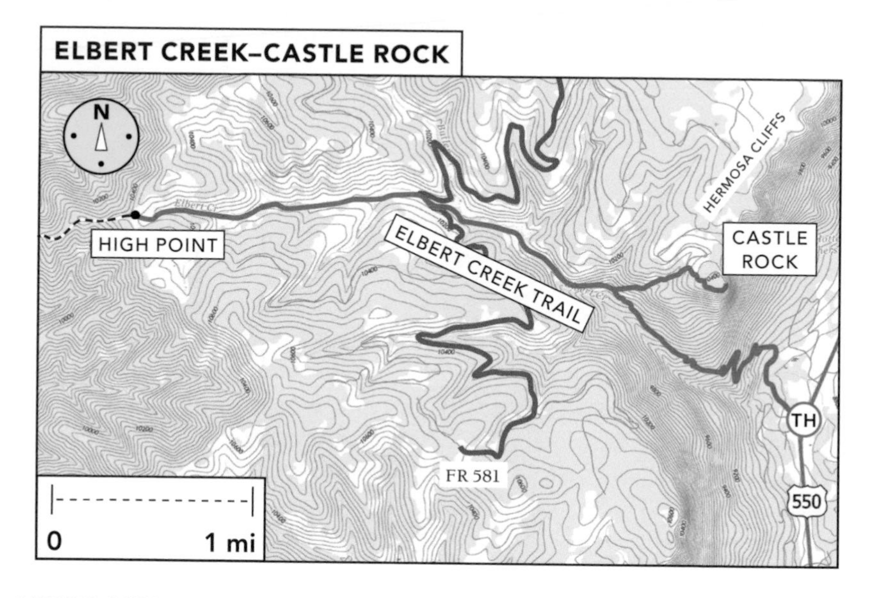

APPROACH: From Thirty-Second Street and Main Avenue in Durango, go 22 miles north on US 550 to Needles Country Square, a small business area with a gas station, liquor store, and more. Park at the far south end of this business area, within spitting distance of the highway; there is limited trailhead parking adjacent to a wooden fence that is part of a corral (N 37 35.542, W 107 49.458, 8,800 feet).

HIKE: Head around the corral to the left and find the gate on the other (south) side. Go through and head west on the trail into a fir-dominated forest. In 0.2 miles ford Elbert Creek, which is not difficult most times of the year, other than spring and early summer.

The trail turns north, and at 0.3 miles you'll pass near a large house owned by someone with great views of the Needle Mountains—Pigeon and Turret Peaks are distinct from here. The trail then turns south and west, with aspen the dominant tree now, rising through some long switchbacks and soon entering a deep canyon that makes its way through the Hermosa Cliffs. Stop to enjoy views of Electra Lake and Missionary Ridge on the way up.

Break through the cliffs, and at 1.7 miles after a long, steady climb you will reach an old herders' cabin (N 37 35.953, W 107 50.346, 9,728 feet). At 1.8 miles, you'll come to an unsigned Y-intersection at a large, open meadow. It's decision time (N 37 36.024, W 107 50.444, 9,875 feet).

Go left at the Y and continue above Elbert Creek. This trail climbs gradually through big timber. It is a good trail most of the way. At 3 miles it joins and follows a road for a few hundred yards. It follows along the south side of the creek at this point. You should be able to pick up the trail again where the road turns north to cross the creek. It is another 1.5 miles to the top of the ridge that separates the Elbert Creek drainage from the Hermosa Creek drainage.

A view of the West Needle and Needle Mountains from Castle Rock.

This hike description takes you only to the top of this ridge; the return is by the same route. The trail, however, turns south along the top and eventually follows Little Elk Creek down to the Hermosa Trail in 6 miles.

OPTIONS: Your other option from the Y-intersection at 1.8 miles is to head right uphill toward Castle Rock on a well-defined trail. In about half a mile you'll begin to run across some faint, abandoned roads in this area. It's fun to wander around on them, and at some point if you continue north on the right one you'll get to Purgatory Resort. Just don't get lost.

Continue up on the well-defined trail. At 2.4 miles you'll come to the edge of the Castle Rock promontory, equally impressive from below or above (N 37 36.054, W 107 49.970, 10,400 feet). Feel free to wander along the ledge, just don't… go… too… far…

PURGATORY FLATS

DISTANCE: 8.4 miles round-trip

ELEVATION: Start at 8,750 feet, low point is 7,700 feet at Animas River (1,050-foot drop)

RATING: Easy

TIME ALLOWED: 3½ to 4½ hours

This hike is one of those reverse climbs: You begin at the top, hike down to the Animas River below (a drop of more than 1,000 feet), then reverse your path and climb back out of the canyon. It's a good half-day hike, but the views, which are great by many standards, are not quite so dramatic as those afforded by the Molas Trail into the same canyon several miles upstream. Cascade Canyon is deep and narrow with a rugged beauty all its own.

APPROACH: From Main Avenue and Thirty-Second Street in Durango, go 25 miles north on US 550. The main entrance to Purgatory Resort is on the left. Just opposite of that is the entrance to Tacoma Village; go that way, east off the highway, and follow signs 0.2 miles to a parking area along a paved road. You should be next to a small lake.

Retrace the road to the other side of a rushing stream (a lake outlet that feeds Purgatory Creek), and find the trail next to a private driveway, going east (N 37 37.782, W 107 48.390, 8,750 feet).

HIKE: The trail heads eastward, dropping down along little Purgatory Creek and soon crossing the creek. You'll begin to get views of the Twilight massif (West Needle Mountains) to the northeast and Purgatory Flats below. After 1.3 miles the trail reaches the flats (N 37 37.793, W 107 47.608, 8,060 feet) and heads almost due south, now following along Cascade Creek. Spots in this area can be marshy in the early summer and present a challenge if you're hoping to keep your boots dry.

At 2.1 miles the creek enters its narrow canyon in its final plunge to the river. Most of the hike is close to the west side of Cascade, but it sometimes moves up to 250 feet above the stream in search of an adequate bench. At the end, the trail zigzags back and forth down to the Animas River just below the mouth of Cascade Creek.

There is a nice flat area on both sides of the Animas River for resting and picnicking. The east side is larger than the west and has some good tree coverage. There is a good bridge across the Animas (N 37 35.869, W 107 46.574, 7,700 feet) for hikers and horses at mile 4.2.

OPTIONS: At the river crossing, the planned half-day hike returns back up the same trail, but the trail continues, quickly crossing the train tracks and heading northeast

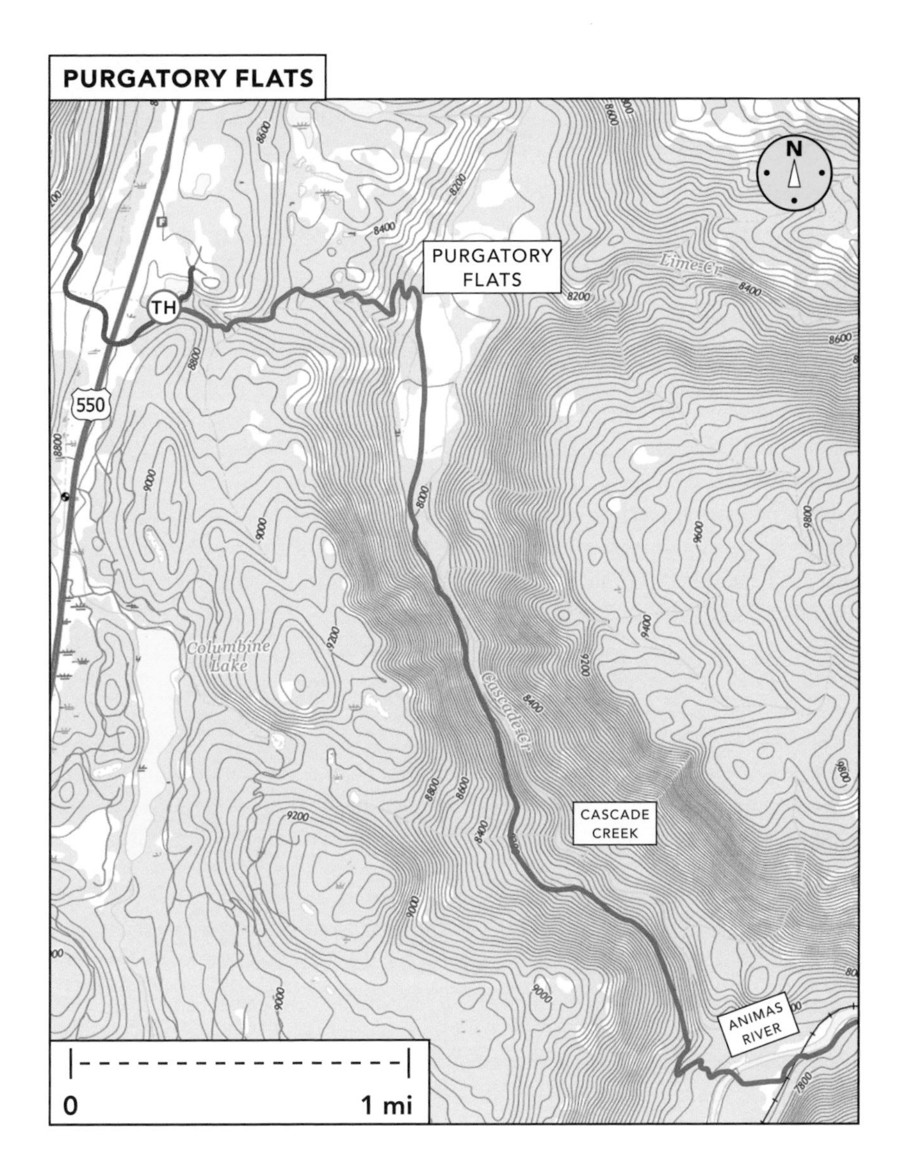

along the east side of the river for another 5.5 miles. There it joins a trail heading up Needle Creek and into Chicago Basin for access to fourteeners Eolus, Sunlight, and Windom. This trail continues on up past Chicago Basin to cross Columbine Pass, then down into the Vallecito Creek drainage. Many people, instead of taking the train, use this access to Chicago Basin and the vaunted fourteeners.

CASCADE CREEK

DISTANCE: 10.2 miles round-trip

ELEVATION: Start at 9,080 feet, turnaround at 9,680 feet (600-foot gain)

RATING: Easy, with a few short and steep climbs

TIME ALLOWED: 4 to 6 hours

This is an excellent walk in a deep, wide valley, with plenty of water stops for you and your dog, a fair amount of shade, a waterfall, and perhaps a couple of surprises. This hike description begins near a US Forest Service work center. An option is to drive up Cascade Road, or FR 783, part of the way or to the end at the gate. This will save some distance; however, the road is rough, slow, and not a lot of fun to drive. The Cascade Creek Trail was extended a couple of decades ago to the work center to avoid this rough stretch and the private cabins along the road.

The reality is that many people will choose to drive up the road, and this description below discusses that route.

APPROACH: Take US 550 about 30 miles north of Durango, 0.8 miles past where the highway crosses Cascade Creek. Watch carefully for a left-hand turn onto a gravel road. It's poorly marked, if it's marked at all. Drive west 0.2 miles to a parking area on the right (N 37 39.606, W 107 48.023, 9,080 feet). If you keep going, you'll quickly reach the work center.

HIKE: The trail heads west, going south of a small pond. At a Y-intersection, go left on the Cascade Creek Trail; the right-hand trail is the Engineer Mountain Trail, and it switchbacks up toward the base of Engineer Mountain.

Cascade Village can be seen to the south, and soon you'll also see Grayrock Peak and Graysill Mountain high on the horizon to the west. In less than a half-mile you'll dive into an aspen forest dotted with a few spruce.

The trail was designed to contour, and that it does. In 1.9 miles you'll gain an overall 40 feet of elevation, joining at that point the FR 783 (N 37 40.359, W 107 49.577, 9,120 feet). You shouldn't have any trouble finding the trail on your way back, but make a mental note of it. At 2.1 miles, you'll reach the road closure; there's room for a few cars to park at this turnaround point (N 37 40.517, W 107 49.672, 9,125 feet).

The road soon turns into a trail. There are some climbs to it, as it rises to skirt some steep, rocky sections next to the creek. You'll ford a couple of unnamed rivulets, perhaps on logs, before coming to Engine Creek Trail at mile 4.5, where there's a nice, solid wooden bridge (N 37 42.311, W 107 50.473, 9,550 feet). Just past the bridge, at

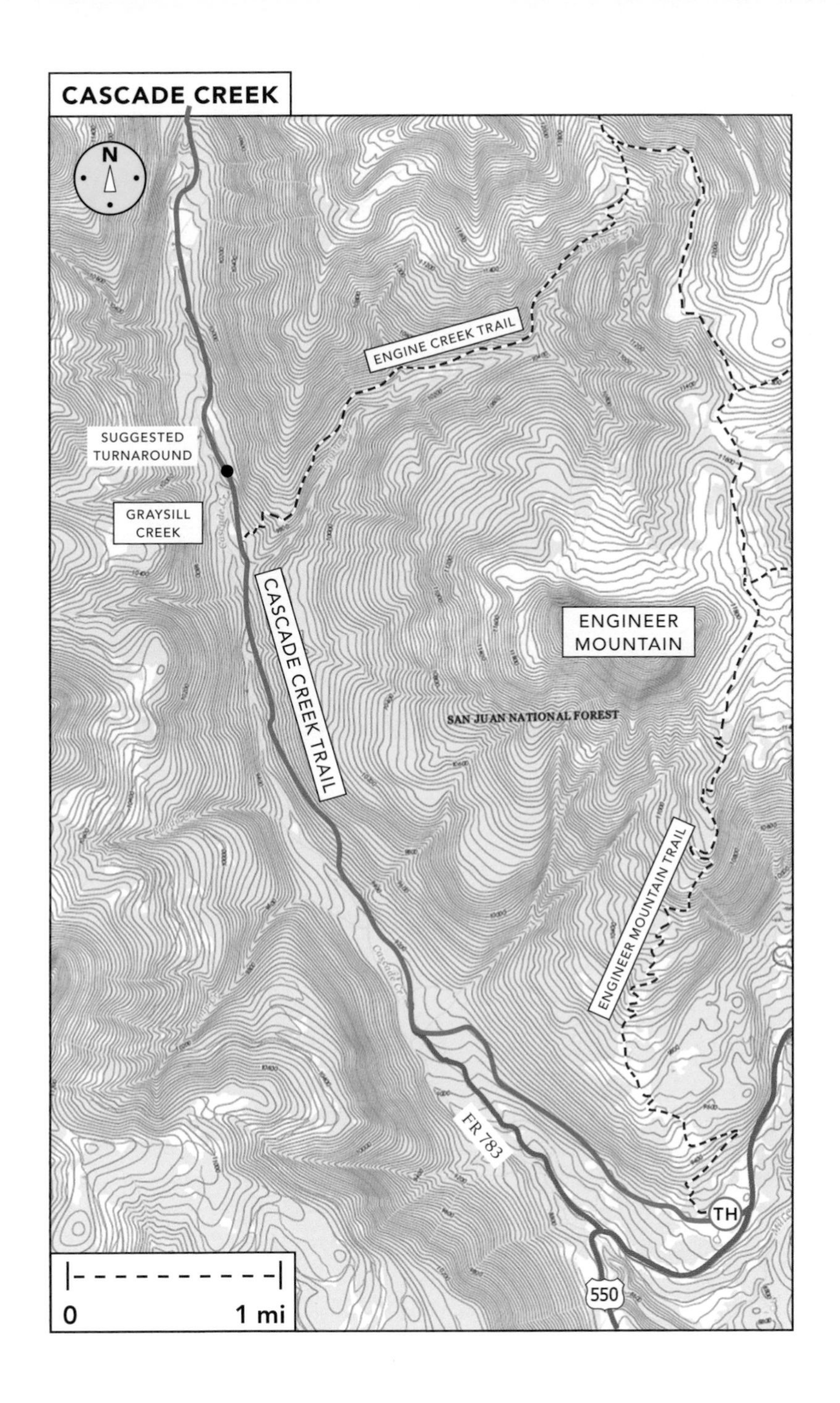
CASCADE CREEK
N
ENGINE CREEK TRAIL
SUGGESTED TURNAROUND
GRAYSILL CREEK
CASCADE CREEK TRAIL
ENGINEER MOUNTAIN
SAN JUAN NATIONAL FOREST
ENGINEER MOUNTAIN TRAIL
FR 783
TH
550
0
1 mi

The Engine Creek Trail takes off up to the right at this intersection along the Cascade Creek Trail. Grizzly Peak looms in the distance.

mile 4.6, is a junction where the more heavily used Engine Creek Trail takes off uphill to the right (northeast), and the Cascade Creek Trail continues north. (The Engine Creek Trail, accessed via the Engineer Mountain Trail, seems to have come on mountain bikers' radar.)

At mile 5.1, just after a steep uphill section, the valley opens up nicely to the north and there's an unofficial junction (N 37 42.766, W 107 50.655, 9,680 feet). Notice Grizzly Peak towering not that far away. At this point an unmaintained trail continues up Cascade Creek. The more official trail crosses Cascade Creek; you may have to search a bit for a good crossing, but you'll likely notice a trail on the other side. You will get your feet wet. This trail heads uphill on the north side of Graysill Creek, reaching the Cascade Divide Road in about a mile. At this unofficial junction, you may notice you are at the top of a nice waterfall. Make your way down either side of Cascade Creek for a better view.

This split is the turnaround point for this hike. The trail along Cascade Creek becomes less and less defined, but it does continue. If you decide to venture on another 2 miles, your efforts will be justly rewarded (you'll understand if you make it that far). In another mile after that, you'll hit the Colorado Trail.

POTATO (SPUD) LAKE

DISTANCE: 2 miles round-trip

ELEVATION: Start at 9,360 feet, lake at 9,800 feet (440-foot gain)

RATING: Easy

TIME ALLOWED: 1 hour

Potato Lake, also known as Spud Lake, is a short, easy hike and a rewarding one. Rising as a steep cliff out of the north side of the lake is Potato Hill, or, of course, Spud Mountain.

APPROACH: From Thirty-Second Street and Main Avenue in Durango, take US 550 north about 27 miles. In 2.3 miles after passing the entrance to Purgatory Resort, and just as you finish making a sweeping right-hand turn to cross Cascade Creek, turn

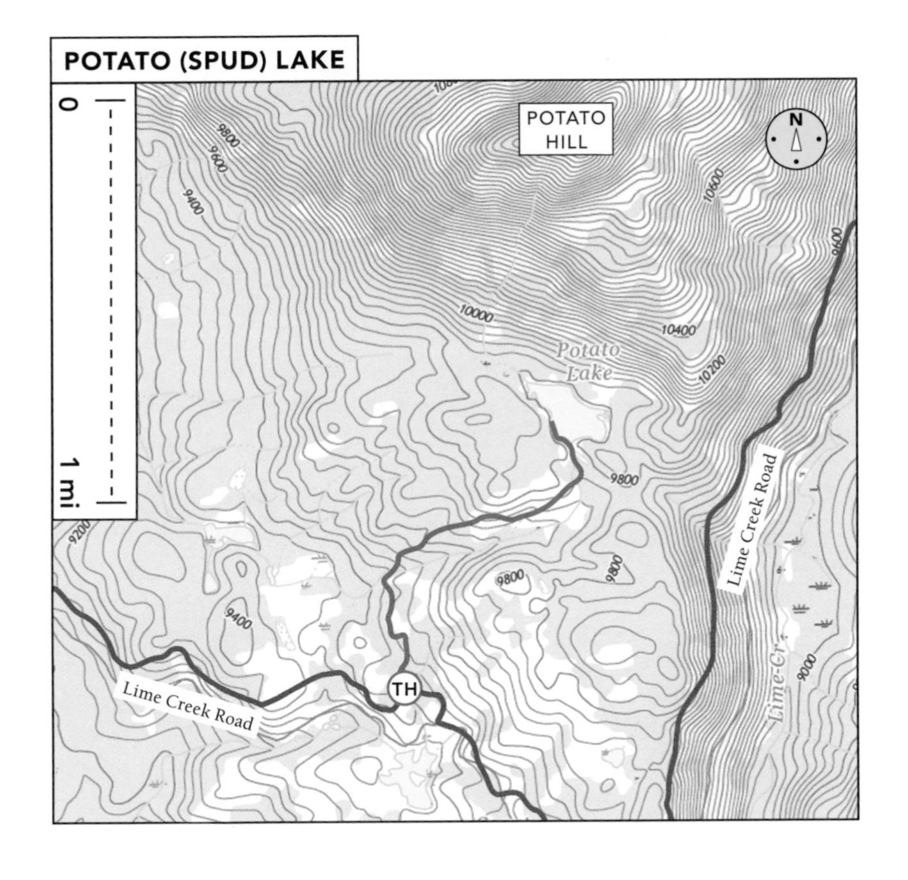

Spud Lake makes a fun, easy and beautiful hike for the whole family.
(Photo by Max Hutcheson)

right onto Lime Creek Road. The road is rocky in places but can be driven in a two-wheel drive if you go carefully.

Take Lime Creek Road 3.5 miles to where the road passes a lily pond. Just as the road turns sharply east to go by the north side of the pond, there is a turnoff big enough to park two or three cars. You can find other parking nearby along the road if necessary. The trail begins there (N 37 39.153, W 107 46.403, 9,360 feet).

HIKE: The trail bears generally north and a bit east. It passes through aspen trees and, shortly before the lake, goes past several interesting beaver ponds, some still active.

The lake (N 37 39.731, W 107 46.004, 9,800 feet) provides several acres of good fishing. It is a scenic spot, with 11,871-foot Spud Mountain towering above to the north, the Twilight Peaks to the east across Lime Creek, and Engineer Mountain to the northwest. Engineer Mountain cannot be seen from the lake, but it can be viewed from several points along the trail. This is a beautiful hike during the summer, but it is especially beautiful during the early fall, when the aspen leaves are in full color. The peak of fall color is usually around October 1, but the trees are likely to be beautiful 10 days before and after this date.

OPTIONS: There is another smaller but beautiful (unnamed) lake nearby for those who have time to explore a little more. To find it, start up the same trail from the parking lot. In 100 yards, veer left off the trail, following the remnants of an old trail for 0.2 miles (count from the parking area). At that point the old trail (it's the former trail to Spud Lake) swings to the right and starts up steeply; for the other lake, turn left at this point on an old road and follow it generally west and gradually downhill for about a half-mile to a nice opening where the lake and surrounding meadow are located. It is a quiet spot, not often visited.

When you're done hiking, you might consider driving along Lime Creek Road all the way around to its northern terminus, which is the lowest spot between Coal Bank Pass and Molas Pass on US 550. This takes you steeply down to Lime Creek, then back up again to rejoin the highway. If you're careful, in a good year you might be able to do it with two-wheel drive.

POTATO HILL (SPUD MOUNTAIN)

DISTANCE: 5 miles round-trip

ELEVATION: Start at 10,600 feet, summit at 11,871 feet (1,271-foot gain)

RATING: Difficult

TIME ALLOWED: 3 to 5 hours

Spud Mountain is low compared to its neighbors, Engineer Mountain to the west and the West Needles to the east, but it stands stubbornly alone and prominent, and makes a good half-day hike—with a big *if*.

If you're seeking a casual and gentle stroll with tremendous vistas along the way, then this hike is *not* for you. Turn the page right now. This is a rugged hike with little or no trail through a thick spruce and fir forest, with many fallen trees in your way. In other words, a lot of the times it's not that easy to get to where you're not exactly sure you're going. A compass may help.

You may find trails briefly and they may help you for a while, but they will almost assuredly pitter out. You will zigzag, you will serpentine, you will hike down and up steep ravines along an ill-defined ridge. You have been warned.

Spud Mountain is best climbed from the north, from the top of Coal Bank Hill. From the top, the view south is impressive, with a long look down the glacially carved Animas Valley and a nice view of Cascade Creek valley. Electra Lake is visible far below. Purgatory Resort is to the southwest.

APPROACH: Take US 550 north from Durango to the top of Coal Bank Hill—33 miles from Thirty-Second Street and Main Avenue, and 5.5 miles from the crossing of

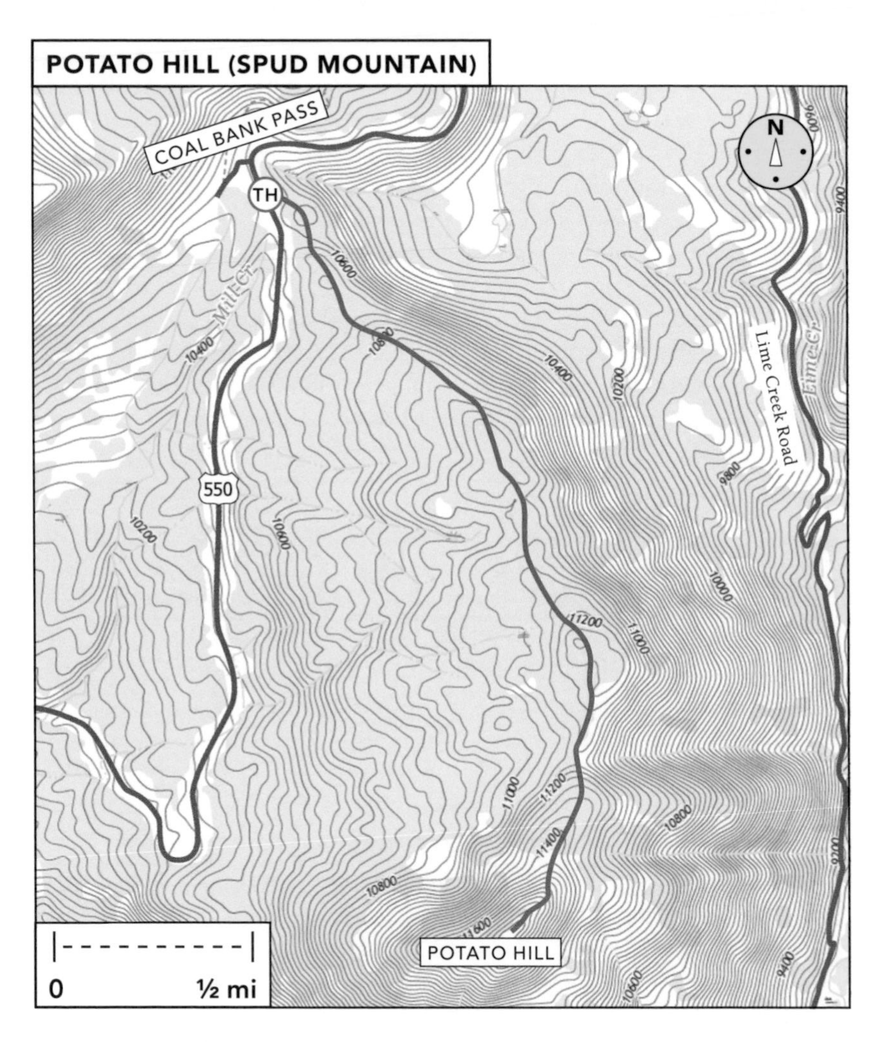

Cascade Creek at the bottom of the hill. Park at the rest stop at the top of Coal Bank, out of the way of tourists, if possible.

HIKE: From the parking area (N 37 41.937, W 107 46.630, 10,600 feet), strike out in a general south-southeast direction, keeping as high as you can on the expansive ridge. There are two barely detectable humps on the ridge. Go right (west) around the second hump to reach a saddle (N 37 40.734, W 107 45.805, 11,140 feet) at the base of the mountain at 2 miles.

Continue and then make another slight drop at 2.2 miles (N 37 40.533, W 107 45.865, 11,410 feet). From here you are looking up at an open, rocky slope. This slope heads up the last 460 feet south—with a little bit of fun scrambling on a narrow ridge—to the summit at 2.5 miles (N 37 40.350, W 107 45.993, 11,871 feet).

Enjoy the view. You've earned it.

Pink moss campion and white prairie phlox cling to the rocks just below the summit of Spud Hill. Engineer Mountain is seen in the background.

OPTIONS: You can also climb Spud Mountain from the west, beginning at a switchback in the highway (N 37 40.543, W 107 46.805, 10,040 feet) just after you pass the sign that tells you you're at 10,000 feet. Park the car near here and begin a steep ascent through down timber. This is by no means an easy ascent, although it is shorter.

Head almost due east to the 11,100-foot saddle previously described, or just to the south of that saddle at the base of the rocky slope. Good luck.

ENGINEER MOUNTAIN

DISTANCE: 7 miles round-trip

ELEVATION: Start at 10,660 feet, summit at 12,968 feet (2,308-foot gain)

RATING: Difficult

TIME ALLOWED: 4 to 6 hours

Engineer Mountain is one of the most photographed peaks in the San Juans. As you approach from Durango, it appears as a symmetrical cone rising straight ahead as if out of the highway. From Jarvis Meadows, the area just south of Cascade Village, it totally dominates the northerly view.

The cone, or cap, is the result of an intrusive volcanic layer bursting through sedimentary layers above. The distinct vertical columns, seen prominently on the eastern flank, are the result of this volcanic action. The volcanic rock breaks down easily and its remnants have formed a huge rock glacier under the nearly vertical northern face. Rock glaciers have interesting characteristics, and, mixed with ice, are actually slowly but steadily on the move. During the glacial age, Engineer Mountain's summit was one of the few points to stick above the ice.

What all of this means for the climber is that from the often flower-covered meadow below, you must ascend a steep ridge on which the rock is not always totally set in place.

APPROACH: The shortest and easiest way to climb Engineer Mountain begins at the top of Coal Bank Pass. Take US 550 north from Thirty-Second Street and Main Avenue in Durango 33 miles to the top of the pass. Just north of the large parking and rest area on the right, turn left (west), then drive about 200 yards to park near the trailhead labeled "Pass Creek Trail." There is parking here for a few cars (N 37 41.956, W 107 46.751, 10,660 feet), but it gets very busy on summer weekends, and you may have to go back down the road a ways or even park at the rest area.

HIKE: Start north on the trail. It moves up a steep grassy slope northeast into the big spruce-fir timber. Once inside the timber, it swings back gradually westward. Two pretty little lakes lie on the left side of the trail at 0.9 miles (N 37 42.306, W 107 46.782, 11,140 feet).

At 2.5 miles, the trail emerges out of the timber onto the tundra and you reach a trail junction with the Engineer Mountain Trail, which goes south and north here (N 37 42.228, W 107 47.904, 11,680 feet). At about this point, hikers should leave the trail and head for the northeast ridge of the mountain. There are many braids of the trail, but to avoid damaging this area, please stay on the main branch. The tundra area here has many beautiful wildflowers.

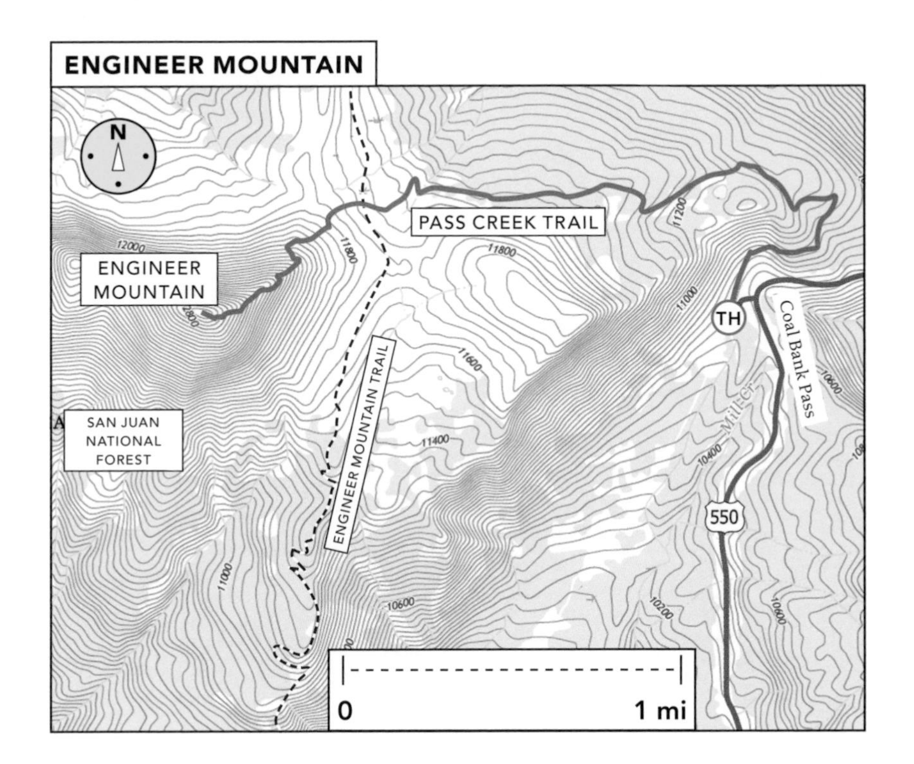

As you move up the beginning of the cone, the tundra rises steeply, later giving way to rock: mostly talus with a few small ledges. Take the right side of the ridge at first, then move up onto the ridge itself. The ridge is narrow—2 to 4 feet wide in places. Much of the rock is loose, and there is much exposure here. Therefore, you must test each handhold before trusting it. A little higher up, you emerge out on the cone itself. The top (N 37 41.957, W 107 48.392, 12,968 feet) is not far beyond.

Because Engineer Mountain stands alone, even though it is a little less than 13,000 feet, the panorama of peaks and valleys to be seen is great in all directions. The north face of Engineer is a sheer drop of 800 feet. The rock glacier seen in this direction lies at the head of one of the branches of Engine Creek, which flows into Cascade Creek.

OPTIONS: If you have an extra couple of hours, you might want to go west from the top, over the small shoulder peak, and around to the north side and back to the tundra and trail across the rock glaciers. The west descent beyond the shoulder is over steep talus but is doable. Hiking the waves themselves involves some up-and-down work, all on loose rocks. Be particularly careful crossing leading edges of the waves, because the rocks are typically at the maximum angle of repose; hiking over them can start a hazardous rockslide. At several places along this area you can hear underground streams gurgling through the rocks.

As mentioned before, there is an Engineer Mountain Trail that approaches from

Working up toward the summit of Engineer Mountain.

the south. It is about twice as long as the Coal Bank Pass route and involves 3,920 feet of altitude gain. This has become a favorite trail for mountain bikers, and some elk hunters still use it in the fall. Hikers might be interested in it as an alternate or a return route, keeping in mind that the south end of it joins US 550 some 5 miles down from Coal Bank Pass, at the Forest Service's Engineer Mountain Work Station.

Going south from the intersection described above, it soon drops into heavy timber and goes mostly south 4 miles to a junction with the work station road, 200 yards west of US 550.

If you want to start up this route from the south end, measure up 0.8 miles from where the highway crosses Cascade Creek and turn left for that 200 yards. If you are approaching from the north, it is the first right turn a little way below the runaway truck turnoff. This turn is not well marked.

GRIZZLY PEAK

DISTANCE: 7 miles round-trip

ELEVATION: Start at 11,200 feet, summit at 13,738 feet (2,538-foot gain)

RATING: Difficult

TIME ALLOWED: 6 to 7 hours

Grizzly Peak is a challenging and rewarding climb with the toughest section up through a couloir of loose dirt and rock. It rises out of the west side of the Cascade Creek valley a few miles northwest of Engineer Mountain. It is a long way from the highway and can best be seen from US 550 just before Cascade Village.

It can be climbed from Cascade Valley, but this is a long route and involves 2 days for most humans. The easiest route is described here.

APPROACH: Turn west at the ski area entrance 25 miles north of Thirty-Second Street and Main Avenue in Durango. As you're heading up toward the ski area, turn north and connect with a gravel road (FR 578). This road soon climbs back to the west and overlooks the ski area. At the top of the climb, the road turns north and descends slightly; in 0.5 miles from the top of the climb the main road makes a 90-degree turn left and heads downhill to Hermosa Park. Go straight instead onto FR 579, the Relay/Cascade Divide Road.

Continue 1.3 miles past that intersection and veer right onto Cascade Divide Road at a well-marked split. (Going left is the Relay Creek Road.) You're now on a former logging road that is in good shape at first, but soon narrows and gets rougher and rougher, and slower and slower. It's bumpy with huge potholes and big dips for stream crossings, and a 4WD is highly recommended.

The road hugs the shoulder of Graysill Mountain, with Cascade Creek far below and Engineer Mountain beyond to the northeast. Go all the way to the end of the road, about 11 miles. The drive from Durango to the trailhead may take 2 hours or more. Many people drive in, camp along this road, then hike the next day.

HIKE: Take the well-defined path off the end of the road (N 37 43.523, W 107 51.705, 11,200 feet) another couple hundred yards to where you strike the Colorado Trail. Take it right (north) to a crossing of an unnamed creek, where the trail swings sharply right (east). At this point it is beginning to contour around a high, steep ridge that comes off the south side of Grizzly.

Soon there should be a fairly obvious route leaving the Colorado Trail to the left, and perhaps a cairn to mark the spot (N 37 43.786, W 107 51.689, 11,200 feet). Take this trail uphill at first. Eventually it levels out, even drops a bit, and heads almost straight north. For a while this trail nearly parallels the Colorado Trail, which keeps losing elevation.

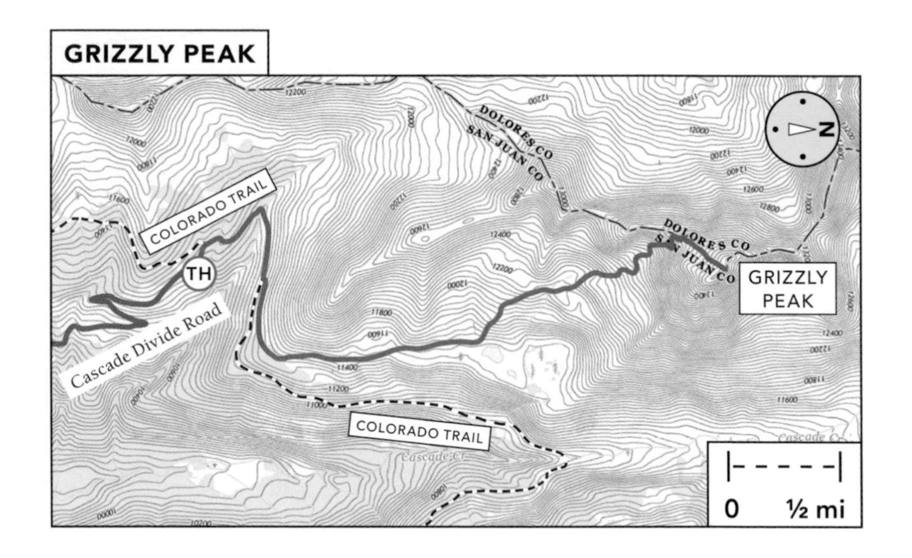

There's a shale-rock area to get through where it sounds like you're stepping on panes of glass. In about a mile off the Colorado Trail you'll come to a picturesque shelf with some small lakes and marshy areas. A stream fills this area from above and another drains it, plunging over the side down to Cascade Creek. Backpackers out to climb Grizzly often camp around this area.

From here the climbers' trail makes its way through rocks and willows to connect up to a steep couloir coming southeast (more or less) from just south of Grizzly's summit. From the southwest side of the lake area, climb steeply upward on the defined trail through the rocky scree and talus toward the northwest and the couloir. Once you're a couple hundred feet above the lake you'll leave the scree and be on tundra with big, scattered rocks. If you just want to laze on or near one of these big boulders for a couple of hours, you will still have had an awesome day.

If you continue, you'll reach the steep couloir, which is filled with big rocks with cliffs on each side. The right side of this is a shoulder of Grizzly Peak, the top of which you cannot see from here. Climb the couloir, still bearing northwest. It's steep and takes some work, but your biggest challenge will be to avoid dislodging rocks and sending them careening down toward your climbing partners. When there's snow in the couloir it adds another degree of difficulty, and climbing early in the summer may require an ice axe, perhaps with crampons as well.

At the top of the chute you will find yourself on a rocky ridge; turn right for a fairly easy quarter-mile climb over talus to the top of Grizzly (N 37 45.370, W 107 51.717, 13,738 feet).

The top itself is very rocky, but it affords excellent views of many rugged peaks that lie north between Trout Lake on the west and South Mineral Creek on the east. The near peaks, looking northwest to northeast, are Sheep Mountain, San Miguel Peak, and Rolling Mountain. A bit farther north, to the left of Rolling Mountain, are

From the Grizzly Peak summit, looking east over the Cascade Creek valley and toward Rolling Mountain on the left.

Vermilion Peak and US Grant Peak above Ice Lake Basin. Almost due northwest, to the left of Sheep, are the San Miguel fourteeners: El Diente, Mount Wilson, and Wilson Peak, as well as Lizard Head with its distinctive shaft rising 400 vertical feet. An eastern view shows the many peaks around Silverton and, farther south, the rugged Needles area of the Weminuche Wilderness.

OPTIONS: For the return trip, the same route is recommended. But for those interested in rock climbing, instead of taking the chute down to the marshy area, continue south along the ridge. This is farther and slower. On this route you will move up and down over various sizes of rocks. At times there is much exposure and slow rock climbing. The route is not recommended for the inexperienced or faint of heart. Once over this tricky ridge, climb to the highest point (still going south) and proceed down the steep south side to a more gentle tundra area. Hike southeast and back to the end of the road.

GRAYROCK PEAK

DISTANCE: 6.8 miles round-trip

ELEVATION: Start at 10,400 feet, summit at 12,504 feet (2,104-foot gain)

RATING: Moderate

TIME ALLOWED: 4 to 5½ hours

Graysill Mountain is a formation in the shape of a horseshoe facing east; its high point is on the southeast corner, and at that point it is called Grayrock Peak. It is not a high peak compared with many others in the San Juans, but because it is the highest point for several miles in any direction, it is impressive and yields fine views. It is located west of Cascade Creek and southwest of Engineer Mountain. If you've skied at Purgatory Resort, you've undoubtedly noticed this peak not far to the north.

The best approach is from the southwest. Done from the east side, this climb demands some bushwhacking and route finding, and slow hiking over rocks. Either way, the hard part is not long, and the summit is surprisingly exhilarating.

APPROACH: Take US 550 north from Thirty-Second Street and Main Avenue in Durango for 25 miles and turn left (west) at the ski-area entrance. Go 0.5 miles on

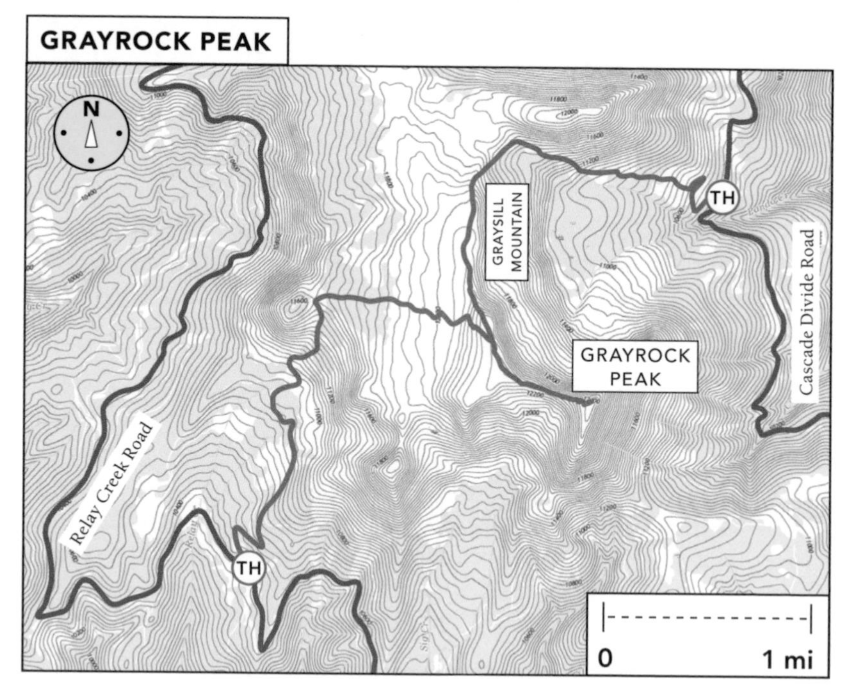

pavement on the main road, then look for a gravel road going right (north), away from the ski area. This is FR 578.

This road is flat as it heads north, but then it heads south and west and climbs in a series of switchbacks. In 3.3 miles it tops out and then turns north (the Elbert Creek Road goes south here). In a half-mile there is a left turn down into Hermosa Park; do not take this, but go straight onto FR 579/580 (the Cascade Divide/Relay Creek Roads). In another 1.2 miles the Cascade and Relay roads split; take Relay Creek Road (FR 580) left; it goes west and northwest, passing under the shoulder of Grayrock on the south side. This is a good gravel road, but it does a lot of switching around.

In 6.2 miles there will be a huge, manmade cleared flat area on your right. Park here.

HIKE: Find the abandoned road that heads north, just west of the cleared area and just off the Relay Creek Road (N 37 39.684, W 107 53.531, 10,400 feet), and begin hiking up. Several old logging roads wind up the mountain for a while; they're well defined, but it won't be perfectly clear which one to use. Go north as best you can, then northeast up a small valley just left of a pointed rock that stands tall on the ridge above. Reach an obvious green saddle between talus slopes (N 37 40.836, W 107 53.226, 11,550 feet).

From here head east, finally breaking out into the open above timberline. Now the choices seem limitless, but continue generally east, maybe just a tad south, uphill. You'll be on grass and then talus, and the going gets steeper as you head toward a high ridge, which perhaps you'll reach somewhere around 12,300 feet (N 37 40.716, W 107 53.099). It's obvious you don't want to go farther east at this point, because of that large abyss before you. You're on the rim of the horseshoe that is Graysill Mountain, looking down onto Pando Creek.

Turn right to go south, and keep gaining altitude. Stay fairly close to the steep drop-off. The going gets rockier and the ridgeline turns southeast, then east, and drops to a saddle (N 37 40.485, W 107 51.998, 12,260 feet) just below Grayrock Peak.

The ridge narrows, and from a distance this looks kind of hairy. But fear not: It works out when you reach it. Hike up the last 250 feet of elevation to the summit. The rocks underfoot are small and noisy, sometimes with a musical sound and sometimes with just a clunk. The summit is marked by a large cairn (N 37 40.437, W 107 51.771, 12,504 feet).

Grayrock Peak features its own special thrill: a sheer cliff on its north side practically straight down for a thousand feet. After recovering from the sight of this plunge, you will want to enjoy the more distant views. Engineer Mountain rises as a fine, stalwart warrior out of Cascade Canyon a few miles northeast. Grizzly Peak is a sharp and dominant point several miles north, even higher than Engineer. Northwest are Hermosa Peak and, farther beyond, Lizard Head and the Wilsons. On the southwest skyline are the La Plata Mountains, and you can even see Sleeping Ute Mountain, which is southwest of Cortez.

The return should be made by the same route as the climb.

OPTIONS: Grayrock can be climbed also from an eastern approach. The access road is the same until the junction of Cascade and Relay roads. For this approach head right up the Cascade Divide Road, which gets rougher and rougher the farther you go. It's nice to have 4WD. In 5.3 miles from the split, the road swings northwest and tends slightly downhill. (At this point you are northeast of Grayrock Peak, which only helps if you know what the peak looks like and can get a glimpse of it way above.) The road crosses two braids of Pando Creek, then swings back uphill toward the northeast. Keep going a couple hundred yards to where the road turns almost due north, and park at the junction of an abandoned road (N 37 41.236, W 107 51.145, 10,400 feet). Interestingly, the starting elevation is identical to that of the western approach.

Start up the abandoned road. It tends northwest, then switchbacks west. Ultimately you want to go nearly due west up to a ridge that's part of Graysill Mountain, but for this lower part, these roads can help you get started and avoid the thick forest by going around it to the north.

When it looks like the roads aren't helping, head west. You'll have to bushwhack, going over down timber and through some thick brush. About 0.8 miles from the start, a slope of shale rock comes down the mountainside above you to the north. There may be another way, but you can walk carefully across the shale and skunk cabbage, keeping the saddle on the ridge as your goal.

There are plenty of pleasant spots to hang out and enjoy the day on the west side of Grayrock Peak.

At 1.5 miles from the car, you'll reach the ridge at 11,700 feet. Head southwest, then south up a mellow, tundra slope on the ridge of Graysill Mountain. Keep gaining altitude and you'll soon link up with the route described on page 147, heading south, southeast, and then east up to the summit.

HERMOSA PEAK

DISTANCE: 3.6 miles round-trip

ELEVATION: Start at 11,520 feet, summit at 12,579 feet (1,059-foot gain)

RATING: Moderate

TIME ALLOWED: 2 to 3 hours

Hermosa Peak involves traveling some backcountry roads, but it is one of the easiest and quickest high-altitude climbs in southwestern Colorado. It offers fine views of even higher peaks from its top; even driving the road to the trailhead is worthwhile, particularly if you've never been that way.

The climb is quite short but is rated moderate because it is high and because some 250 yards of it are steep, with one short hazardous spot.

APPROACH: Access is via the Bolam Pass road; it is 4WD, but it is usually in better condition than many such roads. Under dry conditions, two-wheel-drive cars and trucks can usually make it if they have good clearance and a good low gear for the steep hills. You'll also need to ford Hermosa Creek at one point; pick a good route and keep your momentum.

This hike may be approached on FR 578 from the east from the Purgatory side or from the west from the Rico side. For the eastern approach, take US 550 north of Durango 25 miles and turn left (west) into the main ski area entrance. Go north 0.5 miles and find a gravel road (FR 578) going north. Take that, and stay on it to the top of Bolam Pass.

Drive past the top of the pass 0.7 miles to a left turn onto FR 149. (In all, you're on FR 578 for 18 miles.) Take FR 149 for 0.8 miles to a barrier (N 37 42.963, W 107 55.511, 11,520 feet). Hermosa Peak dominates the southern skyline.

HIKE: Hike down the road 1 mile. You will be following the Colorado Trail, which joins the route just beyond the barrier. The place to leave the road/trail is a point approximately northwest of a saddle between Hermosa Peak and a smaller unnamed peak southwest of it.

It starts up an easy, grassy slope. (There may be a few trees at first, depending on your choice of where to start up.) The grassy slope heads toward the saddle at 1.4

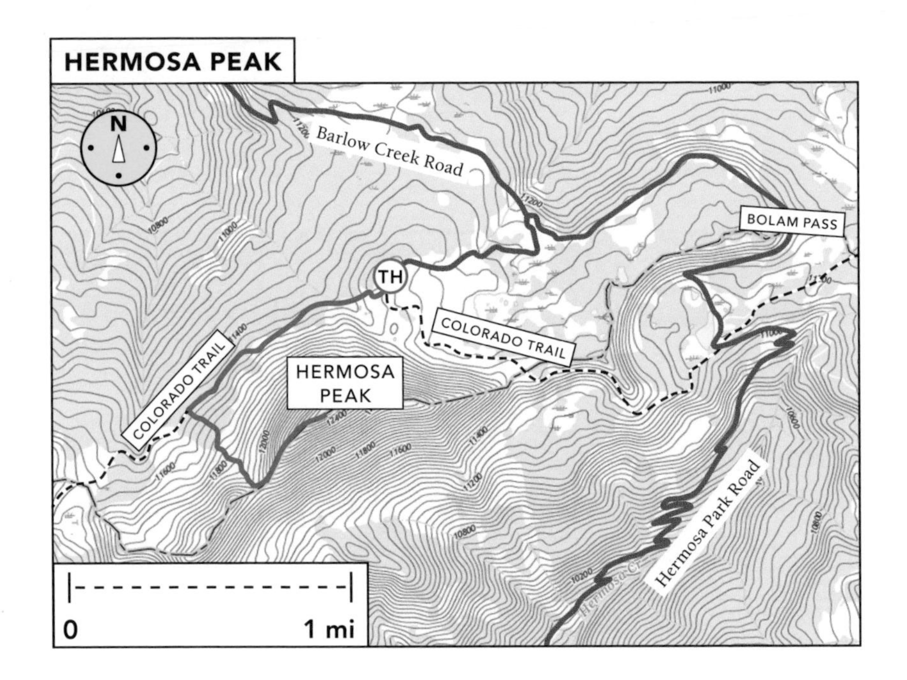

miles. This is quite easy climbing except just below the saddle, where it gets steeper and becomes talus.

At the saddle (N 37 42.364, W 107 55.991, 12,010 feet), go left (northeast) toward the summit. A hundred yards above the saddle there is one small cliff to get over, but most anyone can make it with care or a little boost from a companion. Once above this, it is a short but steep climb to the ridge; the top (N 37 42.599, W 107 55.711, 12,579 feet) is a few hundred yards beyond at 1.8 miles.

For those with experience on peaks, Hermosa Peak is not a huge deal. But if it's, say, the first time on a mountain for someone from the Midwest who is really keen to get some great pictures during the foliage color season, well, that can be interesting. On a recent visit, when we got to the steep part near the top, my hiking partner insisted on crawling on his hands and knees because he was so frightened of the height and steepness. There really was no serious risk; going down he was braver.

The top of the mountain does furnish some beautiful views. All the same mountains that you can see from Bolam Pass can be seen even better from here, plus more. There is a fine view of Engineer Mountain to the east. Blackhawk is the nearest to the southwest. The La Platas loom on the southern horizon. The north face of Hermosa Peak is practically straight down. (Hint from experience: Don't set a pack too close to the edge; it could roll down and disappear over the steep face, necessitating a hairy rescue up from the steep north side.)

JURA KNOB (COAL CREEK–DEER CREEK)

DISTANCE: 9.6-mile loop, plus climb of Jura Knob

ELEVATION: Start at 10,300 feet, Jura summit at 12,614 feet (2,314-foot gain)

RATING: Moderate, with one tricky scramble spot

TIME ALLOWED: 5 to 6 hours

Coal Creek and Deer Creek Trails each provide fine half-day hikes into big timber, but this description combines them into a very good full-day hike that includes a climb of Jura Knob. The trailheads are both on US 550 and are 1.6 miles apart; therefore, this highway distance will need to be provided for in hiking or an arranged shuttle. This road mileage is in addition to the time and mileage given above. Good parking space is available near both trailheads.

The easiest way to do this is to have a car at each end and begin at Coal Creek, seeing as it is 500 feet higher. This high-altitude hike involves considerable altitude gain. Otherwise, it is easy, with only one spot (near the top of Jura Knob) where rock scrambling is involved.

APPROACH: Coal Creek is the first drainage north of Coal Bank Pass. Just below where US 550 crosses the creek, 1.2 miles from the top of the pass, park on the south side of the road (N 37 42.513, W 107 46.204, 10,300 feet) and walk down the highway about 200 yards to where the trail starts sharply upward to the east.

If you have a second car, shuttle it another 1.6 miles to the Deer Creek trailhead, where there are a couple of parking spots at a small pullout. If that pullout is full or you miss it, just continue another 0.2 miles down to where Old Lime Creek Road turns off to the right (south) from the highway. There is plenty of parking in the vicinity.

HIKE: The trail soon angles northeast into the trees, then curves back around westward. At 2 miles, the trail emerges into a grassy clearing. Engineer Mountain, with its sheer north face and the rock glacier below, is unmistakable to the southwest. To the north, the timberline can be seen a few hundred yards above.

You may find two or three trails in this area. What you want to do is head basically north to a saddle on the ridge at 11,640 feet (N 37 43.094, W 107 47.329). You should be able to follow one fairly distinct trail leading up this way. At the ridgetop you'll find a trail running east-west along the ridge, still the Coal Creek Trail.

Upon reaching this high point at 2.4 miles, look northeast across Deer Creek Valley, hundreds of feet below, to two peaks about the same size. Neither of these is

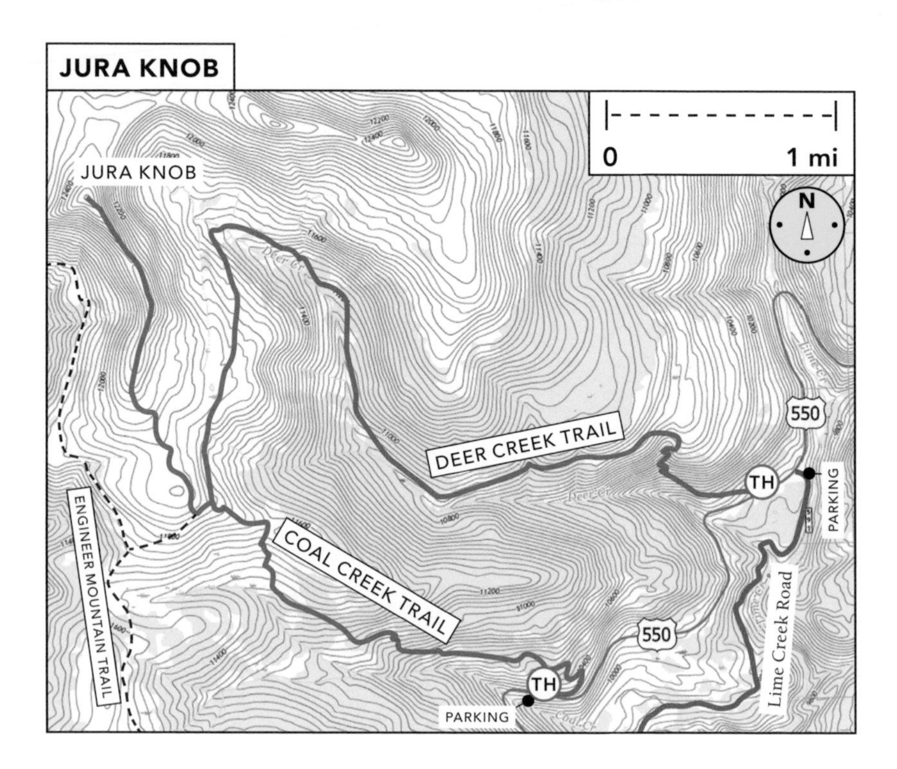

Jura Knob. Continue up west on the ridge, following the sometimes-rutted trail to the junction of the Coal Creek and Deer Creek Trails at 2.7 miles. It should be marked, with signs on two tiny trees at a rocky promontory (N 37 43.176, W 107 47.571, 11,850 feet).

Continue briefly on the Coal Creek Trail, but then veer off it to the north, following the easy ridgeline up toward Jura Knob, 1 mile beyond. One obstacle of some difficulty remains. It is a ledge a short distance below the top. There is one shoulder-high vertical climb. Adults with a bit of climbing experience can make this by themselves with proper foot placement. Anyone can make it with a boost from a partner.

The top, lying a short distance beyond the ledge at 3.7 miles, is a smooth roll with small flat rocks for its surface (N 37 44.238, W 107 48.119, 12,614 feet). It is a good place to stretch out for a rest or to eat a sandwich while enjoying views of peaks in all directions. Immediately to the north are the Twin Sisters on the right and Rolling Mountain to the left. Farther north between these is the Ice Lakes area, with US Grant Peak immediately beyond. To the west, Grizzly Peak majestically guards the Cascade Valley, but a low ridge in between hides the valley itself.

Retrace your route from Jura Knob back to the junction of Coal Creek and Deer Creek Trails. Take Deer Creek Trail left (north). From here it's 4.9 miles to the highway via Deer Creek. The trail drops slightly, then climbs again and reaches a high point at a tarn (N 37 43.560, W 107 47.547, 11,950 feet). From here the trail drops,

The smooth ridge leading toward Jura Knob. It's easy other than one quick vertical rock scramble.

gently and then more steeply, north to cross Deer Creek (N 37 44.118, W 107 47.488, 11,500 feet). Just after this crossing a trail goes up to the left, but for now veer right, staying near the creek. There can be a riot of wildflowers along this trail up to where it enters the heavily wooded area. Eventually the trail ends up well above Deer Creek, climbing a bit before dropping steeply back down to the highway. Once you cross Deer Creek, the trail always stays north of it.

The final descent plummets 1,000 feet to the highway in about a mile, entering an aspen grove just before its finish. Once you hit the highway (N 37 43.187, W 107 45.197), it's 0.3 miles downhill to Old Lime Creek Road and your shuttle car.

OPTIONS: Most options are probably fairly obvious: Park at the Coal Creek Trailhead, hike up Jura Knob, and hike back the same way, avoiding Deer Creek Trail entirely. Still, this is a nice hike and is 7.4 miles round-trip.

Or take a stroll up the Deer Creek Trail as far as you wish and return the same way. The upper end of the creek is in a beautiful high valley, with lots of wildflowers at the right time of summer, as previously mentioned.

CRATER LAKE—NORTH TWILIGHT

DISTANCE: 11 miles round-trip to Crater Lake, 14 miles round-trip to summit of North Twilight Peak

ELEVATION: Start at 10,750 feet, Crater Lake at 11,630 feet (880-foot gain), North Twilight at 13,075 feet (2,325-foot gain)

RATING: Easy but fairly long to the lake; very difficult to summit

TIME ALLOWED: 5 to 7 hours to Crater Lake, 7 to 9 hours to the summit

---

This is the best access to the West Needle portion of the Weminuche Wilderness, the portion of the Weminuche on the west side of the Animas River. The hike above Andrews Lake is very popular, but the farther you go, the fewer people you see, and the trail becomes obviously less well worn. A few people make it up North Twilight Peak and beyond, but often as a 2- or 3-day trip with Crater Lake as the base. Climbing North Twilight is a long day trip, but it's very possible. Get an early start.

APPROACH: The trailhead is at Andrews Lake. To get there take US 550 north from Durango about 39 miles, and take a big right turn southeast onto the Andrews Lake access road. It's one lane with pullouts—kind of funky. (If you reach Molas Pass on US 550, you've gone a mile too far.)

Head up Andrews Lake road 0.6 miles to the day parking at the lake (N 37 43.687, W 107 42.635, 10,750 feet). If the lot is full or you're planning an overnight, use the multiday parking area below. There's an outhouse next to the lake.

HIKE: Take the path next to the outhouse and head south around the lake, quickly picking up a trail that switchbacks uphill toward the south and gains 400 feet in 1 mile. At that point you'll come to a junction (N 37 43.263, W 107 42.440, 11,185 feet). The trail left takes you east toward Snowdon Peak. Continue straight, bearing south.

From here the trail goes up and down, never steeply, and in and out of the spruce-fir forest. The most striking views are off to the west, where you'll see the northeast ridge and approach to Engineer Mountain. As you get closer to Crater Lake, the impressive Twilight massif will rise above.

At 5.5 miles, reach the north end of Crater Lake (N 37 40.536, W 107 42.779, 11,630 feet). On placid days the massif reflects beautifully in the water. If this is your destination, find a relaxing spot, throw in a line, and enjoy.

If North Twilight is your goal, then take some time to study the massif to the southwest, towering 1,400 feet above where you stand. From this perspective the highest point is on the left of this massif. That is actually a false summit, or sub-peak, but you want to aim eventually for that ridge that extends from it, coming toward where you stand. North Twilight is basically in the middle of that massif.

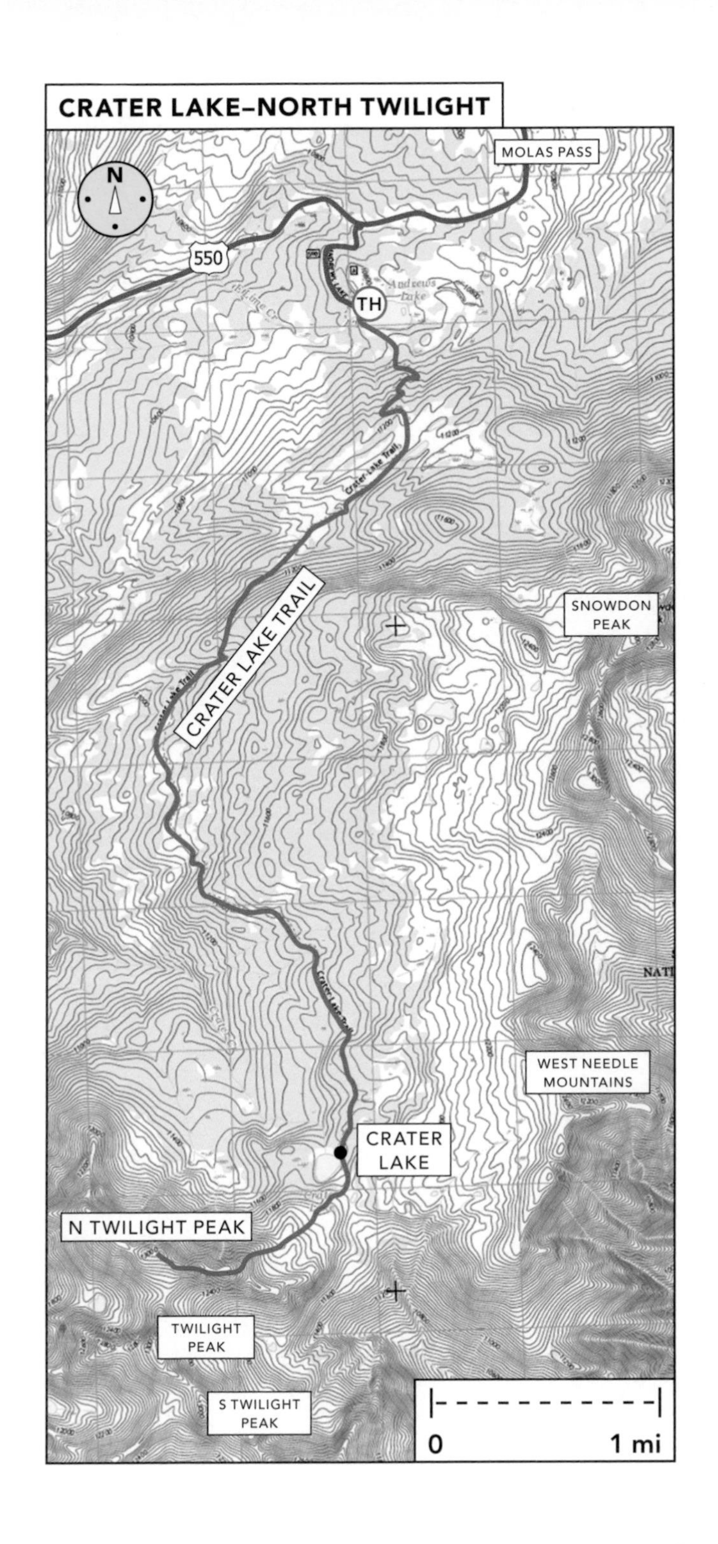
CRATER LAKE–NORTH TWILIGHT
MOLAS PASS
N
550
TH
CRATER LAKE TRAIL
SNOWDON PEAK
WEST NEEDLE MOUNTAINS
CRATER LAKE
N TWILIGHT PEAK
TWILIGHT PEAK
S TWILIGHT PEAK
0
1 mi

The summit ridge on North Twilight Peak, with Crater Lake below and the Needles in the background. (Photo by Peter Schertz)

Take the trail that goes left from the lake and heads up toward the south. First you'll be going toward a saddle, but when you see a clear spot with no willows, at about 5.7 miles, leave the trail and make your way to the aforementioned ridge extending from the false summit. (There is more than one way to skin a cat, as they say, but this seems the easiest.) There probably won't be a trail at first, but eventually you'll see a path scratched onto this ridge, or just below it, and that's the path you want. It'll be steep, but it'll work out, and it'll take you to the high east-west ridge just below and east of the false summit at 6.5 miles (N 37 40.071, W 107 43.284, 12,795 feet).

Now comes the most interesting part of the climb: There is nothing terribly technical, but you'll do some Class 3 scrambling while making your way up and down this rocky ridgeline. Pick your route carefully, and watch your footing on the Twilight gneiss.

Reach the expansive summit at 7 miles (N 37 40.151, W 107 43.641, 13,075 feet) and take your best guess as to where the actual top is. Pile up some rocks and create a new summit if you like.

OPTIONS: From here it's possible to head south to bag Twilight (13,158 feet) and South Twilight (13,090 feet). As you look south from North Twilight, the ridge over to Twilight might look easy. Don't worry, it will provide plenty of challenge, as will the continuation to South Twilight.

SNOWDON PEAK

DISTANCE: 6.2 miles round trip

ELEVATION: Start at 10,750 feet, summit at 13,077 feet (2,327-foot gain)

RATING: Very difficult, due to exposure near summit

TIME ALLOWED: 5 to 7 hours

This dark, often-shiny mountain near the top of Molas Pass captivates the imagination. The area around it attracts winter snowshoers, spring skiers, and summer hikers. One of the climbing attractions is a 360-degree summit view from atop a peak that, as a map shows, has no close neighbors.

Climbing it takes a serious effort and a willingness to accept some risk and exposure. Deep clefts along its north summit ridge are intimidating from below, and just as intimidating up close. But with some careful climbing it all works out.

Best to have some confidence and route-finding experience for this one, or to have a climbing partner with these skills whom you trust. An hour or two of bouldering a day or two before the hike serves as a good warm-up and confidence-builder. (If you're close to Durango, Dalla Mountain Park offers myriad, low-to-the-ground rock scrambles. See City Trails on page 28.)

If you're curious, the name Snowdon apparently comes from a peak of the same name in Snowdonia, a mountainous region of Wales that contains the highest peaks in the United Kingdom excluding Scotland. There may be some debate here, however, as the first man to build a cabin in nearby Silverton in 1874 was Francis Marion Snowden, and there is a Snowden Street in Silverton. Maps since at least 1902 have showed it as Snowdon Peak.

APPROACH: The trailhead is at Andrews Lake, the same spot as the Crater Lake–North Twilight hike. Take US 550 north from Durango about 39 miles, and make a big right turn southeast onto the Andrews Lake access road.

Head up Andrews Lake road 0.6 miles to the day parking at the lake (N 37 43.687, W 107 42.635, 10,750 feet). If the lot is full or you're planning an overnight, use the multiday parking area. There's an outhouse next to the lake.

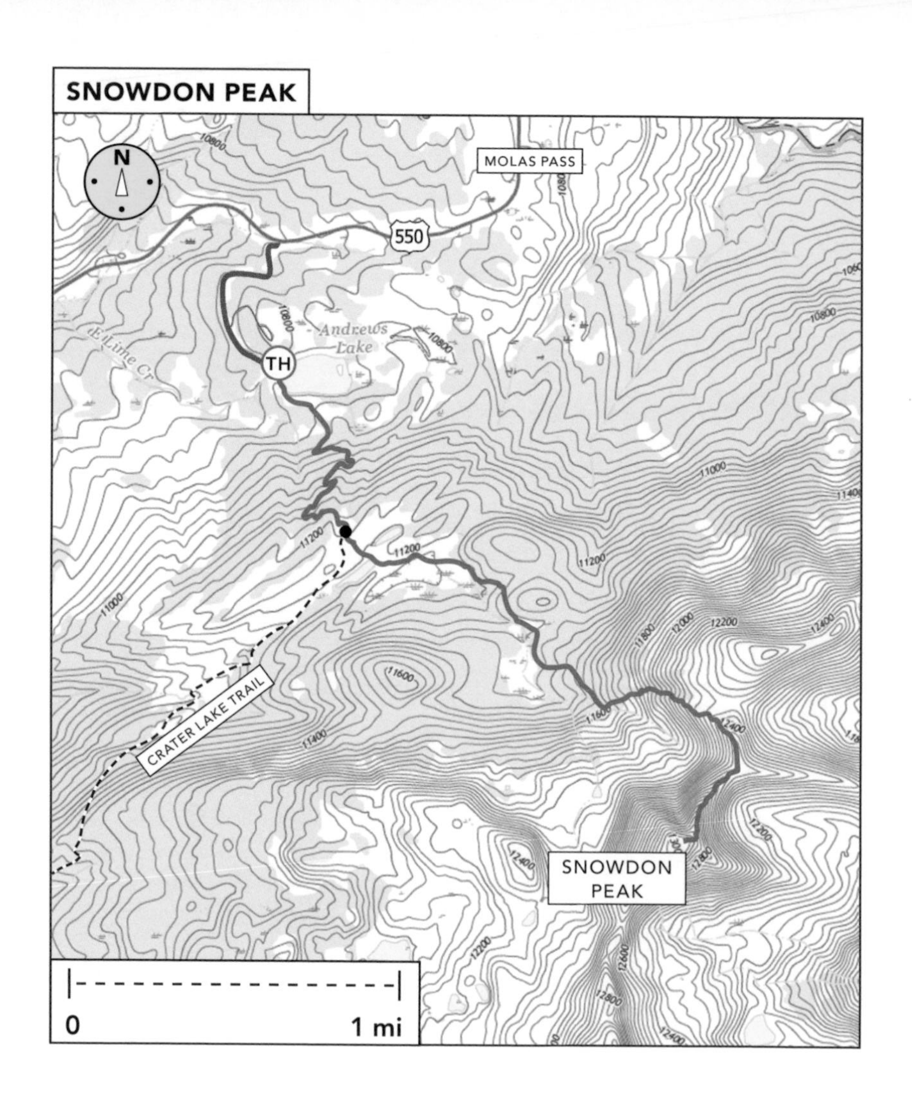

HIKE: Find the trail at the west end of the lake and head south around the lake, quickly picking up a trail that zigzags up a 400-foot rise; just as you reach the top you'll come to a junction at 1 mile (N 37 43.263, W 107 42.440, 11,185 feet). Take the well-defined trail going left (east) toward Snowdon. The other path goes toward Crater Lake.

The trail heads down between two little lakes and then into a large, open, marshy area. In this open area are some geological marvels: potholes into which water drains and disappears! A limestone layer here has eroded, forming underground waterways. The water reappears through the earth miles away.

The trail is well established most of the way through the swampy area; where it braids, try to take the most traveled path.

From the summit, looking south-southeast toward the Needles, with Pigeon the prominent peak on the right.

At 1.8 miles (N 37 42.930, W 107 41.752, 11,370 feet) leave the relative flatness and begin trekking uphill in earnest. Head more or less east toward a saddle between Snowdon's summit and a 12,628-foot hump to the north of it. Up ahead to the southeast is a full view of Snowdon's north ridge and, just north of the summit, a couloir that's been dubbed the Naked Lady. This couloir is a popular path for backcountry skiers looking for a steep challenge. Don't follow the skiers' path heading into the rock field.

The trail continues to steepen. On the way up, it's an Achilles stretcher; on the way down, a toe-smasher.

You can go all the way to the saddle at 2.5 miles (12,340 feet), then hike almost due south to begin the ridge ascent. But the trail pitters out just before this saddle, and it's a bit shorter to head more southeasterly to join the ridge or contour just below it to the right. Aim for a smaller saddle (N 37 42.675, W 107 41.156, 12,555 feet) that serves as a nice gathering spot—a final chance to take a relaxed breath before the summit push.

Head south up the ridge, staying on top or just below it as long as possible. At about 2.9 miles (N 37 42.531, W 107 41.288, 12,890 feet), begin looking for a good path to the left around the approaching cleft in the ridge. This is where the route-finding skills come into play. There may or may not be some good cairns to guide you, and they may be hard to spot. You'll need to downclimb a bit. Test your holds. Be patient in this section, and help your fellow climbers if they need advice on where to plant their feet, or the best route.

Many climbers wear helmets for this climb, as there are a few loose rocks (mostly small), and a few use ropes.

Ultimately you'll come to a spot where it's possible to climb west to the summit. This final short section, which might have seemed daunting a couple hours ago, will now be a breeze.

Enjoy the large, rocky and nearly flat top (N 37 42.477, W 107 41.326, 13,077 feet) at 3.1 miles. On a nice day you'll want to spend some extra time just enjoying your accomplishment and perhaps familiarizing yourself with the expanse of San Juan mountains spread before you. Too many places to name them all, but you have a great view looking east up Elk Creek to the Continental Divide, southeast to Eolus and Pigeon, southwest to the distant La Platas, Spud Hill, and Engineer Mountain, northwest to the Ice Lakes peaks, and almost due north to the fourteener Sneffels.

Yes, going down is a bit trickier, but hopefully you now know the way.

OPTIONS: The return may be varied from the approach. Go south toward the low point between the Snowdon summit and its twin peak (nearly as high at 13,046 feet) a half-mile to the south. There is a break in the rock here, and you will have to do some rock scrambling to get down. At the bottom of this scramble you are faced with some interesting rock pylons. To the right is a steep couloir that can be used with great care. Sometimes there is enough snow here for a good glissade, but the slope is steep, and ice axes are needed for a possible arrest.

A more gradual route down can be found by keeping to the left. At the bottom of this steep area (now 1,000 feet below the north peak), continue north or a little northwest to get back to the flat swampy area from which the approach was made. Westward across this will bring you back to the Crater Lake Trail again. Turn right on it to go back to Andrews Lake.

MOLAS TRAIL

DISTANCE: 7.4 miles round-trip to bridge over the Animas River

ELEVATION: Start at 10,610 feet, Animas River at 8,910 feet (1,700-foot gain or drop, depending on your viewpoint)

RATING: Easy, but save energy for the climb back out

TIME ALLOWED: 3½ to 4½ hours

Along with Purgatory Flats, this is the rare hike that starts high and ends low, more like your typical desert canyon hike. It's fairly popular, particularly early in the summer when the higher-country hikes may be snowed in. And it's always fun to hear the train whistle way down below.

APPROACH: Travel about 42 miles north from Durango on US 550. There's a large parking area and trail access 1.2 miles north of Molas Pass, on the right (south) side of the highway. This is about 6 miles south of Silverton.

HIKE: Find the trailhead (N 37 44.870, W 107 41.250, 10,610 feet) at the south end of the parking area and begin hiking south, slightly downhill through an open, sometimes-boggy area. Check out the nice views of Snowdon Peak due south, with the Grenadier Range to the southeast and Kendall Mountain to the northeast. In 0.2 miles, meet up with the Colorado Trail coming down from your right from Molas Pass.

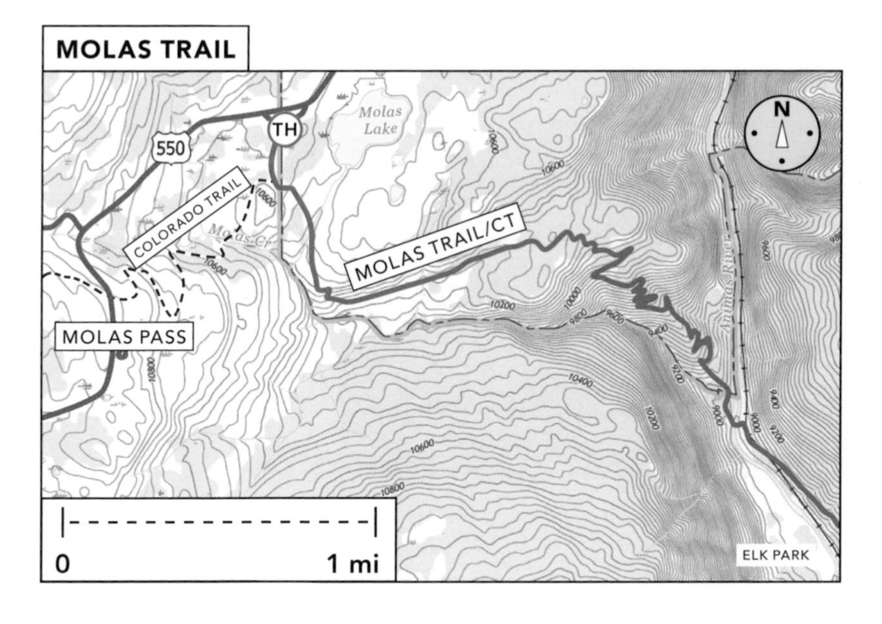

The going gets steeper, and soon you hit a series of switchbacks that drop you down to within sight of Molas Creek, although you never come up next to it. The trail continues downhill in a meadow on the north side of the Molas Creek valley. After crossing this flat meadow, the trail plunges into big spruce-fir timber.

At 1.6 miles from the start (N 37 44.552, W 107 40.244, 10,267 feet), just before the trail begins its steep descent toward the Animas River, watch for an excellent viewpoint at a rocky outcrop to the right of the trail, with a path leading to it. This offers a great view of the Grenadiers, right to left: Garfield, Electric, Vestal, and the Trinitys. Farther south is the impressive Peak Fourteen massif. You can see and even hear the river 1,300 feet below, and you may catch a glimpse of the Durango & Silverton Narrow Gauge Railroad, at this point on the east side of the river.

Head down through the aspen forest on the heavily switchbacked trail. Down. And down. Finally the trail closes in on Molas Creek, and at 3.5 miles crosses it on a bridge of makeshift logs. At 3.6 miles the trail turns toward the Animas River and crosses it on a substantial bridge (N 37 44.013, W 107 39.675, 8,910 feet).

For this view of the Grenadiers, reflected off a pond along Elk Creek, you'll have to hike 3 miles up the Elk Creek Trail.

OPTIONS: If you want to tack on a few more miles, continue across the bridge and pick up the trail going south on the opposite side of the river along the tracks. At 3.8 miles, cross the tracks (look both ways) and head uphill on the Colorado Trail (N 37 43.925, W 107 39.566). This follows Elk Creek up to the Continental Divide in another 8.2 miles. Tremendous avalanches during the winter of 2018–19 left several massive debris of logs across the trail about 3 miles farther on. It might be a bit of a challenge to get through, but thanks to some hearty trail workers, paths through should be obvious.

You could start this hike on the Colorado Trail at the top of Molas Pass, but that does add some distance and 300 feet of elevation at each end of your trip. Park at the overlook and head north downhill briefly to connect with the CT.

Or you could enter the Molas Trail from Molas Lake—not to be confused with Little Molas Lake, which is nearer the top of the pass. This is a recreational spot owned by the town of Silverton that offers camping, fishing, and supplies. From here you would reach the trail by going south-southwest from the lake until you strike the main trail going southeast.

SULTAN–GRAND TURK

DISTANCE: 8.6 miles round-trip to Sultan, 9.8 miles if Grand Turk is included

ELEVATION: Start at 10,900 feet, Sultan summit at 13,368 feet (2,468-foot gain)

RATING: Moderate

TIME ALLOWED: 5½ to 6½ hours

This is a good climb, mostly above the timberline; there are no really difficult spots. Most of it is on tundra and loose rock. You will do a bit of route finding, as there is not a trail the entire way.

This trip can include either Grand Turk or Sultan, or both. The main description for this 8.6-mile round-trip hike takes Sultan only, but Grand Turk is included below as an option.

Although they are not nearly the highest, Sultan and Grand Turk are two of the most prominent peaks in the region, and it is great to get the vantage point from their summits. If you live in Silverton, they tower above every day.

APPROACH: The hike starts near Little Molas Lake, which cannot be seen from the highway. To get there, take US 550 north from Durango 40 miles; from the top of Molas Pass it's another 0.4 miles north to a left-hand turn (west) onto a gravel road.

Follow this road 1.1 miles. It heads around Little Molas, then turns south and ends at a trailhead. There is adequate parking and an outhouse where the Colorado Trail meets up with this road at its terminus (N 37 44.556, W 107 42.720, 10,900 feet).

HIKE: Take the Colorado Trail, which tends west through the forest. In a short time you'll reach an open area caused by an ancient burn. In 1 mile the trail veers right (north-northeast) along a wide, open ridge. Enjoy the excellent views from here, including a look toward the Grenadiers and, farther in the distance, the Needles.

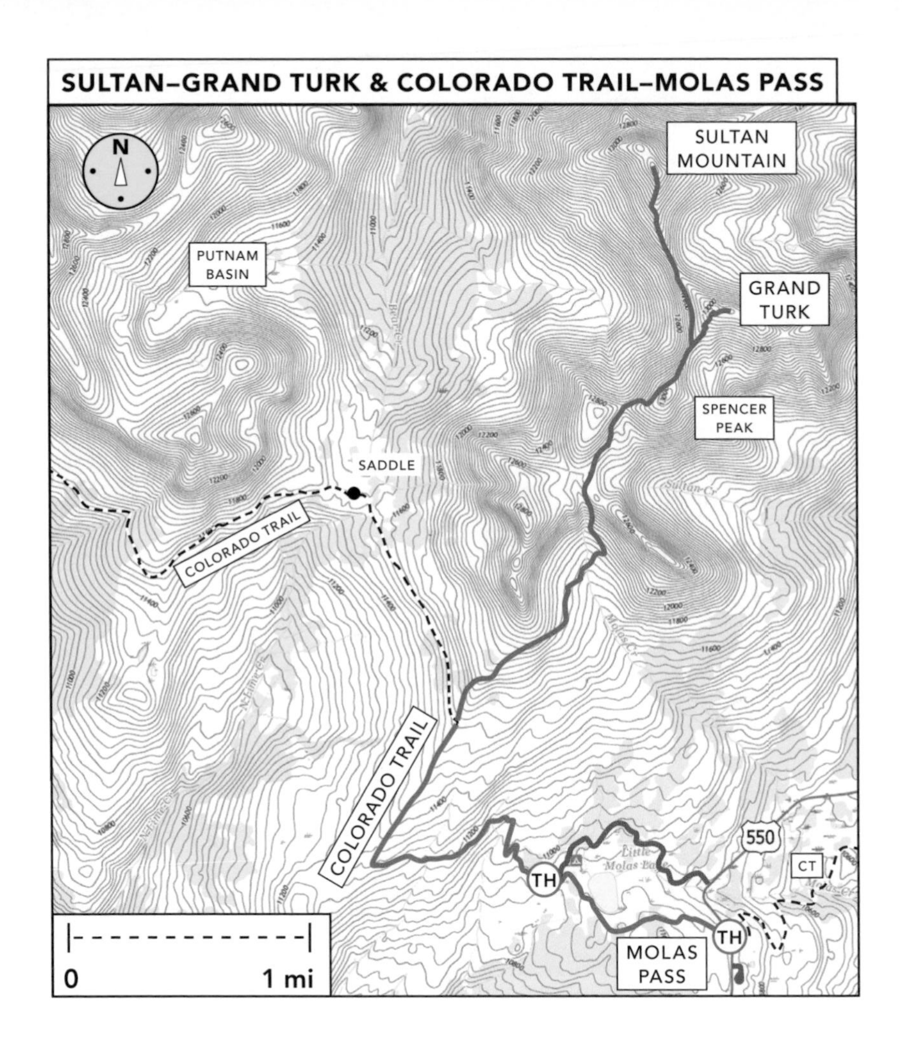

At 1.7 miles the Colorado Trail veers northwest (N 37 45.144, W 107 43.138, 11,610 feet), and you'll likely notice a closed-off trail coming up from your right. Leave the Colorado Trail and head off trail northeast along the top of the ridge toward the rocky bluffs straight ahead. Use your own judgment, but at some point you'll want to veer right and contour under the bluffs, staying fairly high. There's a narrow path along here if you can find it.

Eventually you'll need to drop northeast into the Molas Creek drainage. You should find a trail along here. Cross the creek and hike to the head of the valley, sometimes on slippery hard-packed dirt, and on up, again following a fairly good trail. As the steep climb eases (N 37 45.995, W 107 42.572, 12,450 feet), veer northeast along a fairly gentle meadow. At this point you're walking almost directly toward Grand Turk, and you should see it.

You can see what's up in Silverton from the top of Sultan Mountain.

Traverse up the east side of a steep mountainside; again, you should find a trail, or maybe two. Follow it another quarter-mile to a small saddle at 12,720 feet (N 37 46.299, W 107 42.364). The trail heads northeast around the top of the 13,097-foot-high ridge to the east, whose top in 2008 was named Spencer Peak in honor of mathematician Don Spencer, recipient of the National Medal of Science and a lover of these mountains. (How many peaks have been named for mathematicians?)

Drop down to the next saddle (still headed northeast). You are now at the base of Grand Turk. You should notice a trail heading almost due north from here (N 37 46.508, W 107 42.074, 12,820 feet), contouring over to a saddle below Sultan. To climb Grand Turk, see Options on page 166.

To continue on to Sultan from the saddle, head north along the rocky mountainside to the next saddle, at 12,776 feet. Follow up the ridge north to the top of Sultan (N 37 47.153, W 107 42.236, 13,368 feet).

Sultan provides a fine view northeast down on Silverton, 4,000 feet below. North of here is Anvil Mountain, which connects with Red Mountain. In the valley, US 550 leads on up toward Ouray. To the west below is Bear Creek, and just beyond is Bear Mountain (12,987 feet). Beyond this is Ice Lakes country, with many rugged peaks and ridges.

OPTIONS: To climb Grand Turk, which adds 1.2 miles round-trip, just continue northeast up the ridge from the 12,820-foot saddle, and when you get to a spot where it begins to spread out a bit, veer off to the right. Grand Turk has trouble deciding where to peak out. Actually, it has three peaks close together that are about the same height. The topographic map labels the one farthest east at 13,148 feet (N 37 46.590, W 107 41.749) and does not give heights for the others. Grand Turk also has twin peaks still a little farther east, but these are 100 or more feet lower than the other three. These twin peaks are what you see as the distinctive split-topped mountain that is most frequently viewed from the highway and the train.

COLORADO TRAIL—MOLAS PASS

DISTANCE: 7.8 miles round-trip to saddle above Bear Creek

ELEVATION: Start at 10,900 feet, high point at 11,610 feet (710-foot gain)

RATING: Moderate, due to altitude

TIME ALLOWED: 3½ to 5 hours

This trail heads west from the top of Molas Pass. It is mostly above trees with great views. It is easy to get to, and is a good introduction to the Colorado Trail. For 1.7 miles it follows the same path as the Sultan–Grand Turk hike (see page 163). There is no great defined turnaround spot. Just get out there and enjoy the day.

If you want to go east on the Colorado Trail, you can do that from here, but a better suggestion is to take Molas Trail (see page 161). If you start from there it's a 300-foot drop and a mile to Molas Trail.

You could make the same argument that it's better to begin this trail segment going west from the west side of Little Molas Lake, saving 1.3 miles of hiking. However, if you're just out for a nice day, beginning at the pass starts you out on a nice, mellow grade.

APPROACH: The Colorado Trail crosses US 550 a couple hundred yards north of the top of Molas Pass, which is located 7.5 miles south of Silverton, about 40 miles north of Durango. There is a good rest stop at the top of the pass which has a nice overlook to the north (Silverton area) and east (Grenadiers). A paved parking area and restrooms are also available.

HIKE: Cross the highway carefully and go north and find the Colorado Trail climbing west off the highway. After climbing some, the trail tends back downhill and around the south end of Little Molas Lake. It heads the west side of the lake, then meets up

You may find a register atop Grand Turk. Sultan Mountain looms in the background.

with a gravel road and goes past a parking area with an outhouse at 1.3 miles (N 37 44.556, W 107 42.720, 10,900 feet).

The trail starts a steady climb to the west, zigzagging upward, swings south and then back north, climbing gradually all the while. It turns sharply to follow a ridgeline north-northeast with great views until veering northwest to leave the ridge at 3 miles (N 37 45.144, W 107 43.138, 11,610 feet).

At 3.9 miles the trail swings west along a saddle (N 37 45.969, W 107 43.631, 11,600 feet) that separates Bear Creek drainage to the north and North Lime Creek to the south. Shortly before the saddle, it passes under a high unnamed point that is part of the massif that becomes Grand Turk and Sultan Mountain farther north. After leaving the saddle the trail dips and climbs, but doesn't gain much overall altitude as it passes under some more high unnamed points, eventually passing under Twin Sisters and, later, Grizzly Peak on its way to cross the Bolam Pass road at 20.8 miles.

Hopefully you've stopped your day hike by now, or you've got a long way to return. This stretch makes a good 2- to 3-day backpacking trip.

HIKES OUT OF SILVERTON

Silverton is a popular summer attraction for a reason. The mountains are high and spectacular.

Modern development began in the mid- to late-nineteenth century with eager miners digging into the rock and under the ground, looking for valuable metals. A very few got rich; many made a living; and some went away thinking: "This is a cold, miserable place most of the year, and this hardrock mining is killing me."

Stop at the San Juan County Historical Society's Mining Heritage Center in Silverton, or tour the underground Old Hundred Mine in Cunningham Gulch for a better understanding of the "glory days" of mining. The legacy lives on. Some want to revitalize the mining industry. Others are working to keep toxic minerals from entering the watershed—a huge environmental disaster in 2015 turned the river orange and led to the creation of the Bonita Peak Mining District Superfund site.

In any case, summers are nice and cool, and the hiking opportunities are numerous. You'll find turquoise lakes, mining ruins, challenging peaks, and high country vistas that will take your breath away.

Left, top: Prolific columbine just south of Hematite Basin. Left, right: One of several waterfalls decorating Cunningham Creek in the first mile of the Highland Mary Trail. Left, bottom: Columbine Lake after a late September snowstorm. Below: A small trail leading away from upper Ice Lake, heading up to Island Lake.

HOPE LAKE

DISTANCE: 6.6 miles round-trip from east side

ELEVATION: Start at 10,740 feet, pass at 12,445 feet (1,705-foot gain)

RATING: Moderate

TIME ALLOWED: 3 to 5 hours

Hope Lake lies at the center of its own high basin a little above the timberline. It is surrounded by dramatic sharp peaks well above 13,000 feet. There is a breathtaking ruggedness about this place. Some of the peaks are very colorful, with a mixture of reds, oranges, and grays. The lake can at times provide good fishing. The hike is on the easy side of moderate.

An interesting aspect of this lake is that it is a part of the water supply for the Ames power plant. Hope Lake, at 11,850 feet, is at the headwaters of the Lake Fork of the San Miguel River. Its water flows into Trout Lake. The varying demands of water for power can make Hope Lake beautiful when it's full and less attractive when it's drained down. This can also affect the fishing.

From Trout Lake, the water passes through a flume to the power plant. Ames is where the first commercial alternating current in the United States was generated. The motivation here was to get power more conveniently to the high-altitude mines in the area. There were many doubters, but the Ames plant was put into operation in 1892.

One other tidbit: The USGS map calls it Lake Hope, but the same map also calls the trail the Hope Lake Trail, and a Forest Service district ranger swears it should be Hope Lake. You decide if it makes a difference.

APPROACH: From the Silverton Visitors Center, drive 2.1 miles northwest on US 550 to a left-hand turn (west) on the gravel South Mineral Creek Road. After 4.4 miles on that road you'll come to the South Mineral campground. From here the road gets rougher; it's doable without 4WD, but a vehicle with some clearance is recommended; it can get pretty rough.

From the campground it's 2.3 miles to the Bandora Mine ruins (N 37 47.182, W 107 48.076, 10,750 feet). Although the road continues from here, park near the mine ruins and look for a narrow abandoned road heading southwest uphill.

HIKE: This route is not maintained and is rocky in places, but it is easy to follow and not too steep. Make sure that in 0.8 miles you take the switchback uphill to the right (N 37 46.813, W 107 48.828, 11,340 feet); soon the road switches back again to the west.

At 2.3 miles from the start, begin snaking your way on a trail up toward the pass (it might be tempting to continue left on the level road, but don't). At 2.6 miles, after

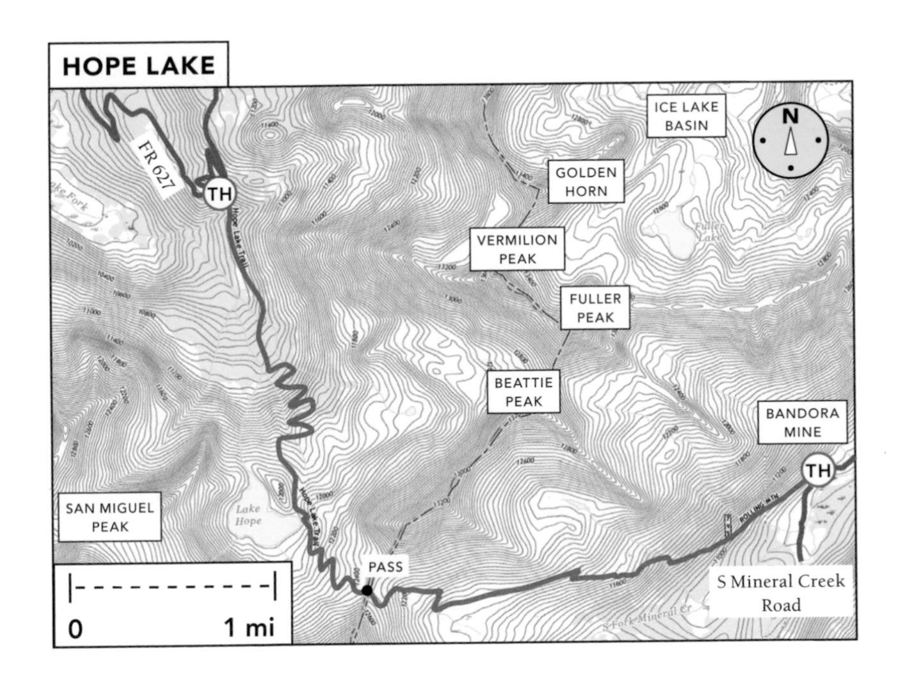

some steep climbing, you'll hit the top of the pass (N 37 46.704, W 107 50.340, 12,445 feet). The view at the top of the pass is dramatic as you first glimpse the sharp peaks, Hope Lake below, and Trout Lake still farther down. From here it's 0.7 miles and 595 feet elevation down to Hope Lake at 11,850 feet.

A truer total elevation gain for this hike, including the trek up to the pass from Bandora and the hike back up to the pass from the lake: 2,300 feet.

OPTIONS: The route to Hope Lake from the west side is via CO 145. Trout Lake is on the east side of the highway 2 miles north of Lizard Head Pass between Telluride and Rico. This is about 12 miles south of the Telluride turnoff from CO 145. At Trout Lake there is a good gravel road (FR 626) along the north side of the lake. Take it 1.8 miles from the highway, then watch for a turn left uphill on FR 627. This climbs steeply at times but is fine for ordinary cars, at least when dry. After 2.6 miles the road switches back sharply to the left but there is good parking here for several cars, and the trailhead (N 37 48.298, W 107 51.101, 10,700 feet) is well marked.

As you may discern from above, this hike is also a spectacular one. It crosses tiny tributaries and larger creeks, with great views looking back toward Trout Lake and the Wilson range beyond (Lizard Head, Mount Wilson, Wilson Peak). The first mile is fairly flat, but then the trail switchbacks steeply uphill. At 2.6 miles you reach the lake (N 37 47.033, W 107 50.713). The trail continues on above the lake another 0.7 miles to the pass at 12,445 feet.

ICE LAKES

DISTANCE: 7.6 miles round-trip to Ice Lake, 8.8 miles round-trip to Island Lake (via Ice Lake)

ELEVATION: Start at 9,850 feet, the lake at 12,257 feet (2,407-foot gain), Island Lake at 12,380 feet (2,530-foot gain)

RATING: Moderate, with a couple of small creek crossings that can be a bit tricky if you want to keep your feet dry

TIME ALLOWED: 4 to 6 hours to Ice Lake, 5 to 6 hours if Island Lake is added

---

Thanks to social media, the popularity of Ice Lake Basin has exploded. Visitors post photos on their favorite apps, and others follow to experience the grandeur. Now, the lake and its beautiful surroundings—turquoise water, waterfalls, cascading creeks, sublime wildflowers—are in danger of being overloved. In the summer of 2019 a group of concerned backcountry folks, including nonprofit organizations, businesses, and people who work for the San Juan National Forest, banded together and set up a "tiny house" at the trailhead. Volunteers stationed at the tiny house coach visitors on "leave no trace" ethics, everything from not cutting switchbacks to packing out toilet paper.

Hopefully this tack will help, and hopefully the Ice Lake craze will die down somewhat. Otherwise, the Forest Service may have to do something drastic such as set up a permit system. Forest Service officials ask those who find the trailhead parking area full to go somewhere else to hike. This book concurs and also advises: Get there early, and try to avoid weekends.

With all that said, this is a fantastic, magical place, and in addition to a hike to Ice Lake Basin, there are many options to explore.

APPROACH: From its intersection with Greene Street in Silverton, take US 550 northwest 2.1 miles and head left (west) onto South Mineral Creek Road. After 4.4 miles on this gravel road you'll see South Mineral Campground on your left; on the other side of the road, to your right, find a spot in the large trailhead parking area (N 37 48.406, W 107 46.450).

HIKE: Begin west from the parking area, climbing slowly at first. It seems the trail becomes steadily steeper. At 0.9 miles a spur trail goes off to the right and quickly makes what can be a dangerous crossing of Clear Creek (N 37 48.705, W 107 46.674, 10,081 feet). This trail connects with the Clear Lake Road.

Continue on the main trail west. At the top of a good climb at 2.4 miles, you may see a cairn and a trail heading to the north (N 37 48.755, W 107 47.493, 11,477 feet).

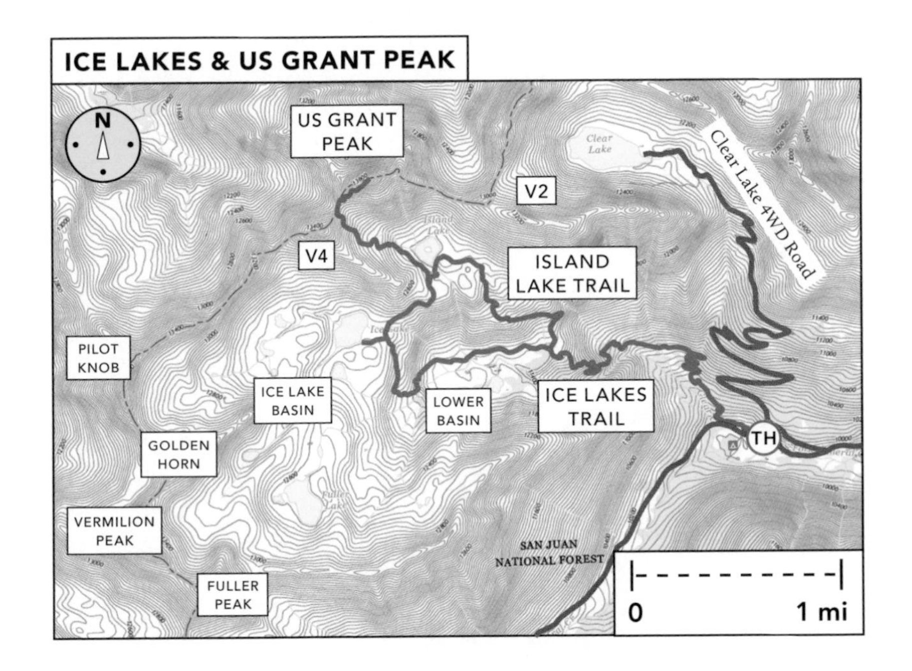

This is a 1.2-mile shortcut trail to Island Lake. Continue west into the Lower Ice Lake Basin and check out the rocky peaks in front of you: Fuller, Golden Horn, and more. After crossing the creeks coming out of Island Lake and upper Ice Lake, begin the hike out of the lower basin at 3 miles.

At 3.7 miles (N 37 48.794, W 107 48.350, 12,250 feet), as you crest the last big climb, a trail takes off north toward Island Lake. From here it's only another 0.1 miles to Ice Lake (N 37 48.787, W 107 48.485, 12,257 feet).

Back at the junction, the trail going north crosses the creek out of Ice Lake and contours up a grassy slope another 0.5 miles to Island Lake (N 37 49.083, W 107 48.131, 12,380 feet). Island Lake, as you may guess, has the unique feature of an island in its midst, resembling a volcano in the way it erupts from the lake floor. Both above-timberline lakes are surrounded by craggy peaks rising well above 13,000 feet. The highest peak in the area is Vermilion at 13,894 feet. Golden Horn (13,780 feet), US Grant (13,767 feet) and Pilot Knob (13,738 feet) are a mite shorter.

OPTIONS: Well, where to start? There are so many choices.

You can head around Ice Lake and strike out south and up toward Fuller Lake (12,585 feet). Fuller is at the base of Fuller, Vermilion, and Golden Horn.

From Island Lake you can head up US Grant, a thrilling hike featured on page 175. If you just want to bag a quick and fairly easy peak, your best bet is a mountain called V2, which is north of Island Lake. Head up the steep trail going toward the pass north of the lake and take a right on the ridge at the pass, referred to as Grant-Swamp

The spectacular upper Ice Lake, with Pilot Knob in view at the right.

Pass. V2 is the mound along the ridge with a top elevation of 13,309 feet. That trail heading to the pass, by the way, is the course of the Hardrock Hundred, one of the country's—make that one of the world's—most revered endurance running events.

If you want to make a loop, that's easy and you've probably already figured it out. A trail from the Island Lake outlet heads north briefly, then east. In 1.2 miles, this cutoff trail dumps you into Lower Ice Lake Basin and onto the Ice Lake Trail at the 2.4-mile mark mentioned above (N 37 48.755, W 107 47.493, 11,477 feet).

Enjoy, soak in the beauty, and please respect the fragile basin and leave no trace.

US GRANT PEAK

DISTANCE: 7.2 miles round-trip to Island Lake (via cutoff trail), 9.2 round-trip to summit

ELEVATION: Start at 9,850 feet, Island Lake at 12,380 feet (2,530-foot gain), US Grant at 13,767 feet (3,917-foot gain)

RATING: Very difficult, with a nearly vertical rock scramble and exposure near the summit

TIME ALLOWED: 4 to 6 hours to Island Lake, 6 to 8 hours to summit

---

Make no bones about it, the last part of the climb is a challenge. You should have some basic rock scrambling experience before attempting this. If you decide not to attempt this crux, the climb is still worthwhile for the lofty perch you have achieved. Make the summit early during monsoon season; the last thing you want is to be scrambling down on wet, slippery rock with lightning crashing around you.

It's a fun, rewarding, and most memorable climb. As you rise, the Ice Lakes and peaks of the basin, Island Lake, Ophir Pass, the Grenadiers, and more in the eastern distance all come into view. Hopefully it doesn't all take your breath away, because you'll need it on the way up.

APPROACH: The approach to this hike is the same as for Ice Lake Basin: From its intersection with Greene Street in Silverton, take US 550 northwest 2.1 miles and head left (west) onto South Mineral Creek Road. After 4.4 miles on this gravel road you'll see South Mineral Campground on your left; on the other side of the road, to your right, find a spot in the large trailhead parking area (N 37 48.406, W 107 46.450).

HIKE: Refer to the directions on page 172 for the Ice Lake Basin hike until the 2.4-mile point, where there's an unsigned split in the trail; there should also be a cairn (N 37 48.755, W 107 47.493, 11,477 feet). You can save time and distance by heading right (north) at this Y, although the going is a bit steeper. This is a 1.2-mile-long cutoff to Island Lake and avoids Upper Ice Lake Basin.

Assuming you take the cutoff, at 3.6 miles you'll reach Island Lake, well above the timberline. Go south of the lake (N 37 49.083, W 107 48.131, 12,380 feet) and contour around, heading for the steep gully and the pass between US Grant Peak and a smaller peak, known as V4, to the southwest of US Grant. Pick the best route and head west-northwest up this steep incline of grassy slopes, dirt, rock, scree and maybe snow. You're aiming for the pass.

The pass, at 4.3 miles, is at 13,170 feet (N 37 49.334, W 107 48.608). Take a look over the pass down toward impressive Waterfall Creek, which leads directly to the tiny establishment of Ophir, and check out the views of the Wilson fourteeners, then head right (northeast) up the ridge. The best path should be fairly easy to follow and shouldn't give you too much difficulty, although you'll be watching your footing on some pebbles and rock here and there.

At 4.5 miles, on the ridge about 150 vertical feet from the top, the real fun begins. There's no good way around it: There's a 10-foot nearly vertical section to scramble up. There is a good crack, and there are handholds and footholds, but you'll want to be sure of them before trusting them with your full body weight. In climbing parlance, this is called a crux. If you have something heavy in your pack, you might consider leaving it here and retrieving it on the way down. Carefully make your way up the crack, and don't smack your head on the overhang when you do reach the ledge above. (This move is more difficult on the way down. Better climbers should go first and act as spotters.)

The next thing to negotiate is this ledge you're on. Trust the ledge and cozy around it to the right. In about 100 feet you will come to a gully. This gully is relatively steep, but the rock is solid and shouldn't give you a problem. Keep going up to the ridge, and once you're back on it, the rest of the way is a breeze.

Take some deep breaths at the summit (N 37 49.468, W 107 48.440, 13,767 feet), and enjoy the exhilarating view!

Hugging the ledge on the way down US Grant Peak.

COLUMBINE LAKE

DISTANCE: 6.6 miles round-trip

ELEVATION: Start at 10,390 feet, lake at 12,685 feet (2,295-foot gain)

RATING: Easy to moderate, with steep climbing up to the pass

TIME ALLOWED: 3½ to 5 hours

This well-known secret gem just northwest of Silverton and just north of Ice Lake Basin has been discovered, so it can get a bit busy on summer weekends. Go early if you can to avoid crowds. It's a rewarding hike the entire way, with the ultimate reward of a picturesque, turquoise-blue lake in a high mountain cirque.

APPROACH: From the intersection of US 550 and Greene Street (the main drag) in Silverton, go north on 550 for 5 miles and turn left off the paved highway onto the Ophir Road. Cross Mineral Creek, make a left-hand switchback, then look for a road (maybe unmarked) heading to the right 0.4 miles from the highway. Go up this narrow, bumpy road for 0.8 miles to the trailhead (N 37 51.620, W 107 43.681, 10,390 feet). Parking is a little difficult; there is more parking room just north of the trailhead. Parking near the switchback is another good option, but this adds about a mile each way to the hike.

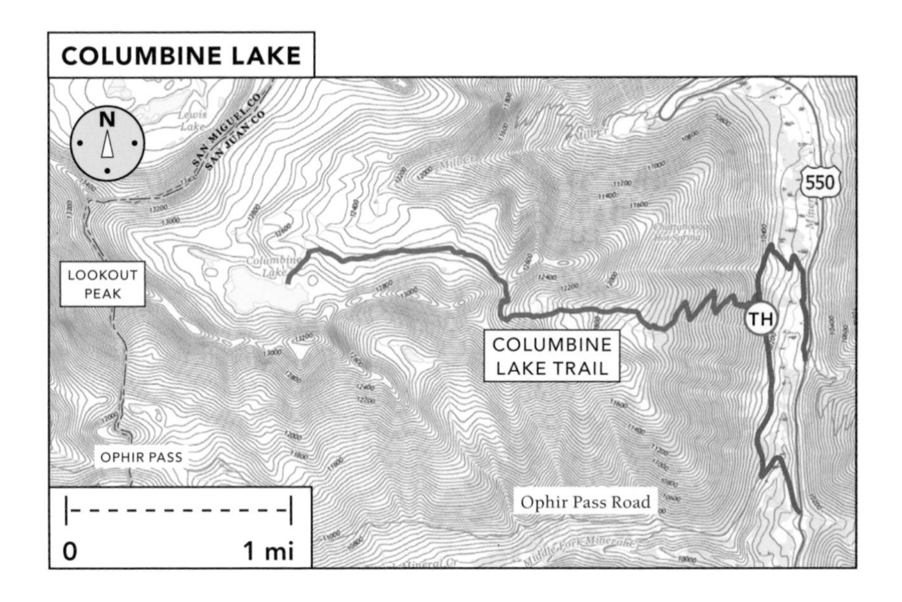

The fascinating shades of turquoise and other blues in Columbine Lake.

HIKE: Be ready to climb. Begin steeply northwest uphill, making several switchbacks as the trail rises quickly through the tall trees. The trail tends west, and the lake is almost due west from the start.

At 1.1 miles, around 11,500 feet, the trail busts out of the trees, and the climb continues steeply up a tight valley. Your goal is that pass up above a rocky escarpment, and you get there by going south around it, traversing above the escarpment.

Hit the pass at mile 2.1 (N 37 51.747, W 107 44.944, 12,504 feet). You've done the tough part of the climb and will actually drop a bit as you contour around the rolling 13,000-foot mountain to the south and head into Mill Creek Basin. This is wide-open tundra country, rife with wildflowers at the right time of year—usually about mid-July through August.

At 3 miles there's one final 200-foot uphill push to the lake. You may find a couple of trails, but one takes you right up to a small dam at lakeside at 3.3 miles (N 37 51.742, W 107 46.005, 12,685 feet).

Marvel at the lake's many hues, caused by rock flour (fine sediment ground up in the surrounding rocks) suspended in the water. If the weather's calm, this is a fine, tranquil place for lunch and a well-deserved nap.

KENDALL MOUNTAIN

DISTANCE: 12 miles round-trip

ELEVATION: Start at 9,300 feet, summit at 13,066 feet (3,766-foot gain)

RATING: Moderate

TIME ALLOWED: 6 to 7 hours

Let's start out by saying you can make this much easier on yourself by driving up the road as far as you like—actually starting not that far from the summit itself.

Kendall Mountain is just over 13,000 feet high and can be seen rising up southeast of Silverton. The hike described here is up a steep rocky road, with a trail scramble up the last part to the top. Four-wheel drive vehicles can go most of the way. Two-wheel drives with good clearance can go halfway or more.

This same route is used for the annual Kendall Mountain Run each July. If you hike it, you will see that it is a grueling race. The best runners make the round-trip in under 2 hours.

APPROACH: Take the main drag, Greene Street, through downtown Silverton and turn right onto Fourteenth Street. This street crosses the Animas River on a bridge, and not long after you reach the other side, it splits; go right onto CR 33, and park in the vicinity. (Going left at the split takes you to the Kendall Mountain Recreation Area.)

HIKE: Start hiking the road south-southwest along the base of the mountain. After briefly staying near river level, the road begins heading up the mountainside, climbing steadily. The road spirals around and up the mountain, at first south, then southeast and east. Most of the route is open so that you'll enjoy many fine views; you'll also see and hear cars chugging up Molas Pass, and perhaps see the train and hear its whistle below.

At 3 miles you'll reach an intersection, where the Deer Park Road (probably unsigned) takes off to the right (south) downhill (N 37 46.984, W 107 39.043, 11,880 feet). Stay left and keep going uphill another 1.8 miles, where a side road (N 37 47.327, W 107 37.824, 12,230 feet) makes a sharp turn left (northwest) uphill toward Kendall Mountain #2, as it's labeled on older topo maps. (This may cause confusion, because some maps don't label Kendall Mountain #2, but instead label the part of Kendall Mountain that's east of Kendall #2 and is higher at 13,338 feet. You want the lower one that overlooks town.) Note that the main road from here goes on up Kendall Gulch to several old mines.

The side road goes steeply uphill, bearing west-northwest. Where it ends you have to scramble up a steep chute (not technical and not exposed), then make your

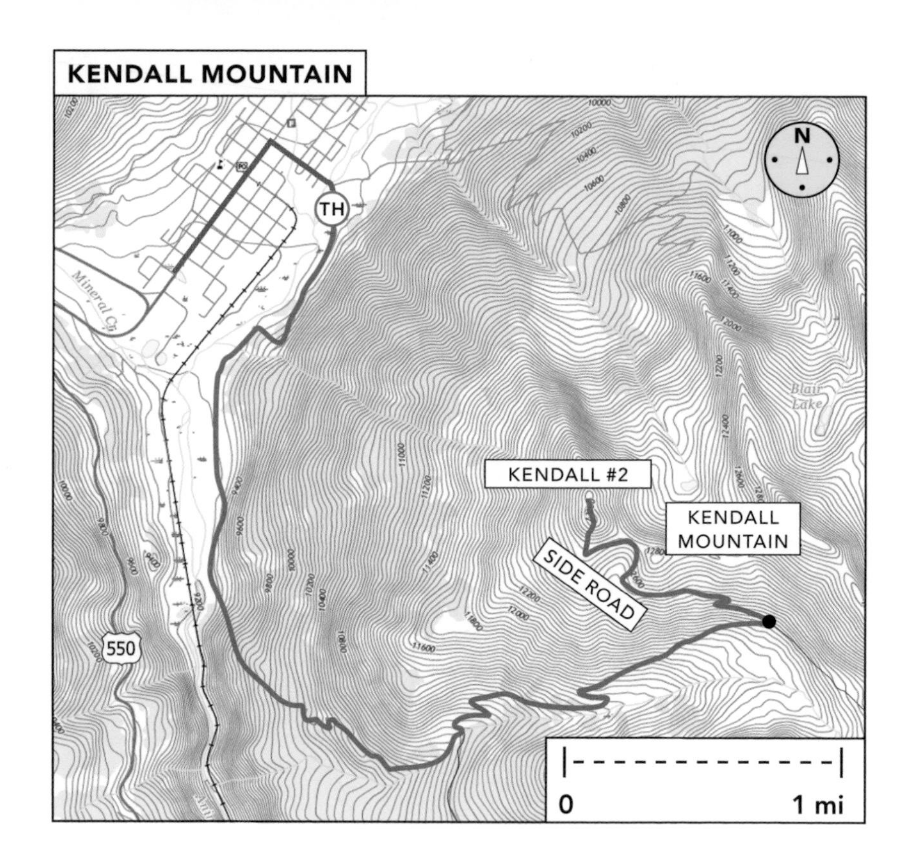

way up a rocky slope to the top. It's 1.2 miles from the sharp left-hand turn to the top (N 37 47.637, W 107 38.519, 13,066 feet). Enjoy the views back toward town, the Animas River Valley and Grand Turk and Sultan Mountains to the west.

OPTIONS: Drive 3 miles up the road to the junction with Deer Park Road. Park somewhere around here to begin the hike. If you do the easy math, you can see that this takes 6 miles off the hike and makes it more of a half-day than a full-day trip. It also takes off almost 1,600 feet elevation gain.

WHITEHEAD PEAK

DISTANCE: 6 miles round-trip

ELEVATION: Start at 10,900 feet, summit at 13,259 feet (2,359-foot gain)

RATING: Difficult, due to steepness and route finding

TIME ALLOWED: 4 to 5 hours

This hike includes a beautiful high-altitude basin at timberline and a peak with good views, particularly of the spectacular Grenadiers. It lies southeast of Silverton off the Kendall Mountain Road. Part of this hike involves a tricky detour around private land. For those who want a better-defined trail (most of the way), see Options on page 182.

APPROACH: Take Greene Street through downtown Silverton and turn right onto 14th Street. This street crosses the Animas River on a bridge, and on the other side it splits; go right onto CR 33. (Going left at the split takes you to the Kendall Mountain Recreation Area.)

Take the Kendall Mountain road up 3 miles from the river bridge, and where there's a split (N 37 46.984, W 107 39.043, 10,880 feet) take the Deer Park Road going right, downhill briefly, to the south. This intersection may not be signed but should be fairly obvious. The road to the right quickly crosses Kendall Gulch.

This often rough road goes south and southeast for 0.9 miles to an open meadow (N 37 46.356, W 107 38.736, 10,900 feet), where it veers left (east). Deer Park Creek runs down the far (south) side of this meadow. There are a few good places to park around this area or just before it, and the hike description starts here.

HIKE: Head up this meadow, and at 0.4 miles the road begins climbing steadily again. At 1.1 miles a side road goes south (see Options on page 182) and the main road soon levels out at a large plateau (N 37 46.308, W 107 37.680, 11,600 feet). From here you can see east up to the head of the basin to a saddle between two high points. The high point to the right is Whitehead Peak, and the higher point to the left of the saddle is Mount Rhoda.

A meadow covers this plateau, and there are camping spots available in the vicinity. The road swings to the north to avoid the meadow, and at this point it gets a little tricky. When the road begins to swing back right (south), you need to scamper up the mountainside where there is little or no semblance of a trail (somewhere around N 37 46.209, W 107 37.450, 11,670 feet). The problem is, if you stay on the road you'll reach a dead end and a "No Trespassing" sign when you come to some old cabins, which are on private property.

So, scramble steeply uphill and after getting through the willows and thick brush, look for a narrow, vague trail that heads basically east, gently uphill. If you scramble

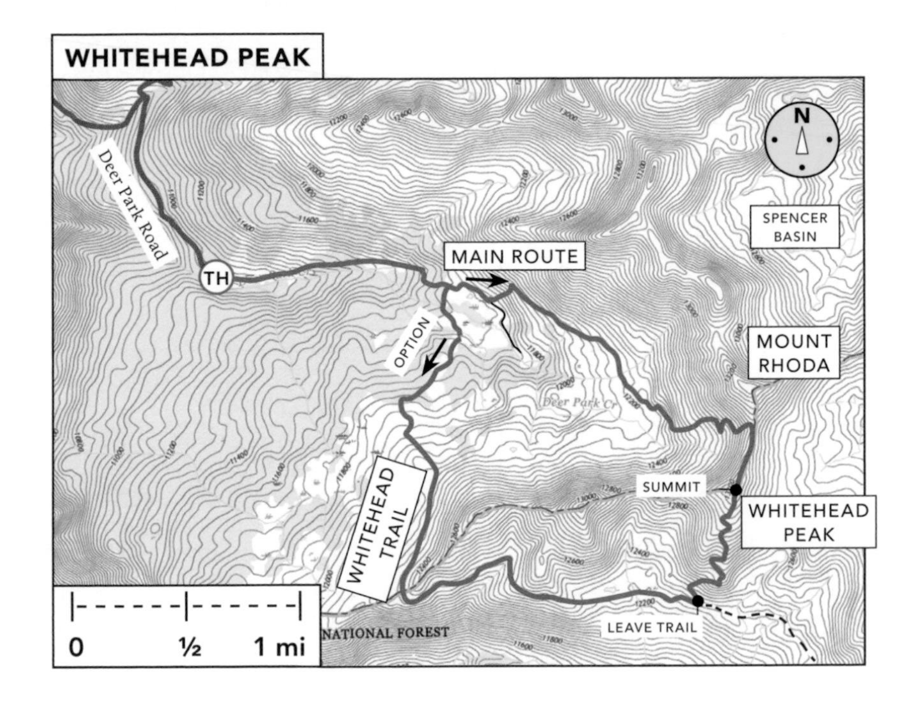

uphill at the point described above, you should be able to head almost due east and find the vague trail at about the 12,000-foot level. As best you can, follow this trail, keeping well above and to the north of a high meadow at 12,200 feet. You'll veer southeast, then have to make your way east up a steep, loose slope with no well-defined trail to the saddle at 2.7 miles (N 37 45.801, W 107 36.306, 13,150 feet). If you do end up at the 12,200-foot meadow, just head almost due east toward the pass. This just means a steeper approach.

From the pass, go right (south) up the ridge 0.3 miles to the summit of Whitehead Peak (N 37 45.584, W 107 36.403, 13,259 feet). From the top there is a good view south to the Grenadiers. The view to the east down across the tundra includes the Highland Mary Lakes.

The return can be made by the approach route, but consider the option below.

OPTIONS: There's a southern approach that avoids the willows and the scramble, and skirts the steep northern side of Whitehead Gulch. This trail continues to Lost Lake and the Highland Mary Lakes farther along, but this description will talk about scaling Whitehead Peak from its southern flank.

At the 1.1-mile mark in the description above, take the side road going south just as you're reaching the plateau (N 37 46.308, W 107 37.680, 11,600 feet). Follow this road to its terminus, about 0.3 miles, and look for a road/trail going up to the south. You may see a chain blocking the route to vehicles, but horses and hikers are allowed.

This trail begins to climb and soon follows a series of wooden posts as it curves

The mighty nice view of the Grenadiers from atop Whitehead Peak.

around to the east above the timberline. Now you've entered the Whitehead Gulch drainage, high above it on a steep mountainside. This trail is called the Whitehead Trail on many maps.

Continue along this route. At about 3 miles from the side road terminus, find a good spot to leave the trail (around N 37 45.174, W 107 36.558, 12,280 feet) and head up the southern slope of Whitehead Peak. It's a steep hill that you might want to zigzag up gradually, but you won't need to use your hands.

In another 0.7 miles or so and 1,000 feet gain, enjoy the summit.

SILVER LAKE

DISTANCE: 4 miles round-trip

ELEVATION: Start at 10,600 feet, lake at 12,186 feet (1,586-foot gain)

RATING: Moderate

TIME ALLOWED: 2 to 4 hours

Silver Lake is surrounded by many old mines. It is not good for fishing because the water is highly mineralized from the mines. It is a great place for mining buffs. It used to be a great place for bottle hunters, but by now most old trophies have disappeared.

There is no road up to the lake and never has been. However, quite an operation took place there, beginning in the 1890s. In the winter transportation was by tram. Several buildings were constructed for mining and milling the ore. Milling it there meant that only the concentrate had to be carried down by tram, or over the steep trail, on the backs of mules. Some buildings are still in fairly good shape, although most have collapsed under the heavy snow, spilling their load of machinery. As a result, rollers and other equipment have mixed in with piles of building materials and a few old shoes, clothes, bed springs, and other junk. It is interesting to study the heaps to try to understand the way of life and work of these miners. The lake and the buildings are above timberline but are surrounded by still higher peaks except on the north side—your ascent route.

APPROACH: Take CR 2 northeast out of Silverton 2 miles to where, just after the pavement ends, there's a turnoff going right downhill and across the Animas River. This brings you into Arrastra Gulch, where a gold discovery in 1872 first ignited the Silverton area mining rush. Follow the road as it heads up the gulch on the east side. From the turn off CR 2 it is about 2 miles of four-wheel driving until you get to a major left-hand switchback above the timberline (N 37 48.309, W 107 36.747, 10,640 feet). Park here, well below the Mayflower Mine, to begin the hike.

There are several side roads where you can get lost on this approach road. The correct road basically parallels an old mining tramway and eventually crosses back (below) to the right side of it. During the time you're above the tramway, one road veers off to the left; it goes up to Little Giant Basin, where there's a small lake just above 12,000 feet.

HIKE: Start northeast up the old road, making one switchback and then coming to the fairly elaborate buildings of the Mayflower Mine high on the east side of the canyon at 0.6 miles (11,200 feet). From the mine, a sometimes-steep and narrow trail leads south on up to the lake in 1.4 miles.

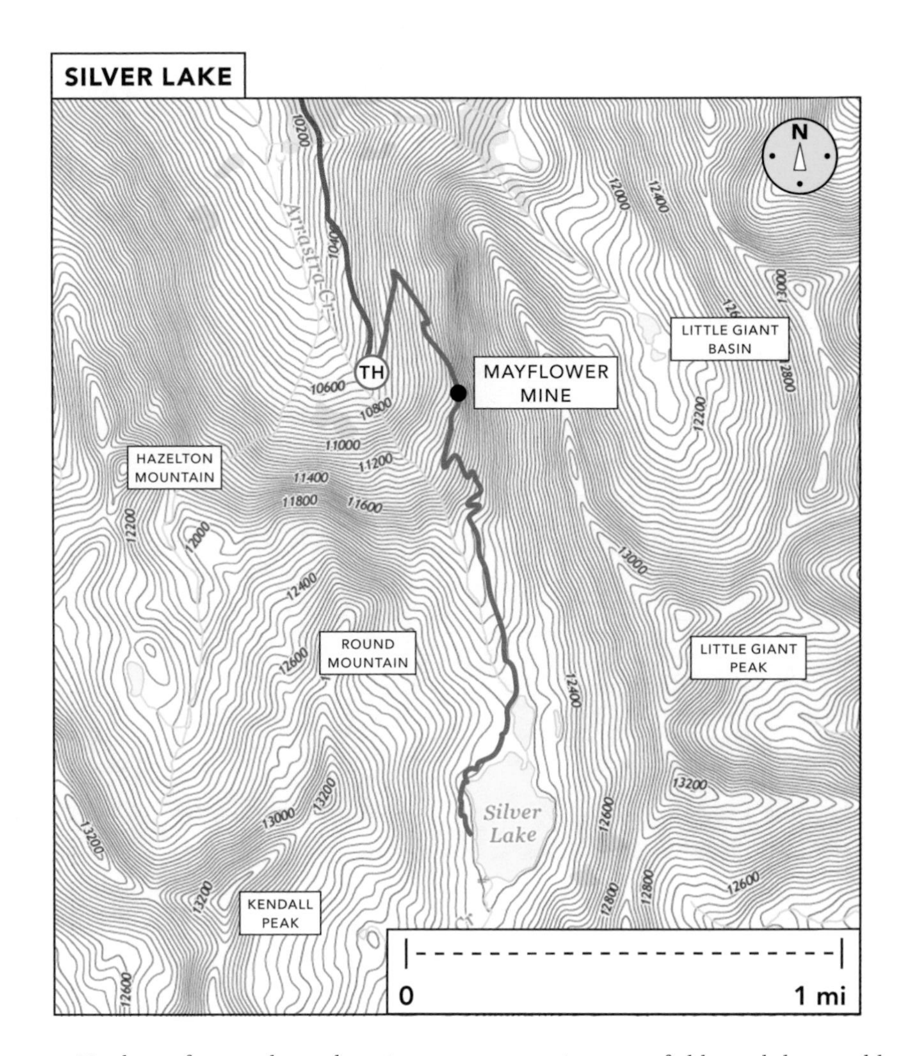

Not long after you leave the mine you may run into snowfields, and they could cause a problem, particularly early in the summer. The snow is from an avalanche path and is likely to be very hard. It might be possible to kick steps into the snow, but the path is fairly steep, so this is risky.

If it seems too risky, another option might avail itself: Where the snow goes over the trail, there is some vertical, solid rock on the uphill side. When summer arrives, the rocks warm up faster than the snow. The warm rocks melt a tunnel under the deep part of the snow next to the rocks. Sometimes it's possible to squeeze through this gap for 10 to 20 yards and find the trail on the other side.

There is one more potentially tricky part where you must cross the gulch. A rope has been set up here to help humans, but if you have a dog with you, this place can be problematic.

The impressive mining ruins around Silver Lake are worth a long look and admiration. Those guys were tough in the old days.

Finally the trail steepness eases and the lake and its ruins appear (N 37 47.532, W 107 36.418, 12,186 feet). To get around on the west side of the lake you have to wade through the old debris. It's nice to have hiking boots around here to avoid accidentally cutting your feet on the old junk, including many nails.

The views are of surrounding hills, some worth hiking up to get views from a higher perch. The lake itself makes a great lunch spot.

HEMATITE BASIN

DISTANCE: 4 miles round-trip to Hematite Lake, 5.6 miles round-trip to Macomber Peak

ELEVATION: Start at 9,660 feet, lake at 11,876 feet (2,216-foot gain), Macomber at 13,222 feet (3,562-foot gain)

RATING: Moderate to slightly difficult

TIME ALLOWED: 4 to 6 hours

This hike is a grunt, as evidenced by the impressive amount of elevation gained in a relatively short distance, but your efforts will be rewarded. The lake is spectacular in an impressive basin, and the additional ascent to Macomber Peak offers a fantastic perspective of the world below.

The trail might be a little hard to find and follow at first, but this and other hikes in the Silverton area continue to increase in popularity, and it is likely that you will have little difficulty. However, like many hikes at this elevation, it may not be easily accessible until July, although the south aspect helps in terms of melting winter snow and possible avalanche paths.

APPROACH: Take Greene Street northeast through downtown Silverton, then turn right onto CR 2. After 2 miles on CR 2 the pavement ends, and at around 3.7 miles watch for a trail heading northwest off the road. There is room for a couple of cars at a pullout here (N 37 50.004, W 107 36.068, 9,660 feet), and space for several more cars 0.2 miles farther on the left, just before CR 2 crosses the Animas River.

HIKE: Find the faint two-track trail (there was no trailhead sign as of this writing) and head slightly uphill into an open meadow. The trail begins briefly toward Brindle Gulch and an abandoned, rusted vehicle with an aspen bursting out of it, but then swings toward the north to cross over a tiny rolling ridge into the Hematite Gulch drainage. (You can also begin up a steep road at the parking near the river, but that way is steeper and you would eventually have to bushwhack a connection to the more defined trail.)

Once you get into the Hematite drainage, it is constant climbing as you stay to the west of and above the creek. Massive Galena Mountain (13,278 feet) hovers behind you as you go in and out of several aspen groves. At 1.8 miles you'll enter the basin and the steepness eases. (N 37 50.766, W 107 36.660, 11,848 feet). If you time it right (generally somewhere around mid-July through August) you'll encounter impressive wildflower displays during this hike, particularly in the area around the basin. The trail may vanish, but tending to the left here works well.

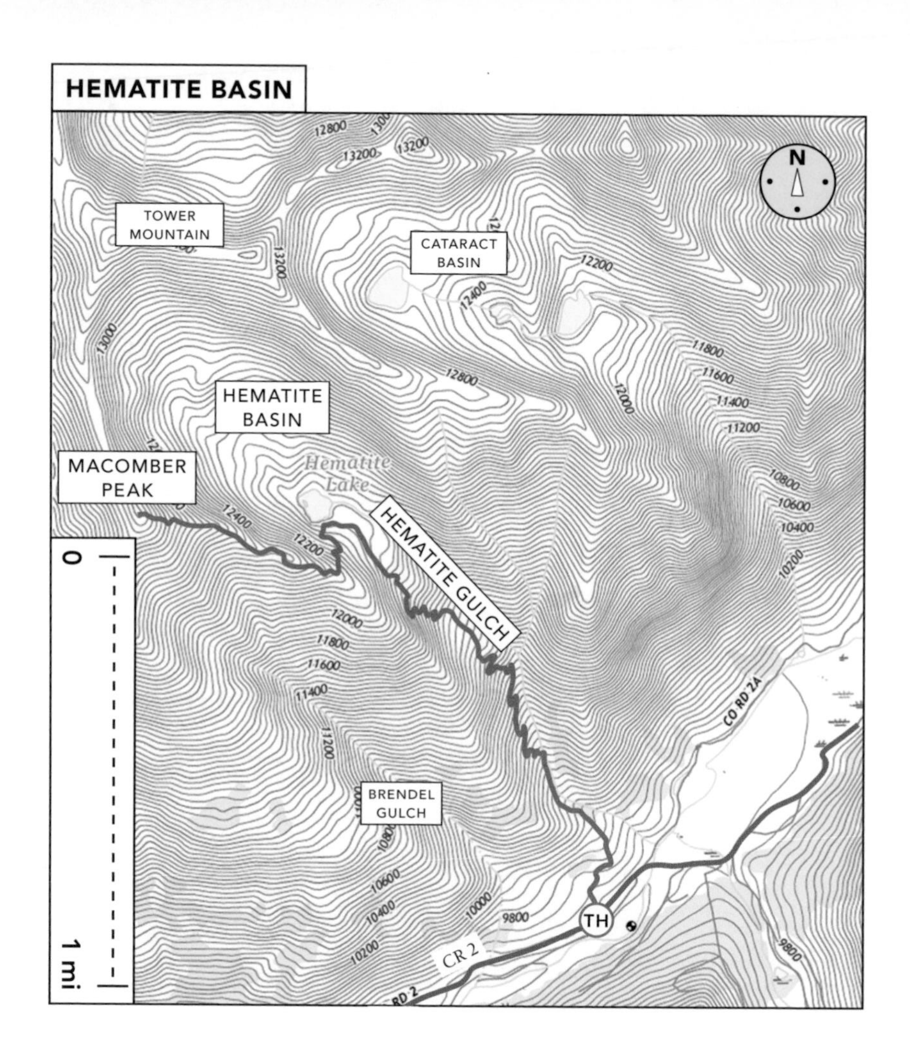

At 2 miles you'll reach the lake (N 37 50.835, W 107 36.790, 11,876 feet). It's one of those special, beautiful, glacial-blue lakes that are rare but found occasionally around the high San Juans. These lakes get their color from rock flour, fine sediment ground up in the surrounding rock that is suspended in the water, reflecting light to give the lake a turquoise hue.

You could stop here, but the hike up to Macomber Peak offers a treat of a different kind: a 360-degree view with a rare vantage point. So head almost due south from the lake, over talus and a grassy slope. You'll end up on a steep contour where footing can be tricky, with loose dirt mixing with bigger rocks and plants. It's possible you'll find a social trail. Pick your way as best you can to reach the ridge (N 37 50.726, W 107 36.755, 12,267 feet) leading northwest to Macomber. (Note: As you head up to the ridge not far from the lake, if it's the right time of season, you may see a massive slope of columbine that could be unparalleled.)

The ridge tends mostly uphill, at times very steeply. Near the top it's particularly steep and easy to misstep, especially on the way down. But anyone in decent shape should be able to make this climb.

At the summit (N 37 50.853, W 107 37.308, 13,222 feet) at 2.8 miles, take a good long time to enjoy your perch. You can view a long way up Cunningham Gulch, with Stony Pass above to the left (east) and Buffalo Boy Mine visible in a basin just east of that. Arrastra Basin with Silver Lake is pretty much due south. The town of Silverton is laid out before you, with Grand Turk and Sultan rising above. To the west are the Ice Lakes Basin peaks.

OPTIONS: Return the way you came, or continue on to Tower Mountain (13,552 feet), the next summit on the ridge to the north. It's a little less than a mile. You can also access Tower, which makes Colorado's highest 100 peaks list, by climbing from Hematite Basin generally northwest to a pass just east of Tower. This way proves a bit more of a technical challenge.

Unusual amount of snowfall on Hematite Lake in mid-August. This was taken from a precipice on the ridge nearing the Macomber summit.

HIGHLAND MARY LAKES

DISTANCE: 4.6 miles round-trip

ELEVATION: Start at 10,770 feet, high point between larger lakes at 12,160 feet (1,390-foot gain)

RATING: Moderate, with talus crossing and possible stream crossing

TIME ALLOWED: 2½ to 4 hours

This is a beautiful high-country hike that takes you to the highlands; imagine you're in Scotland if you like. This is a magnificent, open area above the timberline with fantastic scenery and views.

This hike is close to Silverton, so it does get a lot of use, but unless there's a huge group, you should experience a little solitude, especially if you continue on to Verde Lakes or beyond.

APPROACH: Take Greene Street through downtown Silverton, and at the end of town take a right onto San Juan CR 2. In 2 miles the pavement ends. After another 2 miles on a well-maintained gravel road, take a right onto the Cunningham Gulch Road (CR 4), heading south. In about 0.25 miles, a side road goes uphill toward the Old Hundred Mine, which offers a fun and informative tour, but continue next to the creek.

After 1.7 miles on the Cunningham road, at a Y-intersection, there's a steep left up toward Stony Pass and the Continental Divide. Don't take that either, but continue up the valley. After 3.5 miles on the Cunningham road you'll cross the creek and then make a left-hand hairpin turn and begin very steeply uphill. You probably won't need 4WD, but it's nice to have.

About 0.9 miles past the creek crossing, look for a left-hand turn downhill. In 100 yards you'll ford the creek, which depending on the year and month can be running very swiftly. (Let's just say things get really interesting when you have to carry your dog across a raging, thigh-deep torrent with lightning crashing nearby in a driving rain, with hypothermia coming on.) In another 200 yards you'll reach the end of the road and a fairly large parking area. (N 37 46.856, W 107 34.799, 10,770 feet).

HIKE: Begin south up the Highland Mary Lakes Trail. You'll gain elevation quickly as you hike along the creek and its impressive waterfalls. During the first mile you'll enter the Weminuche Wilderness, so make sure your dogs aren't chasing things and are under control.

At 1.1 miles, keep an eye out for the official Cunningham Creek crossing. (N 37 46.205, W 107 34.579, 11,590 feet). There may be a sign that points the way. There are two or three braids to cross, and if you're lucky there may be some logs thrown

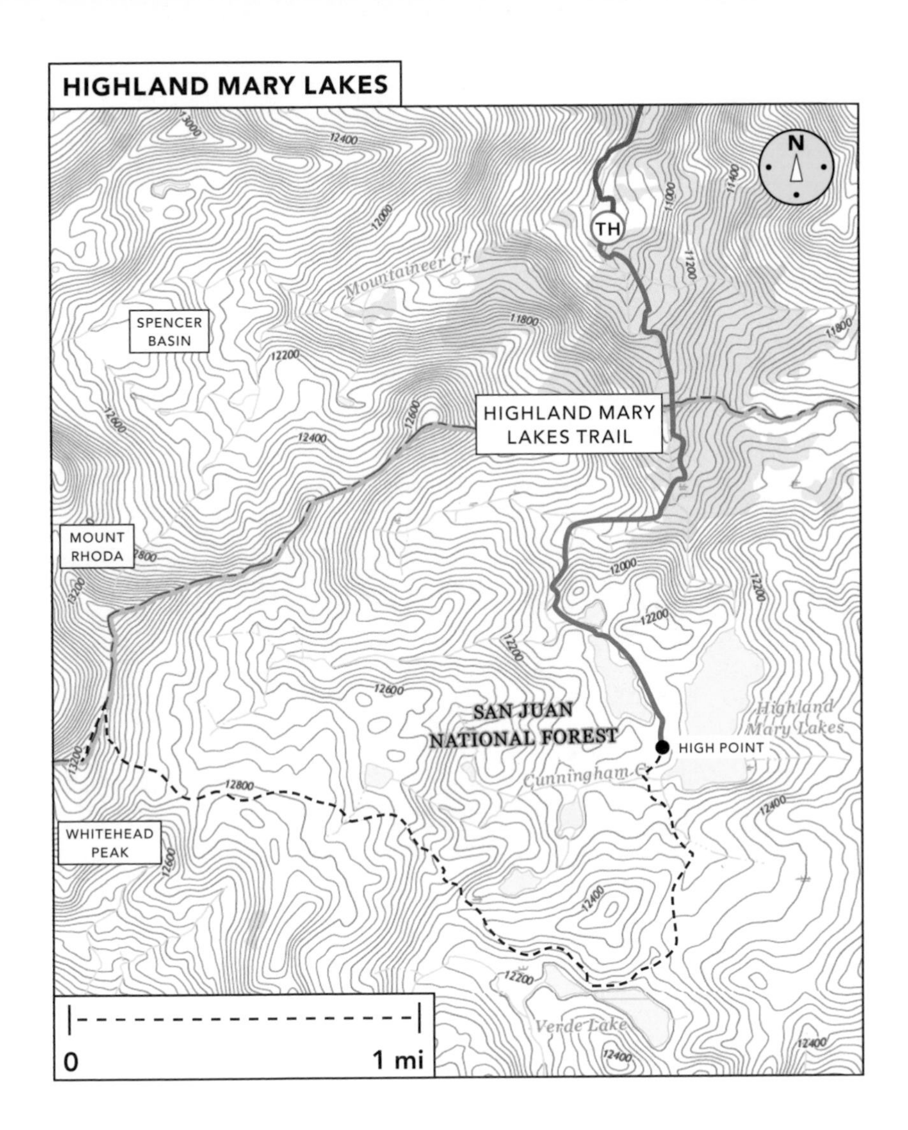

haphazardly into the creek to help. You may have to wade through, but usually by July there are enough rocks to keep from getting wet. Those with hiking poles will be happy.

At 1.6 miles cross a rocky section, and at 1.8 miles you'll find yourself at the first Highland Mary Lake (N 37 45.929, W 107 34.890, 12,120 feet). It's a small one. Another tenth of a mile gets you to the bigger second lake. Assuming you continue, at 2.3 miles you'll reach a high point between the two larger lakes, with the third lake coming into view to the east (N 37 45.596, W 107 34.625, 12,160 feet).

You can hang out around the Highland Mary Lakes, or continue south on the well-used trail to Verde Lakes (see Options on page 192).

Looking north down toward the beautiful Highland Mary Lakes.

OPTIONS: If you continue on the trail you can reach Verde Lakes fairly quickly and easily, and Lost Lake farther on. Plus, this is a reasonably easy method of climbing Whitehead Peak and achieving some great views of the Grenadier Range.

You'll gain another couple hundred feet—follow the wooden posts if the trail is obscured—before dropping down to the Verde Lakes at 3.1 miles (N 37 45.076, W 107 34.668, 12,240 feet). Stay to the right around the lakes. The "upper" lake is only a few feet higher than the lower; they're nearly adjacent. Both should have small but catchable fish.

Curl to the right on a not-well-defined trail and head up a small valley, heading generally northwest. It's easy to lose the semblance of a trail through willows, but at about 4 miles you begin to head more toward the west and continue to climb. You might come near a small lake; stay to the south of that. As you climb higher you'll begin to see a high ridge that includes Whitehead Peak (13,258 feet) and to the north of it Mount Rhoda (13,402 feet). Whitehead is a gentle mound, but Rhoda has a flat top with a rock rib just below it. Head between the two peaks, but tend more toward Whitehead.

After a high point (N 37 45.490, W 107 35.963, 12,880 feet) you'll have to drop a bit to get across a drainage, but then climb again and contour up to the saddle between Whitehead and its higher neighbor. Both are very accessible from here.

That's one way to climb Whitehead Peak. You may find a shortcut, perhaps from the third Highland Mary Lake, and good job if you do. But the way described seems like the most straightforward. See Whitehead Peak on page 181 for two options from the west.

CONTINENTAL DIVIDE

DISTANCE: 13.4 miles round-trip

ELEVATION: Start at 10,760 feet, high point at 12,720 feet (1,960-foot gain)

RATING: Moderate, due to length and altitude

TIME ALLOWED: 8 to 10 hours

This is rather ambitious for a 1-day hike, but strong hikers can make it. The trip is well worthwhile. It is one of the highest and most scenic hikes in the state. The Continental Divide raises its spiny back across the entire width of the state north to south; a trail or route of some sort follows nearby the entire distance. This particular chunk is east of Silverton, where much of the best in the San Juan Mountains can be seen. Fortunately, most of the ascent is made in the first 3 miles.

Along the Continental Divide, the east side looks down into the headwaters of the Rio Grande River. The west side looks into the Highland Mary Lakes basin and, near the end of the hike, into the deep Elk Creek Canyon. But the most dramatic scenery is to the south and southwest, where the Grenadiers rise in many sharp and jagged peaks, their sheer cliffs plunging straight down along the north sides. Beyond the Grenadiers are the Needles. This is truly wild country!

APPROACH: Follow the route described for the Highland Mary Lakes hike, but just after you ford Cunningham Gulch in your vehicle, look for the Continental Divide connector trailhead on your left. If you reach the Highland Mary trailhead, retrace your route to find the Divide trailhead. It should be marked with a small wooden sign (N 37 46.938, W 107 34.764, 10,790 feet).

HIKE: Take this trail, which begins north briefly, east and southeast up toward the Continental Divide—a 1,360 feet gain in 2.5 miles—and turn right at the junction onto both the CDT and Colorado Trail (N 37 46.284, W 107 33.498, 12,150 feet).

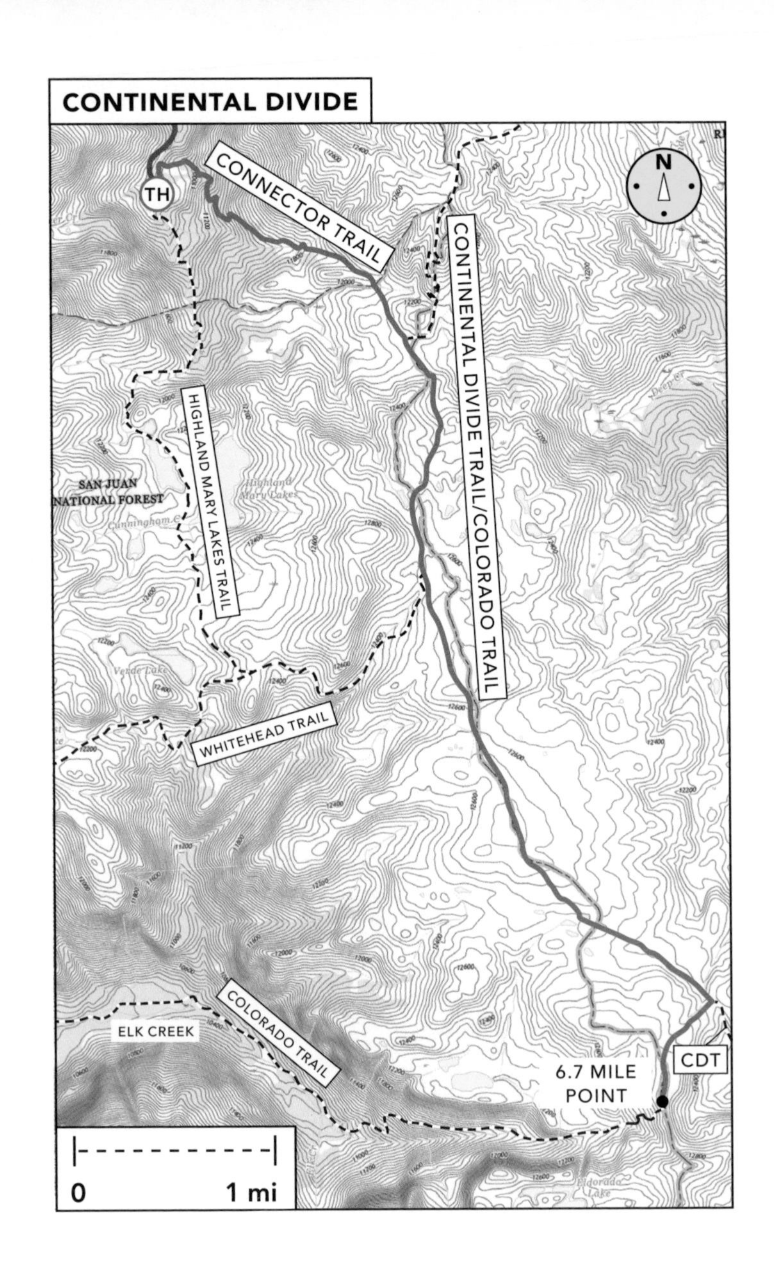
CONTINENTAL DIVIDE
CONNECTOR TRAIL
TH
CONTINENTAL DIVIDE TRAIL/COLORADO TRAIL
HIGHLAND MARY LAKES TRAIL
SAN JUAN
NATIONAL FOREST
WHITEHEAD TRAIL
COLORADO TRAIL
ELK CREEK
CDT
6.7 MILE
POINT
N
0
1 mi

Now you're well above the timberline with great views. You're also exposed to the elements should a storm roll in, so be aware of the weather.

The trail rises quite a bit through here, dipping briefly to match the ridgeline but reaching 12,720 feet. At 3.7 miles the Whitehead Trail, likely unmarked, goes west off the CDT/CT. Continue straight on the CDT/CT (N 37 45.360, W 107 33.414, 12,580 feet).

At 6.2 miles the Colorado Trail leaves the Continental Divide Trail and heads southwest uphill (N 37 43.548, W 107 31.926, 12,460 feet). You could turn back here, or anywhere up to this point for that matter, but it's definitely worth going just a half-mile farther on the Colorado Trail to where it tops out and begins to descend into Elk Creek at 6.7 miles (N 37 43.188, W 107 32.178, 12,690 feet).

Indian paintbrush and other wildflowers near the Continental Divide Trail.

VALLECITO AREA HIKES

This is by all means not an all-inclusive list of the trails in the Vallecito area, but it does highlight a few of the gems.

Vallecito Creek Trail is a popular path and the hiker will quickly understand why. It follows the path of a raging creek up through a narrow valley, sometimes rising well above, then dropping nearly to creek level. To leave this hike out of the book seemed an oversight.

Just like Silverton, the Vallecito area attracts visitors from near and far, many of whom are escaping the oppressive summer heat of the Midwest or the South. Some bring their motorboats or their paddleboards or their OHVs, and some bring their hiking boots.

The Vallecito Creek and Pine River Trails offer access to the Weminuche Wilderness, so it's likely you'll bump into backpackers and horse packers on those.

These trails are great if you're hanging around the Vallecito area for a few days, but they're all easily accessible on a day trip from Bayfield, Ignacio, or Durango.

Left, top: Dollar Lake and Emerald Lake. Left, bottom: The Vallecito Trail offers a spectacular creekside hike. Below: Looking north from the swampy southern shores of Lake Eileen.

LAKE EILEEN

DISTANCE: 3.8 miles round-trip

ELEVATION: Start at 7,740 feet, lake at 8,870 feet (1,130-foot gain)

RATING: Easy to moderate, with a few steep sections

TIME ALLOWED: 1½ to 3 hours

Lake Eileen is not spectacular, but it's easy to get to and is a good quick destination hike. It's a good workout, and it gets you into the Weminuche Wilderness, albeit a portion that was charred severely during the 2002 Missionary Ridge Fire. You'll begin to get some views into the southern peaks of this part of the Weminuche, but the views toward Vallecito Reservoir are more interesting, particularly with the absence of trees.

APPROACH: From Durango, head up Florida Road (CR 240). From the intersection of CR 240 and CR 250 (East Animas Road), drive 11.5 miles and take a right toward Vallecito at Helen's Corner. (If you go straight here you'll end up at Lemon Reservoir.)

Vallecito Reservoir is seen along the Lake Eileen Trail. The 2002 fire ravaged the landscape, but improved the view.

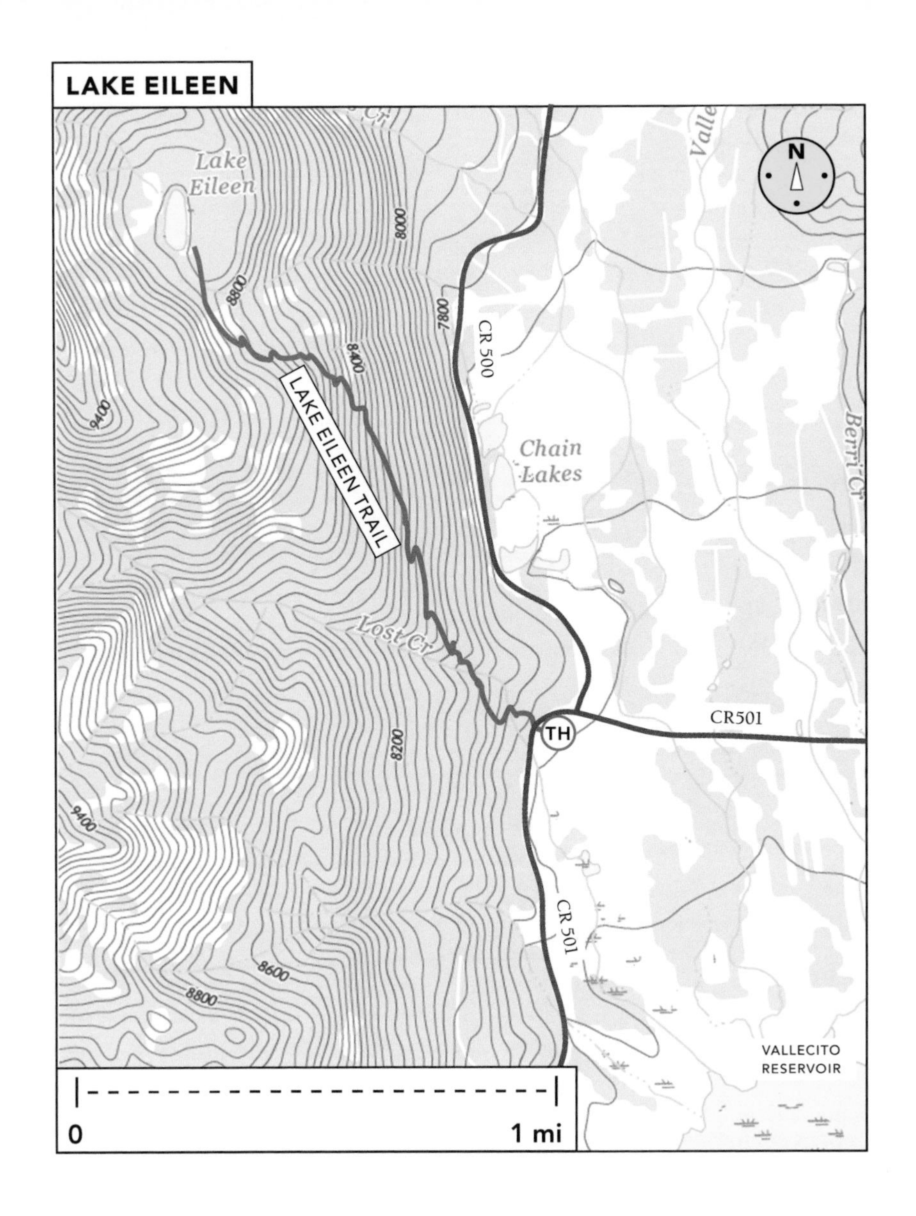

Still on CR 240, go another 2.8 miles up and over a ridge, and then take a left onto CR 501 toward Vallecito.

Drive past the dam and the lake, and then look for a Forest Service work center. This is 9.4 miles from the intersection of CR 240/CR 501. Don't go down the work center entrance, but continue about 50 yards past it and park on the right side along the road in one of several designated spots across from the trailhead. Walk carefully across the road to the start of the Lake Eileen Trail (N 37 26.563, W 107 33.467, 7,740 feet).

HIKE: Begin a steady climb and quickly enter the 2002 burn area. Just past the second crossing of Lost Creek (N 37 26.673, W 107 33.648, 7,950 feet) enter the Weminuche Wilderness at 0.4 miles.

The trail switchbacks up the mountainside, trending north and northwest. The climb is steady, and you'll be sweating on a cloudless summer day. But it's not terribly long, so you won't need huge quantities of water with you.

At 1.9 miles you'll reach the marshy, lily pad-covered lake (N 37 27.447, W 107 34.269, 8,870 feet). It's marshy enough that it's difficult to circumnavigate the lake.

This is a fine hike, but don't expect spectacular views of the mountains from here. Keep this hike in mind for a fall or winter jaunt when it's not hot or buggy.

VALLECITO CREEK

DISTANCE: 6.4 miles round-trip to the first bridge

ELEVATION: Start at 7,910 feet, high point at 8,360 feet (450-foot gain)

RATING: Easy

TIME ALLOWED: 3 to 4 hours

After you've walked a half-mile past the campground, which is sort of annoying, and as you perhaps share the trail with dozens of people and their dogs on a busy summer day, you will enjoy one of the most beautiful creeks in Colorado. The Vallecito gorge is steep and spectacular; the trail is fun and not too difficult. Enjoy.

APPROACH: From Durango, the best way is up Florida Road (CR 240). From the intersection of CR 240 and CR 250 (East Animas Road), drive 11.5 miles and take a right toward Vallecito at Helen's Corner. (If you go straight here you'll end up at Lemon Reservoir.) Still on CR 240, go another 2.8 miles and then take a left onto CR 501 toward Vallecito.

Drive past the reservoir until you reach CR 500, 9.5 miles from the intersection of CR 240 and CR 501. Take a left onto CR 500, and continue 2.8 miles north until the road ends at the Forest Service campground, and turns from pavement to gravel. Take an immediate left into the large trailhead parking area, complete with official pit toilets.

HIKE: The trail for people and horses begins at the southwest corner of the parking area (N 37 28.501, W 107 32.890, 7,910 feet). After 0.5 miles of skirting the campground, go another 100 yards and you'll finally reach the official Vallecito Creek trailhead (N 37 28.705, W 107 32.626, 7,960 feet). Cross Fall Creek (just before it feeds into Vallecito Creek) on a nice bridge and begin a gradual climb. In two places

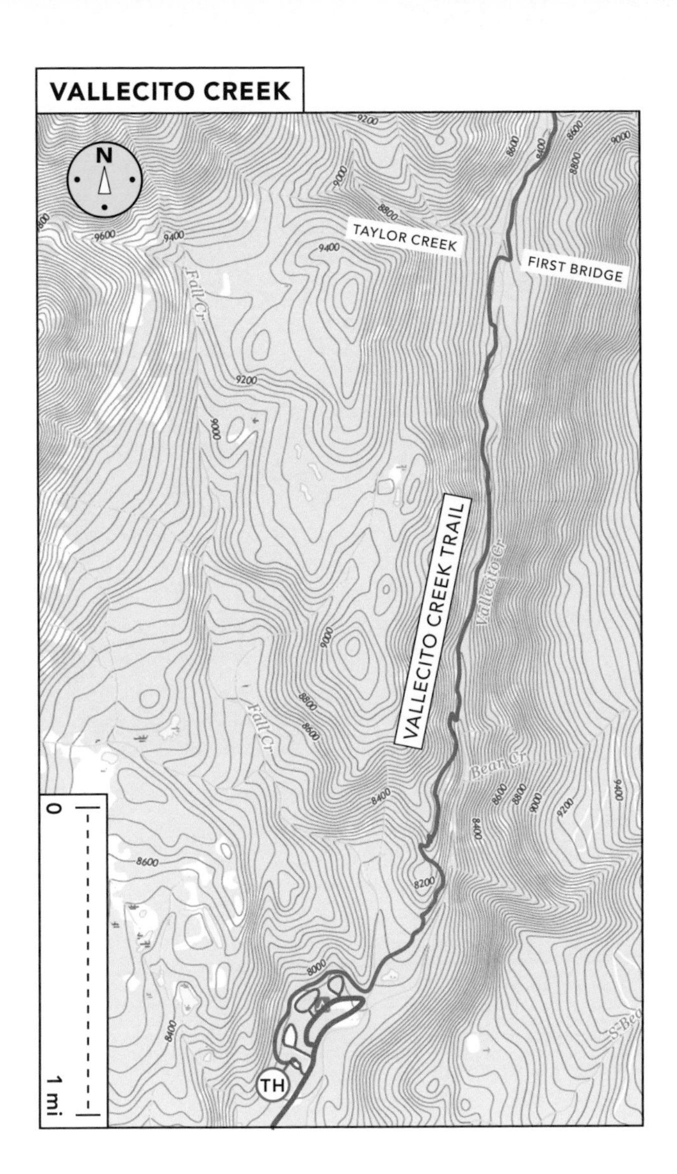

there are separate routes for horses and hikers. If you're hiking, you'll stay right, closer to the edge of the precipice, with Vallecito Creek loud but often invisible below.

At 1.4 miles reach a high point (N 37 29.207, W 107 32.422, 8,360 feet) and begin heading downward to meet up with the creek. You'll find some great vantage points of the rushing waters around here, and again when you reach the creek and begin hiking close to it.

At 1.9 miles (N 37 29.537, W107 32.336, 8,200 feet) you can begin to access the creek. Wade in or fish along the banks if you please, but be careful of the strong current. This might be a good turnaround spot, or you can keep hiking to the first

Looking up the Vallecito valley, which many people use to access the Needle Mountains.

bridge at 3.2 miles (N 37 30.642, W 107 32.178, 8,350 feet). Just before the first bridge you have to wade through Taylor Creek, and if it's running high you may get your feet wet.

The trail continues from here, so don't let me stop you.

OPTIONS: This is a popular access to the peaks and streams of the Vallecito wilderness. If you have a backpack and gear, the possibilities are endless. Just be aware that the third bridge upstream, about 7 miles from the trailhead, has been washed out for a decade or more and you'll have to ford the creek here. This is not an easy task, particularly when the creek is running fast.

CAVE BASIN

DISTANCE: 10.6 miles round-trip to cairn on ridge

ELEVATION: Start at 10,730 feet, high point at 12,330 feet (1,600-foot gain)

RATING: Easy, other than the high altitude

TIME ALLOWED: 4 to 6 hours

With a few minor asterisks, this is a great high-altitude hike with a remarkable vantage point of the Needle Mountains. The finale, with a bird's-eye view in a different direction, is even more spectacular.

So, the asterisks:

* This can be a busy trail. Depending on the time of year, you'll find hikers, hunters, and horse riders. There is quite a bit of parking, fortunately, and people string out fairly well on the trail.
* The gravel road can be very dusty in dry conditions, and it's narrow enough that you'll have to use care to get past oncoming vehicles, which include trailer-hauling trucks and RVs.
* Watch the weather. You're fairly exposed to the elements (rain and lightning), with almost all the trail above 11,000 feet.

All that said, it's an extremely enjoyable hike with plenty of places to hang out.

APPROACH: From Durango, the best way is up Florida Road (CR 240). From the intersection of CR 240 and CR 250 (East Animas Road), drive about 11.5 miles and take a right toward Vallecito at Helen's Corner. (If you go straight here you'll end up at Lemon Reservoir.) Still on CR 240, go another 2.8 miles and then take a left onto CR 501 toward Vallecito.

Drive all the way north around the lake. From the 240/501 intersection it's 9.5 miles to the intersection where CR 500 heads north toward Vallecito Campground. Continue straight (east) here, and go another 1 mile where, just after the road bends southward, you'll come to a turn left onto Middle Mountain Road.

Here you hit gravel, and it's almost exactly 10 miles up winding Middle Mountain Road to the trailhead. You should see it on the left, and there's room for ten to fifteen cars to park on the right side of the road. All in all, it's about 90 minutes from Durango.

HIKE: Start north uphill at the trailhead (N 37 29.803, W 107 30.254, 10,730 feet) on an abandoned road through an open forest. The climb isn't steep exactly, but it's very steady for the first 1.3 miles, at which point the trail enters the Weminuche Wilderness (N 37 30.395, W 107 29.702, 11,473 feet).

Just past the 3-mile mark you'll venture onto a wide, flat area with a limestone base. Beetle-killed trees line the trail at a distance as you move gently uphill. The vista

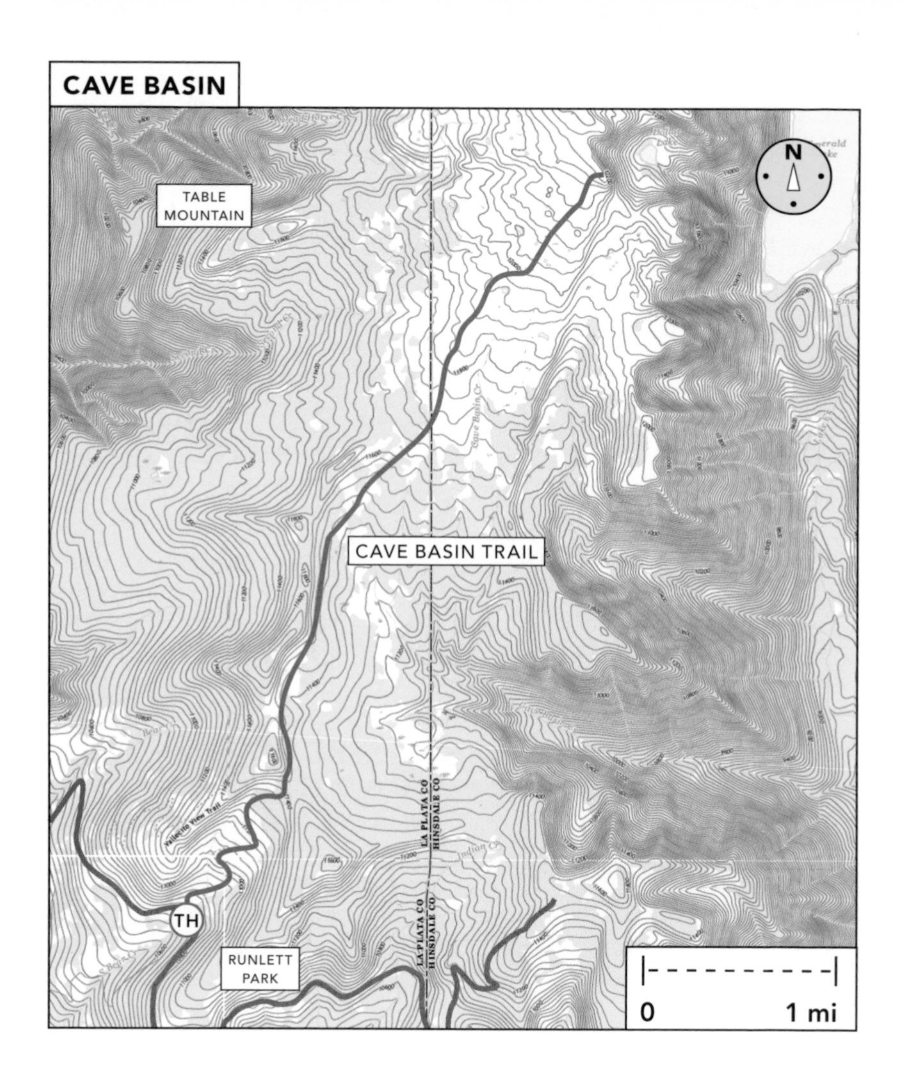

opens up and you'll soon be treated to great views off to the west-northwest of the rugged Weminuche peaks on the other side of the huge Vallecito Creek drainage. See if you can distinguish the fourteeners almost due northwest: rounded Windom Peak, with the Sunlight ridge to Windom's right, and Eolus peeking up behind to the left, barely visible.

At 4.3 miles (N 37 32.569, W 107 28.556, 11,893 feet), the trail begins to rise gently uphill through some willows. There's a good chance you'll lose the trail here through the alpine tundra and become one of the wandering hikers searching for either a trail or the next scarce cairn. Keep trending basically northeast and eventually you'll see a huge cairn up on the high ridge ahead. Head toward that.

After a final climb, find yourself on a promontory suddenly overlooking a couple of lakes well below (N 37 33.054, W 107 27.940, 12,330 feet). Needless to say, watch your footing here. Dollar Lake is about 600 feet below, and Emerald Lake more than 2,000 feet.

OPTIONS: It's possible to hike to Dollar Lake by starting on the Cave Basin trail. You can either make it a continuation of this hike from the cairn or venture east before the final scramble up to the cairn. You'll reach a saddle south of Dollar Lake, then make your way down about 400 feet to the lake. Be prepared for bushwhacking and willows.

Spectacular views of the Needle Mountains await when you reach the tundra along the Cave Basin Trail.

PINE RIVER

DISTANCE: 5.6 miles round-trip to wilderness boundary

ELEVATION: Start at 7,915 feet, wilderness at 8,150 feet (235-foot gain)

RATING: Easy

TIME ALLOWED: 2 to 3½ hours

This is a good family hike to experience a sampling of the Weminuche Wilderness. If you're staying at the campground and aren't up for a huge high-country hike, this is a great option. You'll be walking along a well-traveled trail in a wide river valley, and if you've never been in this part of the country, it'll help acquaint you with that high-country Western pioneer feeling.

This description goes only to the wilderness boundary, but you can keep walking this way for days and days, and many people do.

APPROACH: From Durango, the best way is up Florida Road (CR 240). From the intersection of CR 240 and CR 250 (East Animas Road), drive about 11.5 miles and take a right toward Vallecito at Helen's Corner. (If you go straight here you'll end up at Lemon Reservoir.) Still on CR 240, go another 2.8 miles and then take a left onto CR 501 toward Vallecito.

Drive all the way north around the lake. From the CR 240/501 intersection it's 9.5 miles to the intersection where CR 500 heads north toward Vallecito Campground. Continue straight (east) here on CR 501. The road bends southward just before the Middle Mountain Road turn in 1 mile. Go another 2.2 miles after the Middle Mountain turn and veer left toward the Pine River Campground and trailhead. If you cross the Pine River, you've gone too far.

It's 3.9 miles up the Pine River road to the campground and, at the far end of the road just past the campground, a huge trailhead parking area. The trailhead is easy to spot on the northeast end of the parking area (N 37 26.861, W 107 30.290, 7,915 feet).

HIKE: Begin by passing through a gate. Please remember to close all gates you pass through. This hike travels through private ranch land. The owners are very accommodating, but they do appreciate you staying on the trail.

You're close enough to the river to obtain periodic views. Mostly you'll be wandering through a nice forest in this scenic, wide mountain valley. The elevation gain is minimal, making this a nice, easy stroll, other than scattered rocks and tree roots. Because it is heavily traveled, you'll bump into other hikers, backpackers, and horse packers. Give horses the right of way, and if you have a dog, keep it under control.

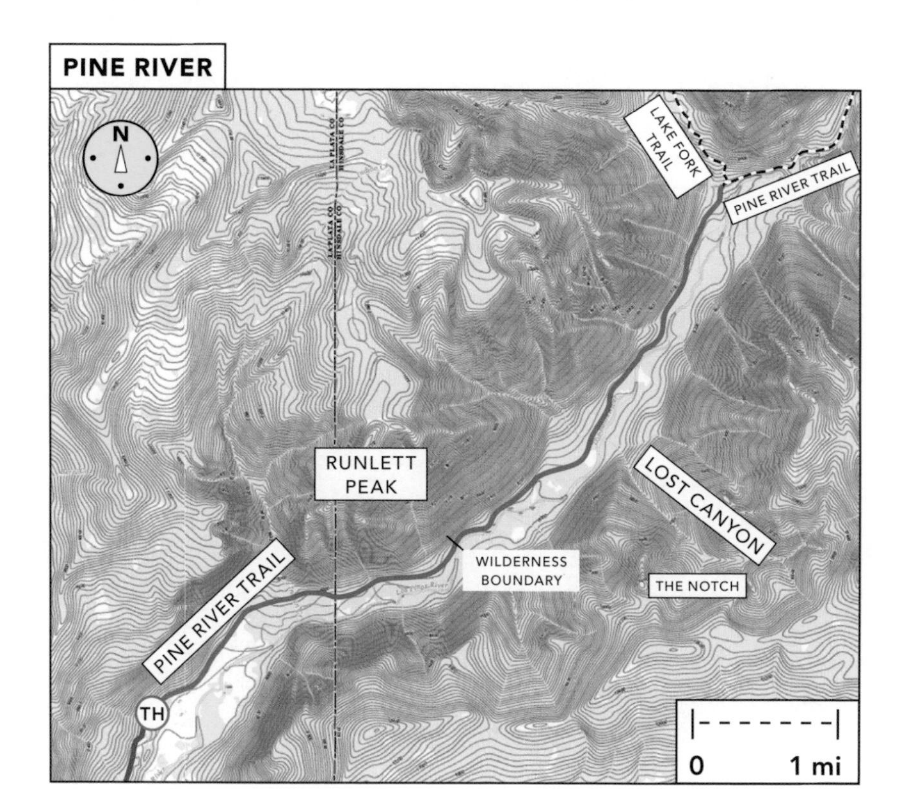

In 2.8 miles you'll reach the wilderness boundary (N 37 27.892, W 107 28.140, 8,150 feet). For an easy, half-day stroll, somewhere around here is a good turnaround point.

OPTIONS: It's quite a bit farther to the fork of Emerald Lake (Lake Fork) and Pine River Trails (N 37 29.994, W 107 26.099), which you'll reach at the 6.3-mile mark. From here, the Pine River Trail continues its slightly uphill trajectory to the northeast. The Emerald Lake Trail climbs at a good grade northward next to Lake Creek. It's 4 more miles to Emerald Lake, pretty much putting it out of reach as a day hike for normal people. (Note: The land around Little Emerald and Emerald Lakes is off limits to camping, but it's open for day use.)

THE AREA FOURTEENERS

Most people with some experience climbing in Colorado sooner or later get bitten by the fourteener bug. By last official count there are fifty-four mountains in the state above 14,000 feet. Sunshine Peak is lowest at 14,001 feet, and Mount Elbert is highest at 14,433 feet. Only Mount Whitney in California, of the other peaks in the contiguous states, is taller than Elbert, and that is only by 65 feet.

Being a fourteener is a blessing and a curse. These majestic peaks are highly overworked, visited 334,000 times a year according to the Colorado Fourteeners Initiative (14ers.org), a nonprofit attempting to preserve the mountains and the routes up them by doing trail work and educating the public.

Fourteeners present a unique challenge to the Colorado hiker. A few are very difficult and are only for the experienced climber. Most are not difficult at all, other than the thin air up there. If you're coming from low elevation or have heart trouble, you may want to think twice. Altitude sickness is a possibility; staying hydrated helps. Obviously it helps to be in good aerobic condition before attempting a fourteener.

Older people in good physical shape are not to be discouraged. People in their seventies and eighties have been known to summit fourteeners.

Twelve of the fourteeners are located in Southwest Colorado. They are: Handies, Redcloud, Sunshine, Sneffels, Wetterhorn, Uncompahgre, the three Needles peaks (Sunlight, Windom, Eolus), and the three Wilsons (Wilson Peak, Mount Wilson, and El Diente). Six of these are easily approachable from the Durango-Silverton corridor and are described here. Some hikers may prefer to car camp for a night if they have had to drive some distance to the trailhead, but none require the extra weight of sleeping equipment to be carried on the trail; day packs and canteens are adequate.

One other caution needs to be given for fourteeners: the snow problem. Unless you enjoy snow climbing and like to use crampons and ice axes, climbing in these mountains should be restricted to July through early September. Some years, snow conditions permit a little earlier and/or a little later climb. However, even during the prime time, you may be called upon to cross some small snowfields. This requires extra care if they are steep. The extra care means kicking good solid steps or using an ice axe if the snow is too hard for steps. If you don't have an ice axe, you may be able to go around the snow above or below.

A good high thirteener can be just as satisfying as a fourteener, and certainly not as crowded. But there is no denying that the perspective from a fourteener summit is intoxicating.

Top: A look south from the Sneffels summit down at Blue Lakes Pass and the cirque (foreground right) above the lakes. On the horizon, following the line made by the pass ridge, are the Ice Lake peaks. Bottom: Wetterhorn Peak, as seen from the west from the Wetterhorn Basin Trail.

MOUNT SNEFFELS

DISTANCE: 2.2 miles round-trip

ELEVATION: Start at 12,430 feet with 4WD, summit at 14,150 (1,720-foot gain); without 4WD, gain about 2,900 feet and hike 5.8 miles round-trip

RATING: Difficult

TIME ALLOWED: 2½ to 4 hours

Mount Sneffels is a pretty straightforward climb. And if you four-wheel it up to the trailhead, it's a short one. That said, there are a couple of aspects that make it just a bit tricky, and there's more about that in the hike description. The climb should test your mettle, unless you're one of those people who bag big peaks for breakfast.

Being the highest point in the area, Sneffels commands tremendous views. It's especially rewarding in late September (if the snows have held off) during the season of aspen foliage color. The north and west sides of the mountain and the lower country to the south are mottled with gold mixed with the dark green of the high-altitude conifers.

To the north way off in the distance you can see Grand Mesa. To the east is 13,825-foot Teakettle Mountain with its unique handle. To the south is Blue Lakes Pass, Gilpin Peak, and the distinctive St. Sophia Ridge. The Wilson range lies to the southwest, and Lone Cone can be seen in the distance to the west-southwest. It's a dizzying array from a small summit top. And it always seems to be really windy, which perhaps adds to the exhilaration.

Yankee Boy Basin, the starting point of the hike—as well as Imogene Pass and Governor Basin, other options from the same access road—has become very popular for all kinds of people and vehicles: 4WDs, off-highway vehicles, motorbikes, hikers, etc. So, this area can become fairly crowded, especially on weekends.

US 550 between Durango and Ouray is one of the most scenic in the world. It takes you over three passes that are 10,500 to 11,000 feet high. The stretch just before Ouray is called "the million-dollar highway," and even historians aren't sure exactly why. One legend is that mine-dump tailing were used as the base of the road in the 1880s, and there's a million dollars' worth of gold in that base. Another hypothesis is that road renovations in the 1920s cost a million dollars a mile. Maybe, another theory goes, the road gives you a million dollars' worth of thrills. It is exciting. Sometimes along this stretch you are riding on the edge of a sheer canyon wall. Lowlanders are known to drive agonizingly slowly; if one is driving in front of you, be patient and don't tail him too closely.

The 25 road miles between Silverton and Ouray are some of the most avalanche-prone in the country, and US 550 gets shut down for a day or even several days almost

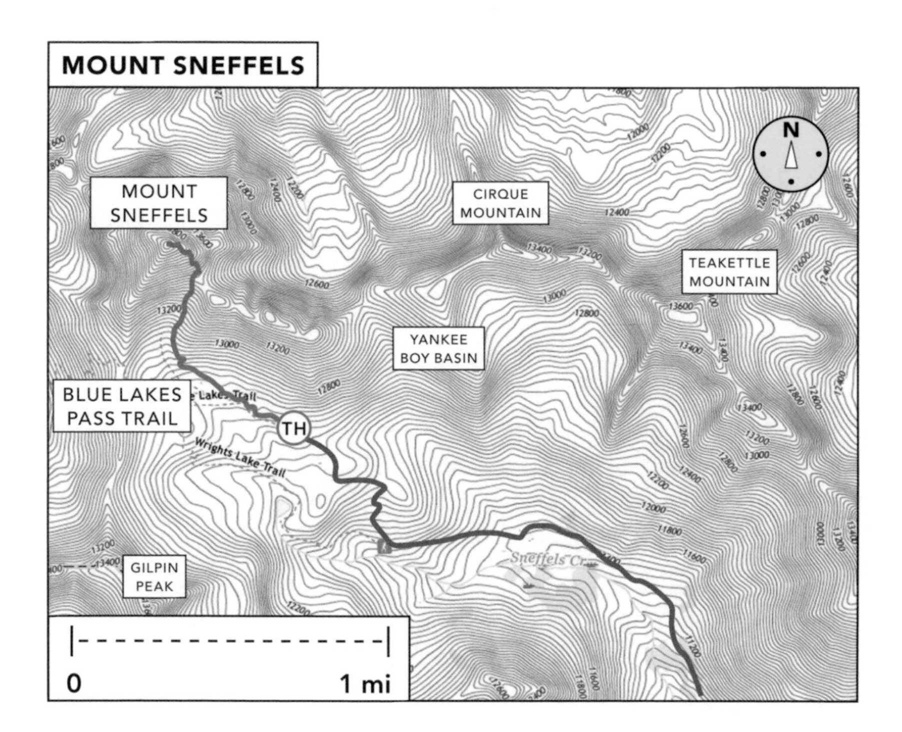

every winter while snow is cleared. Avalanche paths can be recognized in the summer by the treeless strips down a mountain that are surrounded on either side by heavy timber. Early in the summer there will be large hard piles of snow, often containing tree branches, at the bottoms of these chutes.

Sneffels: Where'd *that* name come from? Reportedly it's from Jules Verne's 1864 sci-fi book *Journey to the Center of the Earth*, in which Iceland's volcanic mountain Snaefellsjökull is the entrance to the earth's core. Perhaps there's an entrance on Colorado's Mount Sneffels, but I haven't found it.

APPROACH: The drive to the trailhead is part of the adventure of this trip. Take US 550 north 23 miles from Silverton, and just as you're coming to the last switchback before the town of Ouray, take a left onto the Yankee Boy Basin/Camp Bird Road. It starts out as gravel and is good for several miles; then it becomes progressively rougher. There are a few junctions, but just veer right every time and you won't get lost. Warning: If you stand out of a truck bed at the wrong time, an overhanging cliff will knock you into oblivion; you'll see what I mean.

At 5.9 miles stay right at the turnoff for Imogene Pass. At 6.7 miles stay right at the turn for Governor Basin (10,780 feet). This is where the road becomes four-wheel-drive. The first part isn't too challenging (conditions vary from year to year), and at 7.5 miles you'll reach an area with some parking and a restroom (11,250 feet). After this the road gets much rougher, and if you don't have high clearance, it's time to hike.

Looking down at the approach, with Yankee Boy Basin below.

At 8.2 miles (N 37 59.337, W 107 46.616, 11,660 feet) a sign recommends a short wheelbase only, but this doesn't mean it's just for Jeeps. Regular-sized trucks should be fine, and with good 4WD you should be able to continue up to the small trailhead parking area at 9.3 miles (N 37 59.694, W 107 47.089, 12,430 feet).

HIKE: Begin northwest over well-trod talus. At 0.3 miles the Blue Lakes Pass Trail takes off to the left (N 37 59.843, W 107 47.415, 12,570 feet). Stay right. The climb begins in earnest just a little past this intersection, and up above you will see the scraped-off mountainside you will be scuffling up. This slope used to be filled with scree, which was a blast to run down after summiting, but thousands of users every year have ultimately scraped the scree away. (Nobody's pushing the scree back uphill, unfortunately.)

It is best to keep to the left on the rocks to make your way to the top of the summit ridge. At 0.8 miles, you will reach a saddle on the summit ridge (N 38 00.146, W 107 47.434, 13,570 feet). There you will see the nice protected 400-foot-high rocky couloir going up to the left (northwest) on the left (southwest) side of the ridge. Head up this couloir; most rocks are large and stable, but it's not a bad idea to test the ones that seem questionable. You'll be using your hands at this point. In early summer the presence of snow may complicate things, and you will likely need crampons and an ice axe.

Just a bit (50 yards or so) before reaching the very top of the couloir (N 38 00.226, W 107 47.508, 14,008 feet), look for the best way out of this gully toward the left. Most go through a V-shaped notch. This is a bit of a scramble with some exposure, but be patient and careful and you'll be fine. Once you get to the next gully over it gets easier again, and you can scramble to the top at 1.1 miles (N 38 00.228, W 107 47.542, 14,150 feet).

OPTIONS: To the south side of the summit is a narrow north-south ridge separating Yankee Boy Basin from the Blue Lakes area. You can return this way, or climb up this way if you wish to vary the route, but it's fairly slow going, and be careful of the route you pick. A trail at Blue Lakes Pass (13,000 feet) will take you back down to the basin.

HANDIES PEAK

DISTANCE: 5.4 miles round-trip for American Basin route, 9.8 miles round-trip for Grouse Gulch route, 8 miles round-trip for Grizzly Gulch route

ELEVATION: Start American Basin route at 11,600 feet, summit at 14,048 feet (2,448-foot gain); start Grouse Gulch route at 10,750 feet (3,298-foot gain); start Grizzly Gulch route at 10,422 feet (3,628-foot gain)

RATING: Moderate for American Basin and Grizzly Gulch routes; moderately difficult for Grouse Gulch route, due to a 600-foot drop that you'll have to regain

TIME ALLOWED: 4 to 5½ hours for American Basin route, 5½ to 8 hours for Grouse Gulch route, 5 to 7 hours for Grizzly Gulch route

---

Handies is the most popular fourteener in Southwest Colorado, with an estimated 5,000–7,000 hikers visiting annually, according to 2017 data from the Colorado Fourteeners Initiative. From Durango and Silverton it's the most accessible.

Before you begin, you have a few decisions to make: Do you want the quickest and easiest way up (American Basin)? Do you want the shorter drive but longer hike (Grouse Gulch)? Do you also want to climb Sunshine and Redcloud in one trip and don't mind a bit of steepness (Grizzly Gulch)?

AMERICAN BASIN ROUTE

In any case, Handies has one of the easiest ascents of any of Colorado's fifty-four fourteeners. We'll start with the easiest way, which involves a four-wheel-drive trip to American Basin.

APPROACH: At the northeast end of Silverton's Greene Street (the main street of the town), turn right onto CR 2. This starts as pavement but turns to gravel in a couple of miles. Follow this road 12 miles to a division, where going left leads down along the river to the ghost town of Animas Forks. You should take the right fork uphill (toward Engineer and Cinnamon passes) and shift into four-wheel drive.

At 12.7 miles, the Cinnamon Pass Road turns off very sharply and steeply uphill to the right; it is so sharp that you may have to go past the turn, turn around in the road, and come back to it. This is a picturesque road above timberline, with high peaks and deep glacier-carved canyons. At 14.9 miles, you'll reach the top of Cinnamon Pass at 12,600 feet.

Being careful on a couple of nasty switchbacks, go down the other side at 17.2 miles; shortly after entering timber again, as you are rounding a left-turn

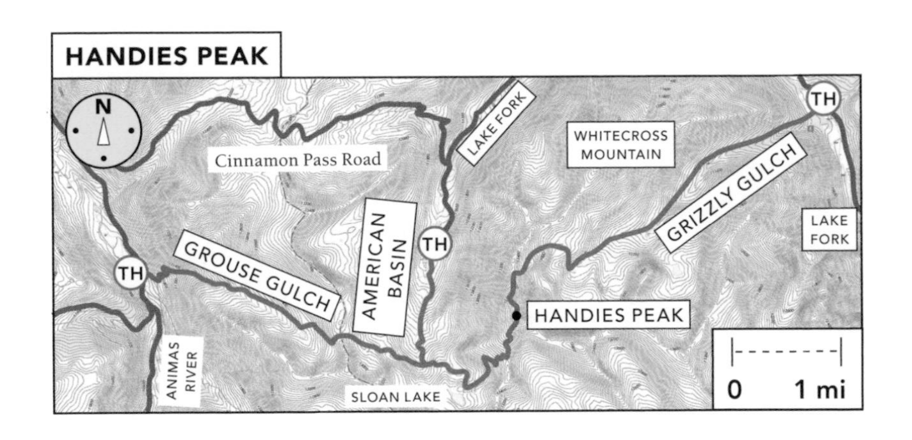

A view from Sloan Lake looking up at Handies Peak's west side. The trail climbs up to a saddle south of the peak.

switchback, a road turns off sharply to the right, downhill. There should be a sign indicating "American Basin." Take this road. About 0.8 rough miles up this road brings you to a roadblock where good parking is available (N 37 55.180, W 107 30.997, 11,600 feet). As you face south to the head of American Basin, you will see it walled off with high, broken cliffs—awesome bastions protecting the valley.

HIKE: The trail heads south uphill, climbing up to Sloan Lake, a nice little gem in a rocky setting at 1.5 miles (N 37 54.285, W 107 30.683, 12,900 feet). The trail does not go directly to the lake, but a short side trail does; it is well worth taking.

The main trail swings back northeast over talus, heading downhill briefly, and in a quarter-mile begins the final ascent, reaching the saddle just south of Handies at 2.3 miles (N 37 54.509, W 107 30.339, 13,480 feet). Gaze down into Boulder Gulch. Then head up the ridge to the north; an S-shaped trail has been etched into the hard dirt. At 2.7 miles the top (N 37 54.778, W 107 30.261, 14,150 feet) is broad and relatively smooth.

There is a steep drop-off northeast into Grizzly Gulch. Looking across this into and up the other side of the Lake Fork of the Gunnison, you will see Redcloud and

The view from near the Handies summit, with Sloan Lake down below. All twelve of Southwest Colorado's fourteeners appear to be visible from here. Note the distinctive horn of Pigeon Peak; Windom, Sunlight, and Eolus are to its left.

Sunshine, both fourteeners. North on the horizon, you can see two more fourteeners: pointed Wetterhorn (14,015 feet) and broad Uncompahgre (14,309 feet). To the west and a bit north, Sneffels (14,150 feet) is the high point on the skyline. To the south are a great host of other San Juan peaks, the most obvious of which is Pigeon with its sheer east face. The Needles fourteeners are east of Pigeon but very hard to distinguish from here.

GROUSE GULCH ROUTE

This route is 9.8 miles round-trip, with a starting point of 10,750 feet (3,298-foot gain). This route is moderately difficult, but the altitude gain is substantial as there is a 600-foot drop that you have to regain both ways. That really makes the elevation gain total more like 4,500 feet. It'll take 5½ to 8 hours.

This route is part of the course for the Hardrock Hundred endurance race held every July. In fact, you are exactly following the Hardrock course all the way to the top of Handies. (This route up Handies has become one of those well-known secrets talked about in the Introduction on page 11.) The Hardrock is a tough 100.5-mile run/hike around the San Juan Mountains that begins in Silverton, goes near Lake City, through Ouray and Telluride, and back to Silverton. Several hikes in this book cross the course or use small parts of it. And if you thought 4,500 elevation was tough, the Hardrock has 33,000 feet elevation gain!

APPROACH: On the northeast end of Greene Street in Silverton, take a right onto CR 2. After 2 miles the paved road turns to very good gravel. At 7.6 miles, just past Eureka, the road climbs steeply and begins to get a little bit rougher. However, pretty much any car should make it to this trailhead with a bit of care. At 10.6 miles the road crosses the Animas River for the first time. There are several parking spots near the bridge (N 37 55.082, W 107 33.493, 10,750 feet) to park for this hike.

HIKE: From the bridge, go 150 yards uphill and take a closed-off road going up to the right (N 37 55.130, W 107 33.488, 10,780 feet). This old road switchbacks up the mountainside above Grouse Gulch, before straightening out and connecting with the gulch.

At 1.9 miles (N 37 54.705, W 107 32.118, 12,470 feet) you will pass by a small lake that is to your right. Climb oh-so-steadily up this well-defined path to a saddle that divides Grouse Gulch basin with American Basin at 3.2 miles (N 37 54.652, W 107 31.779, 13,070 feet). Handies Peak comes into view across American Basin. You're heading eventually, after a slight twist south, toward that saddle just south of Handies.

Cross the pass and drop down into American Basin. At 3.1 miles cross a high fork of the Lake Fork of the Gunnison River, then climb up to meet with the trail coming up the basin at 3.2 miles.

The climb steepens and at 4 miles you will reach Sloan Lake at 12,900 feet; this point is at the 1.5-mile mark of the American Basin route described on page 214.

GRIZZLY GULCH ROUTE

This route is 8 miles round-trip, with the start at 10,420 feet (3,628-foot gain). The route is moderate due to some steepness; the time is 5 to 7 hours.

Many people use this route because it's easy to get to from Lake City and it's across the road from the trailhead for Sunshine and Redcloud, two other fourteeners.

APPROACH: Take the Lake Fork of the Gunnison road (paved at first) that begins about 3 miles south of Lake City off CO 149. This soon brings you along beautiful Lake San Cristobal. It's 16.5 miles from the highway to the trailhead (N 37 56.218, W 107 27.642, 10,400 feet). This is a busy area. The trail for Redcloud and Sunshine goes northeast from here, while the Handies trailhead goes southwest, crossing the Lake Fork on a nice bridge.

HIKE: The route climbs steadily from the get-go, following above and northwest of Grizzly Gulch. It steepens as you climb out of Grizzly toward the ridge between Whitecross Mountain (13,500 feet) and Handies. Once you hit the ridge at 13,600 feet there'll be some loose rock and dirt, and steepness, but the route up is not difficult to follow.

You can also reach the American Basin route from the Lake Fork of the Gunnison road. Continue past the Grizzly Gulch trailhead 3.6 miles to the left-hand turn into American Basin. The road gets a bit rougher past the Grizzly Gulch trailhead but should be doable for most vehicles. It is nice to have good clearance. Alternately, you can get to the Grizzly trailhead from the Cinnamon Pass side.

Handies from the pass between Grouse Gulch and American Basin. The trail climbs to a saddle south of Handies.

REDCLOUD & SUNSHINE PEAKS

DISTANCE: 12 miles round-trip

ELEVATION: Start at 10,420 feet, Redcloud summit at 14,034 feet (3,614-foot gain), Sunshine summit at 14,001 feet

RATING: Difficult, due to the distance and altitude

TIME ALLOWED: 7 to 8½ hours

Redcloud and Sunshine are usually climbed together. There is a 500-foot drop to the saddle between, which is all that has to be regained to get the second peak on the same trip. So here is a fairly easy way to bag two fourteeners in one day. In fact, they are close enough to Handies that very strong parties, bent on making fast time, could potentially do all three in one day. The rating of Difficult is given because of the distance and total altitude gain. However, there is no really difficult spot anywhere along this route.

APPROACH: To reach the trailhead, follow the same directions from Silverton given for Handies Peak on page 214, going 3.6 miles past American Basin to the trailhead; it is where Grizzly and Silver Creek both come into Lake Fork.

From Lake City, take the Lake Fork of the Gunnison road that begins about 3 miles south of Lake City off CO 149. It's 16.5 miles from the highway to the trailhead.

On both sides of the road at the trailhead there is plenty of parking space (N 37 56.218, W 107 27.642, 10,420 feet). Although it's not the quietest spot, the parking area is sometimes used for camping, presumably by those who want to get an early morning start. There's an outhouse and a couple of stabilized historic buildings from the 1800s. There is some private land along the road between American Basin and this trailhead, complicating the task of finding a good campsite. Keep searching; you'll find one.

HIKE: The trail follows an old road uphill. After 1 mile, you'll exit the forest and be welcomed by great views of the valley up ahead, and Silver Creek rushing by below. At 2.1 miles you leave the proximity of the creek, heading steeply uphill to the left; at 2.2 miles the trail levels out again and you'll see the valley ahead, curving around to the right (east and southeast).

At 3 miles from the trailhead, the climbing begins in earnest as you hike up to a saddle at 3.7 miles (N 37 56.766, W 107 24.880, 13,020 feet). From the saddle go southwest along the ridge until the ridge steepens; then follow the trail as it contours more gently and switchbacks up the mountain. You shouldn't get too far from the ridge.

When the ridge tops out at 4.3 miles, you'll turn south and have a relatively easy 0.2 miles to the summit (N 37 56.456, W 107 25.305). Standing on the top, feast your eyes on peaks and valleys galore. To the north are the unmistakable summits of

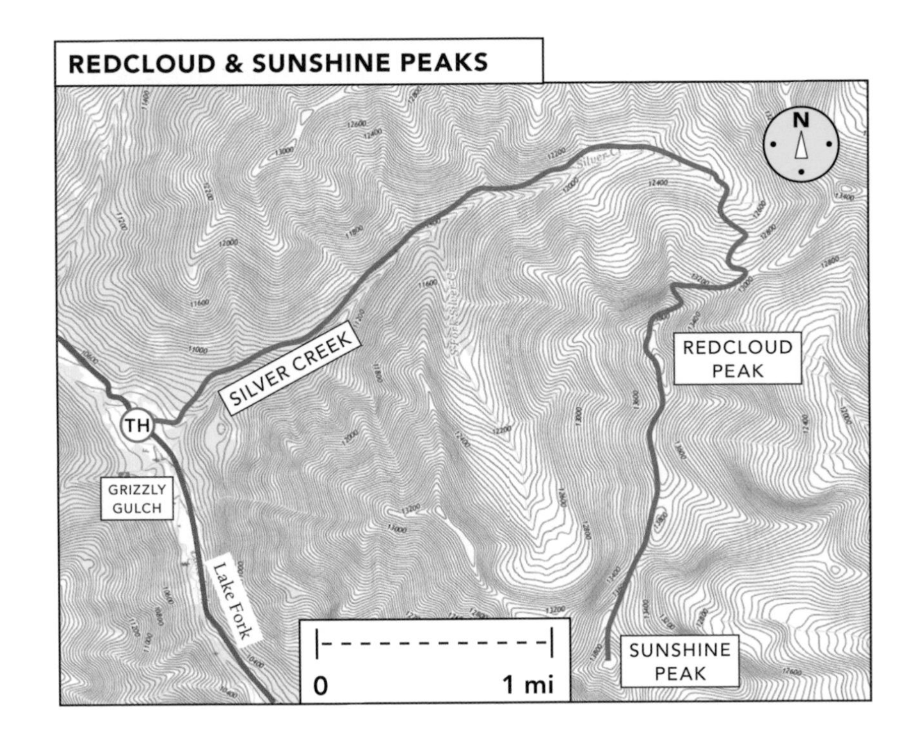

Wetterhorn and Uncompahgre. To the southwest are the Grenadiers and more, and, of course, Sunshine looms large to the south.

Undoubtedly you've seen a marmot by now. Maybe one is chewing your radiator hose just as you're enjoying the summit view. These creatures inhabit much of the backcountry high altitudes (9,000 feet and up). They are furry rodents with bushy tails and weigh about eight pounds. Because of their whistle-like call, they are nicknamed "whistle pigs." They like to sit up on their hind legs and stare at you or peek from behind a rock. Sometimes you can get within a few feet of them, but usually they quickly duck into a convenient nearby hole.

From Redcloud, it is an easy 1.5 miles down into a saddle (N 37 55.710, W 107 25.420, 13,520 feet) and out again up to the top of Sunshine (N 37 55.364, W 107 25.531, 14,001 feet).

For the return trip, it is possible to shorten the distance by going back to the saddle north below Sunshine and down into South Fork. Don't do this for two reasons: First, it causes erosion. Second, it's not that easy, and you can end up launching rocks on your climbing partners. It might save some time, but the going is slower and the trail is much rougher. An alternate route west off Redcloud, then north into South Fork, is recommended by some but is also steep and can be troublesome if you get off course.

Best option: Start early and leave plenty of time to go back over Redcloud and down the same trail you came up.

UNCOMPAHGRE PEAK

DISTANCE: 8 miles round-trip

ELEVATION: Start at 11,450 feet, Uncompahgre summit at 14,309 feet (2,859-foot gain)

RATING: Moderate, due to altitude

TIME ALLOWED: 4 to 5 hours

Uncompahgre Peak is one of the easiest fourteeners to climb. It is the highest point in southwestern Colorado and the sixth-highest peak in the state. The rating is moderate not because there are any big difficulties, but only because of the altitude.

Uncompahgre has a very distinctive top that can easily be recognized from the east, the west, and the south. The top is very large and relatively smooth compared with most high peaks, being something close to 300 yards long and 100 yards wide, and gently sloping to the southeast. The north face is, however, a complete contrast, plunging straight down nearly 1,000 feet. It is awesome!

The name Uncompahgre, first recorded by the Escalante-Dominguez expedition in 1776, comes from the Ute Indians who once dominated this area. It is said to mean "red lake" or "where water makes rock red."

APPROACH: There are two methods, depending on whether you'd rather take the rough four-wheel-drive way (approximately 4 hours' driving from Durango) or the smooth, mostly paved way (approximately 5 hours' driving from Durango). Each brings you to the Nellie Creek turnoff on Henson Creek Road.

If you drive on paved highways to Lake City, go west from town about 5 miles on the Henson Creek Road to the Nellie Creek turnoff, heading north up alongside Nellie Creek.

For the four-wheel-drive method, go 12 miles from Silverton to a division just before you reach Animas Forks. Where there's a split, go right uphill (toward Engineer and Cinnamon passes) and shift into four-wheel drive. At a junction at 12.7 miles, continue straight toward Engineer Pass. Reach the high point at 17.1 miles, where the road veers right (northeast) and actually drops down to Engineer Pass at 17.5 miles.

There are a few slow spots, but generally this road is easy going, particularly when you get a mile or two down from the pass. It's 9.3 miles from the top of the pass to the old site of Capitol City, then another 4 miles from there to the Nellie Creek turnoff (FR 877).

Once you're on the Nellie Creek Road, it's 4 miles of four-wheel driving to the end of the road at the Big Blue Wilderness boundary at 11,450 feet. Park here (N 38 03.790, W 107 25.335, 11,450 feet).

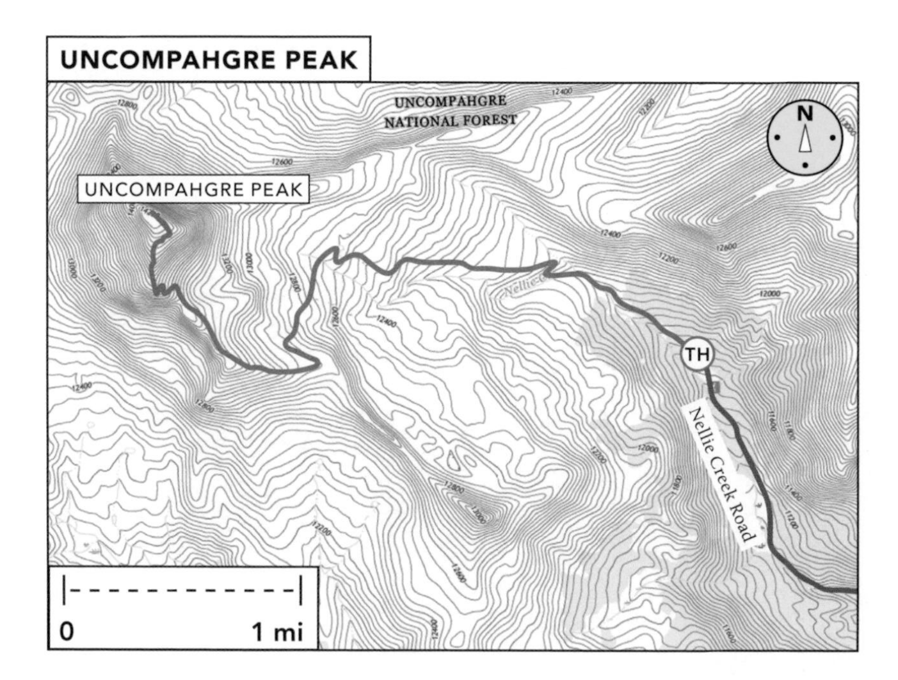

HIKE: The route begins northwest, following Nellie Creek. It eventually bears west toward the peak, then south to reach a ridgeline at 12,930 feet (N 38 03.769, W 107 27.032) at about 3 miles.

Again the trail swings around, this time toward the northwest, and joins a more distinct ridge. The ridge drops off steeply to your left, although there are possible routes up and down this way.

Continue the easy, gradual climb (easy if you can find enough oxygen) a mile along this final distinct ridgeline to the top (N 38 04.303, W 107 27.732, 14,309 feet). There's just a bit of steep, loose rock to get back to the ridge before the final ascent.

Once on top, you are "king of the mountain," and you can see many miles in all directions on a good day, and vast stretches of peaks and big valleys. The nearest peaks, of course, are Matterhorn, which you can now look down on, and Wetterhorn just beyond. To the northwest of Wetterhorn is Coxcomb, so named because of the appearance of its unique top. The Big Blue valley is particularly impressive to the northeast.

The descent is best made by the approach route.

OPTIONS: You could add Wetterhorn and/or Matterhorn to your day by using the North Henson Creek approach. (See Approach for Wetterhorn on page 225.)

Head up the Matterhorn Creek Trail; at a junction at 1.7 miles, veer right. As you reach higher ground in the openness of the tundra, you can begin to see the three high peaks of the area. Wetterhorn (14,015 feet) is to the left; Matterhorn (13,590 feet) is almost straight ahead; Uncompahgre, your objective, is off to the right.

Uncompaghre, the state's sixth-highest peak and tallest in the San Juan Mountains, as seen on the way up Wetterhorn Peak. (Photo by Steve Chapman)

Follow the trail to a saddle southeast of Matterhorn and Uncompahgre (N 38 03.630, W 107 29.219, 12,460 feet), taking the right-hand side where the trails come in from the north. The Uncompahgre Trail swings back southeast for 1.5 miles beyond the saddle, joins still another trail (N 38 03.342, W 107 27.636, 12,150 feet), and then ascends to Uncompahgre's southeast ridge trail at the 12,930-foot mark as described above (N 38 03.769, W 107 27.032).

Matterhorn presents few technical problems. It can be climbed by bushwhacking up the southeast side on the way back from Uncompahgre. It is steep tundra at first; this gives way to large rocks—some loose, some fixed—as you get within 500 or 600 feet from the top. In some locations, Matterhorn would be an impressive peak, but here it is subdued by its two higher neighbors. The most impressive view here is the ridge on the west side connecting to Wetterhorn. This is a jagged knife-edge a mile long. Just looking at it is scary.

WETTERHORN PEAK

DISTANCE: 7.2 miles round-trip

ELEVATION: Start at 10,850 feet, Wetterhorn summit at 14,015 feet (3,165-foot gain)

RATING: Difficult

TIME ALLOWED: 4 to 6 hours

This is a fun climb with enough exposure and scrambling to make it interesting. It's probably not good for a first-time fourteener; it's a good one to get some experience on before attempting the truly harder ones.

APPROACH: At the northeast end of Silverton's Greene Street (the main street of the town), turn right and follow CR 2. This starts as pavement but turns to gravel in 2 miles. Follow this road 12 miles to a division, where the left side leads down along the river to the ghost town of Animas Forks. You should take the right fork uphill (toward Engineer and Cinnamon passes) and shift into four-wheel-drive.

When you get to a junction at 12.7 miles, continue straight toward Engineer Pass; the Cinnamon Pass Road turns off steeply uphill to the right. At 17.1 miles, you'll reach the high point, where the road veers right (northeast) and actually drops down to Engineer Pass at 17.5 miles.

There are a few slow spots, but generally this road is easy going, particularly when you get a mile or two down from the pass. It's 9.3 miles from the top of the pass to the old site of Capitol City, where you make a left turn northwest onto North Henson Road.

Capitol City is a ghost town with a few old buildings still standing in the largest flat spot in Henson Creek Valley (several new houses have been built recently). Its mining founders of a hundred years ago were ambitious and dreamed of replacing Denver as the state capital.

There are several campsites along North Henson Road, which follows the north fork of Henson Creek. After 2 miles take a right-hand turn (N 38 01.394, W 107 29.566, 10,390 feet) off this road onto a four-wheel-drive road that heads up north along Matterhorn Creek to the Wetterhorn/Matterhorn trailhead. This is a very rough road, and it's only 0.7 miles to the trailhead from here; you could hoof this part, but it would mean an extra 450 feet of climbing. There's room for a few cars at the trailhead (N 38 01.839, W 107 29.475, 10,850 feet).

HIKE: Begin hiking north up the closed-off old road. It switches back twice, heading east momentarily, then back north. In 1.7 miles from the start you'll reach an

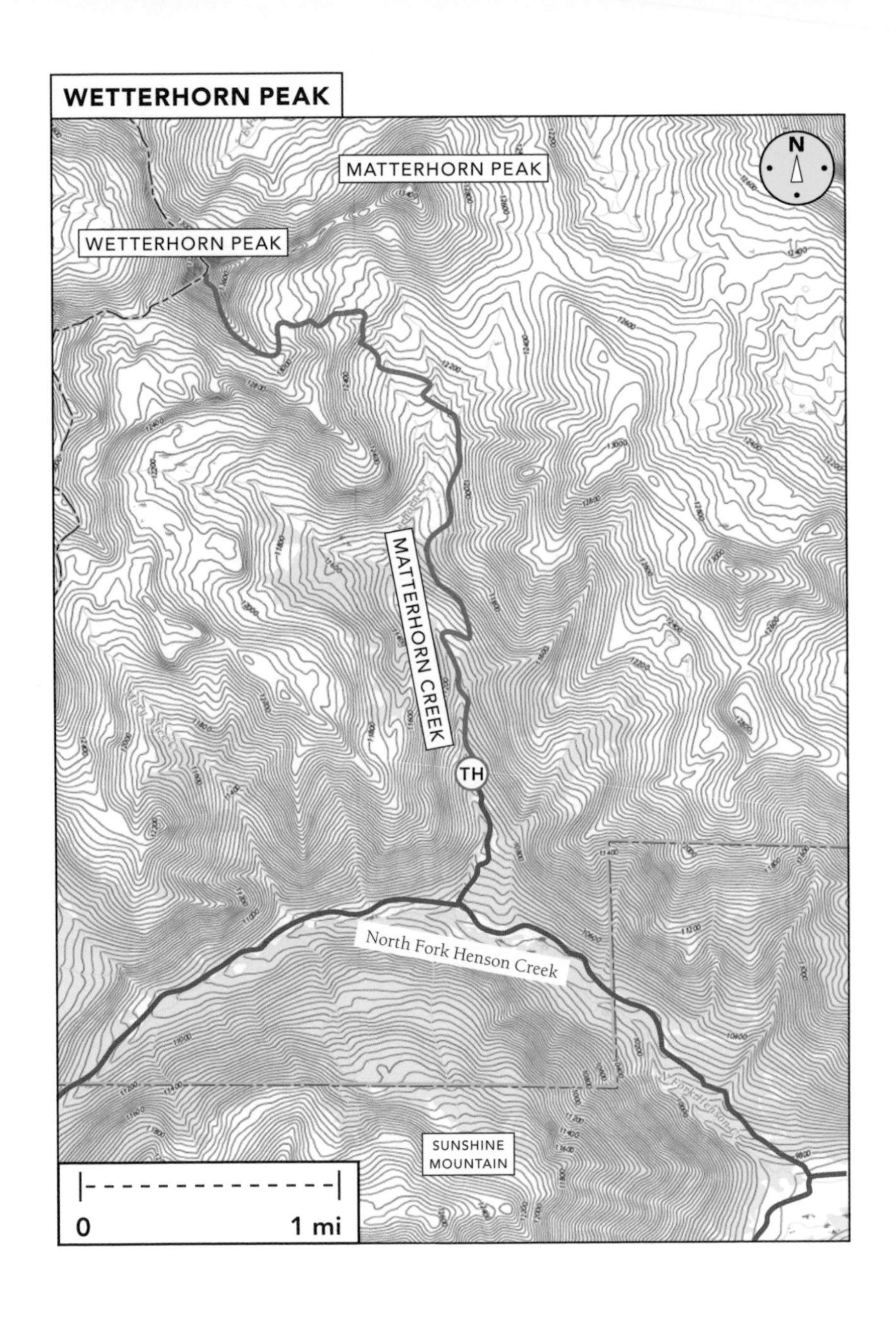
WETTERHORN PEAK
MATTERHORN PEAK
WETTERHORN PEAK
N
MATTERHORN CREEK
TH
North Fork Henson Creek
SUNSHINE
MOUNTAIN
0
1 mi

Looking south down the ridge from near the top of Wetterhorn. Matterhorn Creek is at the left. (Photo by Steve Chapman)

intersection (N 38 03.105, W 107 29.577, 12,000 feet) of the Wetterhorn Trail with the old Ridgestock Driveway. Go left on the Wetterhorn Trail.

From the intersection you get a nice view northwest toward the Wetterhorn summit. Soon you'll see Uncompahgre Peak off to the northeast. The trail is well cairned as it weaves up through a rock field and gets to a point almost due east of the summit. Undoubtedly you'll notice marmots (the porcupine-sized furry animals) and pikas (the tiny mouse-like ones) moving in the rock field.

The trail heads southwest and then west to reach Wetterhorn's southeast ridge at 3 miles. When you reach the ridge you're at 13,100 feet (N 38 03.345, W 107 30.400). It's another 0.3 miles along the ridge to about 13,600 feet, where you'll need to start doing some serious route-finding up the steep rocks. Pick the best way up and don't kick rocks on the person below you. We started up one gully, then crossed over to the next one by going up a short, steep set of rocks and down the other side on an obvious smooth ramp. Follow cairns and use your best judgment, and enjoy your stay on the rocky summit (N 38 03.642, W 107 30.653, 14,015 feet).

OPTIONS: You could make a big day of this by adding Matterhorn and/or Uncompahgre. See Options for Uncompahgre on page 223.

COLORADO PARKS WILDLIFE
STATE WILDLIFE AREA
THIS AREA IS OPERATED AND MANAGED WITH
FUNDS FROM HUNTING AND FISHING
LICENSES
NO VEHICLES
BEYOND THIS POINT
THIS INCLUDES:
Mountain Bikes
Motor Bikes and
All Terrain Vehicles.
COLORADO PARKS WILDLIFE
COLORADO PARKS AND WILDLIFE
DOGS
MUST BE
ON LEASH

ETHICS

We all want to believe that people who are enjoying the outdoors will do the right thing—assuming, that is, they understand what the right thing is. There are bad eggs in every crowd, but if people at least have knowledge and a few ethics by which to abide, they will generally treat the land with the respect it deserves and needs.

However, we all can use a refresher now and then. If you're looking for a more in-depth primer on how to be a steward of the natural world, read Aldo Leopold's "Land Ethic" essay in his 1949 book *A Sand County Almanac*. Or read just about anything from John Muir, a staunch proponent of "places to play in and pray in, where Nature may heal and cheer and give strength to body and soul alike."

The following are three more modern outdoor ethics models to consider while you're out on the trails.

LEAVE NO TRACE

The Leave No Trace Center for Outdoor Ethics researches and educates the public on up-to-date principles, using insights gleaned from biologists, land managers, and other leaders in outdoor education. The nonprofit was incorporated in 1994, and it sprung from a similar program that began in 1987 and is led by the US Forest Service, National Park Service, and Bureau of Land Management.

Although the principles have roots in the backcountry, they can be applied anywhere, from the wilderness to your backyard.

Here are the Center's "Seven Principles of Leave No Trace":

1. Plan Ahead and Prepare.
2. Travel and Camp on Durable Surfaces.
3. Dispose of Waste Properly.
4. Leave What You Find.
5. Minimize Campfire Impacts.
6. Respect Wildlife.
7. Be Considerate of Other Visitors.

For a more in-depth look at the principles, visit LNT.org.

The Dry Gulch Trail is on Parks and Wildlife land, and is accessible only from August through November. Trailhead signs expound on regulations.

TRAIL ETIQUETTE: RULES OF THE TRAIL

Since 1990 Durango-based Trails 2000 has encouraged share-the-trails ethics. Its "Durango Shares the Trails" educational campaign promotes positive interaction on, and stewardship of, the trails. These useful guidelines are as follows:

- Stay on the trail.
- If the trails are wet, it is not your day.
- If another trail user approaches you, say hello, especially if they say hi to you. Grunts do not count!
- Mountain bikers trudge and toil to get uphill. Please let them.
- When runners try to get past you, let them.
- When you see a horse, stop about 200 feet from the horse; announce yourself so the rider and horse both hear you; be clearly visible; pull off to the downside of the trail; and say hello as they pass.
- Please keep your dog on a leash or under voice control.
- When someone says, "on your left," please move to the right and allow them to pass. Hopefully you'll get a thank you.

TREAD LIGHTLY CAMPAIGN

Started by the US Forest Service in 1985, Tread Lightly became a separate nonprofit in 1990. The group works closely with the Boy Scouts of America and other organizations to spread the word. This campaign is geared toward all outdoor users: hikers, cyclists, motorbikers, and four-wheel drivers, just to start.

Here is the TREAD Pledge, geared toward a younger crowd, as presented by Lightfoot the squirrel:

Travel on trails or other legal areas.

Respect animals, plants, and people.

Every time you go outdoors, think safety, bring a friend, and be prepared.

Always leave the outdoors better than you found it.

Discover how fun the outdoors can be when you Tread Lightly!

For more information, visit TreadLightly.org.

RESOURCES

Bureau of Land Management
Tres Rios Field Office
29211 Highway 184
Dolores, CO 81323
970-882-1120
Web: blm.gov/office/tres-rios-field-office
Silverton Public Lands Office (May–Oct.): 970-387-5530

City of Durango Parks and Recreation
2700 Main Avenue
Durango, CO 81301
970-375-7321
Email: rec@durangogov.org
Web: durangogov.org/ParksandRec

Colorado Fourteeners Initiative
1600 Jackson Street, Suite 205
Golden, CO 80401
303-278-7650
Email: cfi@14ers.org
Web: 14ers.org

Colorado Parks and Wildlife
151 E. 16th Street
Durango, CO 81301
970-247-0855
Web: cpw.state.co.us

Colorado Trail Foundation
710 Tenth Street, Suite 210
Golden, CO 80401-5843
303-384-3729
Web: coloradotrail.org

San Juan Mountains Association
PO Box 2261
Durango, CO 81302
970-247-4874
Email: info@sjma.org
Web: sjma.org
Visit the SJMA bookstore at the San Juan Public Lands Center, 15 Burnett Court, in the Durango Tech Center, just west of town.

San Juan National Forest
15 Burnett Court
Durango, CO 81301
970-247-4874
Web: fs.usda.gov/sanjuan
Columbine District: 367 Pearl Street, Bayfield, 970-884-2512
Dolores District: 29211 Highway 184, Dolores, 970-882-7296
Pagosa District: 180 Pagosa Street, Pagosa Springs, 970-264-2268

Trails 2000
PO Box 3868
Durango, CO 81302
970-259-4682
Web: trails2000.org

INDEX

Page locators in **bold** indicate maps; page locators in *italics* indicate photographs.

Facing: An interpretive hike on the Hermosa Creek Trail was held early August 2019 for the public to see how the San Juan National Forest was bouncing back from a devastating fire the previous year.

Following: A view of the summit ridge on the Crater Lake–North Twilight trail, with the wide North Twilight summit at the center.

ABOUT THE AUTHORS

JOHN PEEL grew up exploring the mountains of Colorado. He moved to Southwest Colorado in 1990, and this is one of the first books he bought. He wrote the fourth edition of *Hiking Trails of Southwestern Colorado*, published in 2006. John spent twenty-two years as a writer and editor with the *Durango Herald*, and now runs his own family history research business. He lives in Durango with his wife, Judy, and dog, Buda.

PAUL PIXLER taught philosophy at Fort Lewis College for nearly thirty years and spent much of his spare time hiking and climbing the San Juan Mountains of Southwest Colorado. Paul wrote the first three editions of *Hiking Trails of Southwestern Colorado*, the first of which was printed in 1980. Paul died in 2011, aged ninety.